COLORADO KIDS

Illustration by Kelsey Simpson, fifth grade

A Statewide
Family Outdoor
Adventure Guide

Linda Collison and Bob Russell

PRUETT PUBLISHING COMPANY
BOULDER, COLORADO

Printed in the United States
10 9 8 7 6 5 4 3 2 1

Library of Congress Cataloging-in-Publication data

Collison, Linda, 1953–
     Colorado kids : a statewide family outdoor adventure guide /
Linda Collison and Bob Russell.
        p.   cm.
     Includes bibliographical references and index.
     ISBN 0-87108-862-2
     1. Colorado—Guidebooks. 2. Family recreation—Colorado—
Guidebooks. 3. Outdoor recreation—Colorado—Guidebooks.
I. Russell, Bob, 1948–   . II. Title.
F774.3.C59   1997
917.8804'33—dc21   97-6771
                                                                        CIP

Cover and book design by Kathleen McAffrey, Starr Design
Book composition by Lyn Chaffee
Cover photographs by AIP Photos
Cover illustrations by Cheryl Duff, Patrick McAffrey, Brock Stringham, and Ashley Tait
Interior illustrations by the first, third, fourth, and fifth graders at Leawood Elementary School, Littleton, Colorado

Special thanks to Leawood Elementary School teachers Alicia Cespedes, Tim Chiles, Alan Fettner, Michele Handley, Pam Nims, Claudia Stough, Jeanne Thomas, and Marilyn Tuck.

To our own Colorado kids:
Artie, Sarah, Mindy, Adam, and Matt

Illustration by Patrick McAffrey, third grade

CONTENTS

PREFACE

For centuries Colorado has been a land of adventure. Although today's travelers are more likely to arrive by jet or automobile than on horseback or wagon train, the mountains, canyons, and plains still call.

We, Bob and Linda, heard the call. We met in Colorado while skydiving; both of us were single parents at the time. We soon found we had a lot in common besides free-fall: hiking, camping, and raising teenagers, for example. After a long and adventurous courtship we married, by which time our combined group of five children were nearly adults themselves.

Over the years we've taken our children to many of the places in this book (though not all, as they're certain to point out). Some activities we discovered on our own; some the kids found for us, on their own. Friends gave us tips, and we took trips with nieces, nephews, and neighbor kids to further our research.

Colorado Kids is a collection of what we've found to be the best family-oriented adventures in the state. We've included many free or very low cost activities as well as some expensive ones, some heavily visited places as well as a few obscure amusements you won't find in other guidebooks. We've even left out a few attractions you might find in some guides, attractions that, in our experience, aren't appropriate for most kids. As parents we've written this book primarily for other parents—or for adults who find themselves in charge of young people. We've given what we found to be helpful tips and good advice when adventuring with young ones.

Telephone numbers are included for all activities. It's always best to call ahead to confirm hours, fees, and other pertinent information that can and does change. For more information, check the Activity Resources appendix. Or have your kids call or write for information about activities that interest them. The National Park Service and area chambers of commerce are great sources of free information. Older kids can help plan routes, navigate, choose campsites, and so on. Appendix B: Best Activities for Tots Ages 2–5 can help you plan an adventure designed for kids of those sometimes difficult ages. And although Colorado's weather is generally sunny, if bad weather spoils your outdoor plans, check the In Case of Bad Weather sections included in the material on most urban areas. Here you'll find suggestions for indoor activities we've found to be fun or educational.

Whether you live here or are visiting, we hope you and your family will enjoy the outdoor wonders of Colorado as much as our family does.

Linda and Bob

HOW TO HAVE A GREAT FAMILY ADVENTURE

Adventure to some can only mean taking great risks in extreme places—Cape Horn, Mount Everest, the moon. And others say adventure is the domain of youth, an extravagance for single people in prime physical shape, for daredevils who aren't burdened with mortgages, diapers, their kids' college tuition, or a few extra inches of fat. But we don't believe adventure has any age requirements or such a narrow definition. And although we enjoy sports like skydiving, adventure to us does not mean recklessly hurling ourselves into the arms of Fate. Instead, it is recognizing and accepting a challenge; it is anything that makes our hearts beat excitedly, that makes us feel alive.

Part of the fun of living is the surprise of it all. Whenever events don't turn out exactly as planned the plot thickens, and the possibility for a real experience is born. This Linda learned from her own parents, who seemed happiest, who literally shined, when life threw them a curve ball. Her folks seemed to have the most fun when the camping trip got rained on, when the car broke down late at night on a country road, when money was scarce, when everyone else was bored. This faculty for finding fun, for making an adventure out of the least little thing is one of the most valuable gifts her parents gave Linda; we can only hope we've passed some of that on to our own children.

There's no age limit to adventure. Linda remembers her grandfather Leonard at eighty-four years old planning a road trip with great excitement. He was always ready for an impromptu voyage and could turn the simplest walk to the store into an amazing journey.

Little kids have adventures all the time, and we grown-ups don't even know it. We think they're out in the backyard playing on the swing-set, but they're way off on another continent or in a different galaxy. Adults are usually excluded from the day-to-day adventures of their children, being far too preoccupied with the dull realities of making a living. But if we make the time, we can occasionally find some excitement together.

What makes a family adventure? For a three-year-old it could be a morning at the city park, the playground, the zoo. For a ten-year-old it could be an evening spent looking at the moon through binoculars or an amoeba with a microscope. For some sixteen-year-olds it could be learning to shoot an arrow with a bow, dropping a hundred feet through space tied to a bungee cord, or bouncing down a rocky mountain trail on a fat-tire bike.

How do you guarantee a good family adventure? If you can guarantee it, it's not an adventure! But you can set the stage for one. Be prepared: Fill the tank with gas, pack up the car, and go. Keep your eyes open and leave your expectations at home. If you're bound and determined to have a "perfect experience" with your family, you'll likely be disappointed. Be content to enjoy things as they are—don't try to force fun, and sooner or later you'll find it.

In general, the younger your children are, the shorter your activities should be. Don't try to get your money's worth out of a zoo, an outdoor museum, or a national monument by overtaxing your child's attention span; it's better to leave too soon than too late. Call it a day before the kids are tired or bored so that they aren't turned off to the whole experience.

Many hobbies and interests add a sense of discovery and a sort of mission to an outing. Stargazing, bird-watching, exploring old graveyards and ghost towns—everyone is fascinated with something. Sometimes one person's passion becomes a family pursuit; other families are content to diversify, traveling together with each member remaining true to his or her own delight. (To this day, whenever Linda travels with her daughter they stop for trees and plants. Her daughter touches, smells, photographs, and picks leaves from the ground. Mindy and Sarah both have a fascination for history; old graveyards, historic buildings and such. Bob and the boys are still stargazers; they stay up late watching meteors, identifying stars and planets, discussing the possibility of alien beings. And Linda always stoops to examine the rocks underfoot.)

Whatever your pleasure, Colorado offers a rich setting for outdoor adventures of all descriptions. Our cities' parks and recreation systems are among the biggest and best in the country. Colorado is fortunate to have within its boundaries two national parks, seven national monuments, one national historic site, thirty-nine state parks, and hundreds of thousands of acres of National Forest Service and Bureau of Land Management land. Some of the most popular statewide activities are skiing, mountain biking, camping, river rafting, horseback riding, and fishing. Those who march to a different beat can find nearly unlimited opportunities for rock climbing, trapshooting, snowshoeing, archery, wildlife photography—the list is endless.

The hardest part may not be deciding what you want to do, but choosing the best place to do it. That's where we hope this guidebook will help. There are a million adventures to be had in Colorado—we've written about the ones we think are the best for families with children (and left out those we've found to be adult-oriented).

You don't have to be the Swiss Family Robinson to have outdoor fun with kids. You just have to recognize a good time when it's happening. As a friend once said, "An adventure is anything that will make a good story later."

May you find yourselves characters in many exciting stories to come.

HOW TO PLAN FOR
A SAFE TRIP

The smartest adventurers are prepared for the curveballs nature likes to throw. Most notable can be the weather. There's a saying in Colorado: If you don't like the weather, wait a few minutes—it'll change. Often it's a drastic change. This state's wild beauty is matched only by the unpredictability and extremes of the weather. A sunny shirtsleeve kind of day can become dangerously cold after the sun goes down. Snow often falls in the higher elevations year-round.

The layered approach to dressing works best in any season, in any part of the state. Never go on an outing without a variety of clothes, including hats, coats, gloves, and extra socks made of wool or polypropylene, which will retain heat even when wet. It's a good idea to keep an assortment of these items in the car at all times.

Other natural events can pose dangers to adventuring families. Winter is followed by spring snowmelt and runoff, which means that mountain rivers will usually be deeper and swifter than normal during the months of April, May, and sometimes June. The increased volume and speed of the water as well as its frigid temperature can be deadly to those who fall in. In general, plan rafting trips for midsummer, depending on conditions. Always use the services of a professional rafting company unless someone in your party is qualified as a guide. In addition, check with the Forest Service about river conditions before you go. Merely walking along stream banks can be dangerous during runoff. Even during dry summer months a sudden rainstorm can cause flash flooding, in which case you should climb to higher ground.

Thunderstorms, hailstorms, blizzards, and tornadoes have all been known to occur in Colorado. Pay attention to forecasts, listen to the wisdom of locals, and keep an eye on the weather at all times. If ominous clouds threaten, seek shelter immediately.

Colorado is a big state: Sometimes the sheer distance between where you are and where you want to be can pose safety problems. Fill your car's gas tank when it's half empty; the next service station might be sixty miles away—and closed when you get there. Don't rely too heavily on cellular phones. Mountains can block reception, and large distances delay rescues. Be self-reliant: Keep your car in good repair and know its limitations. If you don't have four-wheel-drive, stay on well-surfaced roads. If you don't have snow tires or chains, stay close to town during the winter and early spring.

Keep your vehicle supplied with what you would need to survive if you were stranded. Make sure you always have in your car:

- Nonperishable snacks and drinking water
- Extra sunscreen
- Handkerchiefs or pre-moistened towelettes
- A bag of assorted coats, hats, and socks
- "Car blankets" that can be used for warmth or shade, and a cardboard windshield sun visor
- Jumper cables, roadside emergency flares, gas can, spare tire and jack
- A shovel during the winter and early spring

Always carry with you:

- Drinking water
- Sunscreen and hats
- A compact first-aid kit
- Warm clothing that can be layered

COMMON DANGERS

EXPOSURE TO THE ELEMENTS

Hypothermia, a lowering of the body's core temperature, can strike even in the summer, especially if you get wet. A layered approach to dressing allows for changes in temperature; always carry extra clothes. Wool sweaters and polypropylene undershirts help keep you warm even when wet. Don't forget to put a hat in your pocket; a substantial amount of body heat is lost through the scalp. Teach your kids to stay put if they get lost and to construct a makeshift shelter out of branches, leaves, or snow to ward off the elements. When someone is lost, their first and most severe risk is hypothermia from exposure.

SUNBURN, DEHYDRATION, AND HEAT EXHAUSTION

Also caused by exposure to the elements, sunburn is a common problem year-round in Colorado. An actual first- or second-degree burn, sunburn is painful and hastens dehydration. The best medicine is prevention, which includes wearing protective clothing, broad-brimmed hats, and sunscreen at all times. Dehydration can sneak up on you. If you wait until you're thirsty to drink, you're probably already dehydrated. Caffeine-containing beverages such as iced tea and cola soft drinks cause water loss through a diuretic effect. If you must have your caffeine, be prepared to drink twice as much water to replace what you'll lose. Children should drink at least a quart of water a day, adults at least two quarts. Carry a water bottle when enjoying outdoor activities, and keep track of how much you're drinking.

ALTITUDE OR MOUNTAIN SICKNESS

If you live at sea level and are vacationing in Colorado, you may notice you tire more easily and become winded at our altitudes. Although caused by "thinner air," these symptoms alone do not constitute altitude sickness. But if your vacation takes you into elevations above 8,000 feet, you may notice more fatigue, restless sleep, a slight headache, or nausea. Mild symptoms of mountain sickness such as these will sometimes disappear on their own and may be alleviated by rest and increased fluid intake. If symptoms persist, return to a lower altitude and consult a physician. In its most serious form, altitude sickness becomes high altitude pulmonary edema or high altitude cerebral edema—life-threatening swelling of the lungs or brain. Not enough is known about this illness, which can affect even young, healthy, athletic people. The only real cure is to get back down to lower ground immediately and seek medical treatment.

GIARDIASIS

Resist the temptation to drink out of that crystal-clear mountain stream without first purifying the water! Even the cleanest, most sparkling rivers probably contain microscopic *Giardia* parasites, which can cause gastrointestinal havoc such as severe cramps, diarrhea, vomiting, fever, and chills. Although water can be made safe by prolonged boiling, the use of special filters, or purification tablets, the easiest and safest way for most families to avoid *Giardia* and other disease-causing microbes is to carry water from home or drink bottled water.

LIGHTNING

Although it's most common during the summer months, lightning occasionally strikes during other seasons as well. It is a very real danger, and we've seen seemingly intelligent people ignore it. A good rule of thumb is to start mountain hikes early in the day and to turn back if dark clouds gather. Seek shelter indoors if possible. If a lightning strike seems imminent, crouch down hunched over in a ball to present as little surface area as possible, preferably in a ditch away from tall trees. The success of this last-minute maneuver depends more on luck than science—prevention and good judgment are the best remedies.

ENCOUNTERS WITH WILD ANIMALS

In spite of the occasional highly publicized story of a bear or mountain lion attack, it is extremely rare for humans even to see these and other potentially dangerous wild animals. Although you'll hear a lot of opinions about what to do in case of an attack, they are often conflicting and confusing. (Let's see—do you avoid eye contact and stand your ground, or do you make a lot of noise and run like hell?) Our advice is to avoid unpleasant encounters altogether by using common sense when exploring the Colorado outdoors. Keep children close at hand; there is safety in size and numbers. Never feed, attempt to touch, or in any way harass a wild animal. If you come across a bear, mountain lion, snake, or other potentially dangerous animal, slowly back away in a respectful manner. Don't make sudden movements, and *don't run.* Mountain lions and bears have been known to chase running humans.

First-Aid Kits

The trouble with most first-aid kits is that they contain items you don't need and probably won't use. The kit we use is stripped to the bare necessities, based on the common injuries and ailments most likely to happen on family outings. It's so compact it fits in a cosmetic bag. Because of its small size and negligible weight it's easy to carry everywhere, and although we're not equipped to do minor surgery or detoxify snake venom, as some explorers are, we've never been in a position to need that sort of intervention. Here's what we carry in our family kit:

- Moleskin and adhesive bandages for blisters, among the most common and annoying outdoor health problems
- Aloe vera gel for sunburn or chafing
- Tweezers for removing splinters
- Several clean white handkerchiefs for washing scraped knees and stanching bloody noses
- A small cake of soap (You really don't need all those tinctures and caustic solutions to clean a wound; the best germicide is soap and water.)
- A small tube of Neosporin or a bacitracin ointment to prevent infection of superficial scrapes and "road rash"
- Ace wrap in a two- or three-inch roll for wrapping sprained ankles or to hold a splint in place
- Compact foil survival blankets (these are available at any camping supply store—they fold up to the size of a wallet)
- An over-the-counter pain reliever that works for you. We use generic ibuprofen or ketoprofen. Children should not take aspirin, nor should it be given to someone who has had a head injury. Keep in mind that most outdoor headaches are caused by dehydration and that the best remedy is to drink more water. High altitude can also cause headaches, in which case the best remedy is to descend to lower ground.

- Diphenhydramine such as Benadryl for mild allergic reactions and hay fever symptoms
- An over-the-counter antidiarrheal medication (Diarrhea can hasten dehydration, which can quickly become serious if not alleviated.)
- An over-the-counter motion-sickness medication for anyone prone to car sickness
- Extra medication for anyone taking it regularly

These are only guidelines—they are what we use in our first-aid kit. Not all medications are appropriate for all people; before taking any of the listed nonprescription medications or giving them to children, check with your own health care provider.

Keep your first-aid kit stocked and ready to go. Unused pills should be discarded when they reach their expiration dates or if the kit becomes wet.

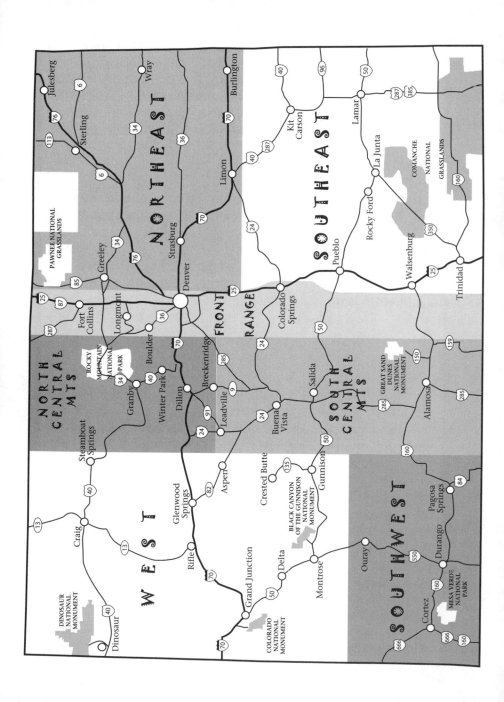

NORTHEASTERN PLAINS

If you want to escape the city, don't head west into the mountains—that's where everyone else is heading. If you really want some peace and quiet, pack up the kids and drive to Colorado's "Outback"—a romantic term the tourism folks are using for the vast plains covering the eastern third of the state.

Ages ago this land between the Front Range of the Rockies and the prairies of Nebraska was a shallow sea teeming with prehistoric life. Later, huge herds of buffalo grazed here and were hunted by Arapaho, Kiowa, Southern Cheyenne, and other Native peoples who depended on them for survival. During the nineteenth century this corner of what is now Colorado was an important source of water for trappers, traders, and ranchers and farmers who depended on the South Platte River for their livelihoods.

Today, northeast Colorado is an area devoted mostly to farming and ranching, but also to recreation and wildlife management. Grasslands and reservoirs provide habitat for many species of prairie and wetland birds, mammals, reptiles, and fish—as well as good opportunities for patient humans to catch a fish, a photo, or just a glimpse of the flora and fauna.

Most families won't choose this area of the state as a vacation destination. If you have a fear of vast open spaces, if you need to spend a lot of money to have fun, if your kids need high-tech entertainment to keep boredom at bay, a trip to the northeast Outback could be a frustrating waste of time. But if yours is the kind of family that takes delight in seeing who can spot the most antelope or the most out-of-state license tags, if you get a thrill from driving roads that follow old trading routes across land where millions of buffalo once thundered, and if you like the feel of dry summer wind blowing on your face from an open car window—you just might enjoy a drive through this country.

11

And although you may not spend a week at a Holiday Inn out here, you could easily spend three enjoyable days on a road trip, with frequent stops along the way.

The Platte River towns of Greeley, Fort Morgan, Brush, Sterling, and Julesburg offer weekend fun during the summer and autumn months in the form of rodeos, festivals, and fairs. Reservoirs and wildlife areas offer picnic and camping spots—and water to play in. Begin just north of Greeley at the town of Ault and follow Highway 14 east through the Pawnee National Grasslands to Sterling. From Sterling, take Highway 138 to Julesburg in the extreme northeast corner of the state, about 160 miles from Greeley. Then travel south on Highway 385 for 123 miles to Burlington, stopping in the town of Wray, at Beecher Island Battleground, and at Bonny Reservoir, just north of Burlington. From Burlington, return to the Front Range area by following I-70 west 160 miles to Denver.

GREELEY AREA

"Go west, young man," quoted nineteenth-century journalist and abolitionist Horace Greeley. And although Horace never went to eastern Colorado, visiting Englishwoman Isabella Bird in 1873 had this to say about the town named for the man: "This settlement is called the Greeley Temperance Colony, and was founded lately by an industrious class of emigrants from the East, all total abstainers, and holding advanced political opinions. . . . A population of 3,000 [they] are the most prosperous and rising colony in Colorado, being altogether free from either laziness or crime."

In this century you can buy a beer easily enough in Greeley, whose population is now about seventy thousand. Home to the University of Northern Colorado, it is still a hardworking, conservative community—except during the annual Greeley Stampede. This week-long Independence Day celebration gives local farmers, ranchers, students, and merchants a chance to kick up their heels and have some fun.

Denver Broncos Summer Training Camp

Football fans, see your favorite Denver Bronco players as they warm up for the season. If you're lucky you might even get an up-close glimpse of your favorite player and an autograph or two. Bring a picnic to eat on the grounds, then stroll around the University of Northern Colorado's campus to inspire your youngsters to work toward that scholarship.

WHERE: Butler Hancock Field, University of Northern Colorado Campus; (970) 351-2007, or call (970) 351-1099 for information about the training camp.

WHEN: Generally mid-July through mid-August; weekdays at 9 A.M. and again at 3 P.M.

ACTIVITIES: Watching Colorado's professional football team as they warm up for the season. No charge.

FACILITIES: Parking, restrooms.

BE SURE TO BRING: Cushions to sit on, sunscreen, hats, and binoculars. Don't forget a pen and something to autograph—just in case.

Centennial Village and Island Grove Park

We're sure we picked the hottest day of the year to tag along behind a day-care class at Centennial Village. Three bedraggled adults herded a class of preschoolers dressed in homemade pioneer costumes through the village to explore the cabins, houses, and tepees. All the dwellings have been relocated, reconstructed, or replicated here to show visitors the history of home life in northeastern Colorado. Most popular with the kids seemed to be the rawhide tepee. The rugged little homesteader's shanty was our favorite; we could easily imagine the hardy people who lived there. The table was set, a charred enamel coffee pot waited on the woodstove—it looked like the family had just stepped out to do the chores.

Visitors can take the regularly scheduled tour given by calico-clad volunteers, or you can just poke around on your own, opening doors to houses and making up stories about the folks who might have lived there. This outing is best suited for school-age kids and adults with an interest in historical buildings. Most families will find an hour's worth of educational activity here, but we advise picking a day when the outdoor temperature is bearable!

WHERE: Greeley, on 1475 A Street; follow signs from Highway 85 to Fourteenth Avenue; (970) 350-9220.

WHEN: Mid-April through early October. During the summer months the park is open from 10 A.M. to 5 P.M. Tuesday through Saturday and from 1 to 5 p.m. on Sunday. Call for off-season hours.

ACTIVITIES: Guided and self-tours of buildings and exhibits depicting the architectural and cultural heritage of northeastern Colorado. A summer series of exhibitions and concerts; holiday programs. A small fee is charged.

FACILITIES: Parking, restrooms, water fountain and soda machine, gift and craft shop. Adjacent to a shady municipal park with picnic tables and swimming pool.

BE SURE TO BRING: A cooler of drinks and a picnic lunch to enjoy after your visit. Bring suits and several dollars if you want to swim in the municipal outdoor pool.

FORT VASQUEZ

It's easy to miss this historic site if you're cruising Highway 85; watch carefully for a small sign 1 mile south of Platteville. Although there's not a lot to do here, there are some good displays of Bowie knives, trade beads, arrowheads, and other implements. The adobe fort is being painstakingly reconstructed, and it's interesting to watch the process. You might want to bring extra money for the small gift shop. There's a great selection of western history books and Indian craft kits designed for children.

A short visit to Fort Vasquez is most enjoyable for school-age kids and adults. If you like this small fort, consider spending a summer touring all of Colorado's historic forts and trading posts.

WHERE: 15 miles south of Greeley and 1 mile south of Platteville on Highway 85; (970) 785-2832.

WHEN: Summer hours, Monday through Saturday from 10 A.M. to 5 P.M. and 1 to 5 P.M. on Sunday. Call for off-season hours. White Line Rendezvous, a historical reenactment, is usually held the last weekend in May.

ACTIVITIES: Touring a reconstructed 1830s trading fort. Donations are solicited.

FACILITIES: Restrooms, water fountain, museum, gift shop.

PAWNEE NATIONAL GRASSLANDS

The grasslands are not everyone's idea of fun. Hot and dry in the summer, often bitterly cold in the winter, this is a land ruled by raptors surveying their domains from telephone poles and fence posts. It's easy to envision the prairie as a shallow sea, the way it was a hundred million years ago, when dinosaurs roamed this land. Low rolling waves of land look like ocean swells. The horizon is circular, as if viewed from the bow of a ship.

Your first stop should be the ranger station in Greeley, just east of Highway 85 at 660 O Street. Ask for the free bird-tour map, which you can take by car or by mountain bike. And be sure to shell out a few bucks for the complete grasslands map. (Don't be a cheapskate, as we were!) The park is pockmarked with private ranches and farmland, which makes it a little confusing to know where to go. You could drive or pedal around all afternoon looking for Pawnee Buttes and end up out of gas or dehydrated in somebody's north forty.

Most people who go to the grasslands visit the Pawnee Buttes—sandstone formations that provide interesting visual relief in the endless swells of prairie. The easy 1.5-mile trail around the buttes is a good way to get you out of the car and stretching your legs. Keep in mind that there are no facilities at the buttes, so stop at nearby Crow Valley Recreation Area to use the restrooms.

Many gravel roads penetrate the grasslands and make good biking routes. Weld County Road 77 at Crow Valley Recreation Area in Briggsdale is a good place to start. Be warned: Although the terrain is rather flat, summer temperatures can climb over 100 degrees! The best weather usually occurs in September through early November. Even so, listen to the weather forecast before you go, because blizzards and thunderstorms can span the seasons.

If you're camping, bring a stove. Don't plan on a campfire, for wood is scarce here, and fires are generally discouraged or prohibited. Be sure to borrow or buy a star map—this is an exceptional place for amateur astronomy. For moonlit nights, bring binoculars to check out the craters. This is also a good time and place to develop an interest in bird-watching. Mountain plovers, horned larks, American kestrels, burrowing owls—over 250 species have been recorded here. Other animals, such as mule deer, coyotes, prairie dogs, jackrabbits, short-horned lizards, and various snakes, including rattlers, are sometimes seen here.

Rock hounds can see good examples of sandstone, shale, chert, and agate. Fossils and arrowheads are here, too, for the observant to spot. The kids might be disappointed to learn they can't take home any artifacts they might find, but such discoveries are important to researchers and should be reported. Who knows? It could be the start of a lifelong hobby or even a career for your youngster.

WHERE: Half an hour's drive northeast of Greeley. Go north on Highway 85 to Ault, then turn right onto Route 14. Grasslands begin about 12 miles east. (970) 353-5004.

WHEN: Year-round. Fall and late spring are usually best due to extreme temperatures and storms in midsummer and winter.

ACTIVITIES: Auto-touring, hiking, biking, archaeology, stargazing, camping. Currently no fees.

FACILITIES: Primitive camping and picnicking at the Crow Valley Recreation Area, .25-mile north of Briggsdale on Road 77. Restrooms and water.

BE SURE TO BRING: Map, binoculars, food and water, sun protection, a full tank of gas. In winter, early spring, or late fall, bring warm clothes.

AREA STATE PARKS AND NATIONAL FORESTS

JACKSON STATE PARK

Northeast of Greeley; from I-76 take County Road 39 north 7.25 miles to Goodrich. Follow signs west on Y5 about 2.5 miles to the park. Because it seems so far from anywhere, you might think you'd have the park to yourself. Wrong! Jackson State Park seems to be the premier vacation spot of eastern Colorado. Camping is popular: There are more than 260 sites with full amenities. Shade is available but scarce. There's a swim beach on this shallow reservoir, but it's not for the squeamish—it can get green and slimy with algae. Water skiing and boating are popular summer activities, and the marina rents equipment. Winter recreation includes camping, ice skating, ice boating, and ice fishing. Wildlife viewing is good any time of year. Among the more unusual species found here are pelicans! Weekend interpretive programs take place during the summer months at the amphitheater. Kids might want to bring their bicycles, or rent them at the marina, and ride around the lake. Bring bug repellent during warm months. A user's fee is charged; (970) 645-2551.

Outdoor Fairs and Festivals

Greeley Independence Stampede

Seven to ten days of professional and junior rodeos, carnivals, parades, fireworks, live bands, and other entertainment. On and around July 4 at the Greeley fairgrounds. Call (800) 982-BULL, or contact the Greeley Chamber of Commerce at (970) 352-3566.

Weld County Fair

Farm animals, 4-H exhibits, carnival and rodeo. In late July at the Greeley fairgrounds; (970) 356-4000.

Fort Lupton Trapper's Days

Three days of historical reenactments and other entertainment at the Trapper Days park in Fort Lupton, about 25 miles south of Greeley on Highway 85, in early September. Contact the Fort Lupton Chamber of Commerce at (970) 857-4474

In Case of Bad Weather

Greeley Municipal Museum

A bit tedious, but for those interested in Weld County history or genealogy, a short visit can supplement a tour of nearby Centennial Village. Tuesday through Saturday, 9 A.M. to 5 P.M.; 919 Seventh Street; (970) 350-9220. Donations accepted.

1870 Meeker Home

A thirty-minute guided tour of Indian agent Nathan Meeker's house might be of interest to those who like to look at antique furnishings, belongings, and memorabilia of a bygone era. Some rooms are of interest to kids. Meeker was killed by Utes in 1879 near the town in western Colorado that is named after him. 1324 Ninth Avenue in Greeley; (970) 350-9220. A fee is charged.

Burlington Area

Most people know Burlington (if they know it at all) as the first Colorado town on I-70 west over the Kansas state line. Burlington, 163 miles east of Denver, is an anticipated oasis for many of us when we're driving the interstate. Gas stations, fast-food restaurants, and truck-stop cafés are highly visible here. But if you venture just a little farther off the highway and spend more than half an hour filling stomachs and gas tanks, you'll find a delightful bit of recreated history in this farming, ranching, and railroad community on the eastern plains.

Be sure to stop at the State Welcome Center, just off I-70. Here volunteers—assisted by hundreds of maps and brochures—can help you plan any vacation or getaway in the state.

Old Town and Kit Carson County Carousel

Old Town sounds a little corny, with its summer weekend street fights and cancan shows, but kids really like it. Most adults (like us) enjoy it too. It's an easy way to visualize a part of history that has perhaps been highly romanticized. Nonetheless, the rowdy action helps prevent those crippling attacks of yawning that take over as soon as you start looking at anything deemed "historical." Serious Old West buffs will want to spend more time touring the turn-of-the-century buildings filled with memorabilia. The rest of us will make a beeline for the old-fashioned soda fountain, followed by a wagon ride from Old Town to the nearby Kit Carson County Carousel—a hand-carved merry-go-round that's been designated a National Historic Landmark. For a quarter you can ride a leaping lion or a horse.

WHERE: I-70 Exits 437 and 438 to 420 South Fourteenth Street; (800) 288-1334.

WHEN: Self-guided tours of the buildings year-round, but more activities (including saloon shows, wagon and carousel rides) are available on summer weekends. From 9 A.M. to 6 P.M. Monday through Saturday and from 12 to 6 P.M. on Sunday; extended hours from Memorial Day to Labor Day.

ACTIVITIES: Indoor/outdoor entertainment and learning, including museums, wagon rides, carousel rides, live performances, and a bit of old-fashioned commercialism. A fee is charged.

FACILITIES: Restrooms, soda fountain, and other concessions, gift shops.

BE SURE TO BRING: A little cash for treats, and pocket change to ride the carousel.

BEECHER ISLAND BATTLEGROUND

Beecher Island is a sandbar in the middle of the Arikaree Fork of the Republican riverbed—a dried-up creek that becomes a true river only in the spring after the snow melts. It's not much to look at now, maybe, but if only the creek could talk. It was here that Major George Forsyth led his ragtag civilian army to a victory against the Cheyenne in 1868. Many men on both sides died in the battle, among them Lieutenant Frederick Beecher, second in command. The Cheyenne leader Roman Nose was killed, too, as he attempted to save a dying way of life for the Plains tribes.

The battle of Beecher Island was one of the last fights between the U.S. Army and the Cheyenne people. A drive to this little-known historic site gives you a chance to discuss with your children the conflicting values and ways of life each side represented. Walk the riverbed and the surrounding valley that was, for a few days long ago, a battleground. Reflect about how the "winning of the West" changed the American frontier forever. Camp out under a harvest moon and wonder what it would have been like to have been a Cheyenne warrior or a private in the United States Army.

This is a minimally developed site, missed by most tourists driving 75 miles an hour on the Interstate. If you have an appreciation for history and aren't expecting to find a miniature Gettysburg battlefield here, it's worth a visit and a campout. A small museum in the town of Wray—17 miles north—houses historical artifacts, memorabilia, and information about the battle and other events that played a part in the history of eastern Colorado.

WHERE: About 40 miles north of Burlington off Highway 385. Contact the Wray Chamber of Commerce at (970) 332-5063.

WHEN: Year-round. Beecher Island Reunion in mid-September features a black powder shooting demonstration, races, music, and a craft show.

ACTIVITIES: Historical education, hiking, primitive camping, nature viewing, picnicking. No fee charged.

FACILITIES: Water, picnic area, primitive campground (no electrical hookups). Museum in Wray.

BE SURE TO BRING: A cooler of food and drinks, sun protection, and insect repellent during the warm months.

Area State Parks and National Forests

Bonny State Recreation Area

Year-round camping on two hundred sites, including one campground with full amenities. A marina rents equipment for most water sports. Landlubbers can enjoy horseshoe pits, bike riding, or nature walks around this 7,200-acre park. Excellent birding opportunities are to be found here, for Bonny is a destination for migrating geese and a year-round home to dozens of species, including ospreys and greater prairie chickens. In the spring you might see wild turkeys at Foster Grove Campground. Look for sandhill cranes in October, as well as loons, snowy egrets, tundra swans, and screech owls. During the summer butterfly-watchers can enjoy a multicolored variety here where the tall-grass and shortgrass prairies meet. Go east on I-70 to Burlington, then north on Highway 385 for 23 miles; (970) 354-7306.

Outdoor Fairs and Festivals

Little Britches Rodeo

This nationally sanctioned event features kids, maybe the age of your own! In June, at the fairgrounds in Burlington. Contact the Burlington Chamber of Commerce at (719) 346-8070.

Kit Carson County Fair and Rodeo

A typical old-fashioned county fair in Burlington, early August. Contact the county extension service at (719) 346-5571.

COLORADO'S FRONT RANGE

The eastern range of the Rocky Mountains is the longest continuous geologic uplift in the state. Stretching across more than 200 miles from the Wyoming border south to Canon City, Colorado, this dramatic range overlooks the most populated areas of our state. Longs Peak, Mount Evans, Mount Bierstadt, and Grays Peak—all these 14,000-foot peaks stand shoulder to shoulder along the Front Range. The most famous of them all is Pikes Peak, which casts its shadow on Colorado Springs. At one time easterners referred to half of Colorado as Pikes Peak Country; "Pikes Peak or Bust" was the slogan of gold seekers and fortune hunters in 1859. The discovery of gold around Pikes Peak prompted a migration of people who came, saw, and settled.

Although the lofty mountains hold opportunities for adventure, plenty of outdoor fun can be found without ever leaving town. The Front Range cities boast a large number of urban parks, open space lands, and multi-use trails—some of the finest in the country—all with a view of the much-loved peaks that rise abruptly from the plains.

The semi-arid weather along the Front Range is great for outdoor activities. On the average there are only eighty-eight days of precipitation a year along this populated corridor. Gloomy, rainy days are few. Snow might bury a Front Range city a couple of times a year, but it generally melts away after a day or two of warm sunshine that invariably follows.

If you live in or are visiting one of the Front Range cities and don't have the time or the means to drive to the mountains or the plains, there are countless outdoor adventures waiting to be had virtually in your own backyard.

FORT COLLINS AREA

"But Daddy, where's the fort?" an observant child might ask. Actually, there hasn't been a fort in Fort Collins since 1871, when a military encampment was set up here to protect new settlements near the Overland Trail. The growing community soon discarded the fort but kept the name. Throughout the twentieth century, Fort Collins developed first as a supply center for miners, farmers, and ranchers—and as home to the Agricultural College of Colorado, now Colorado State University.

Today, Fort Collins, 60 miles north of Denver, is a sports-loving college town of about one hundred thousand residents with just enough arts and culture available to make a healthy balance. A good system of multi-use trails and bike lanes crisscross this sprawling community both for outdoor enjoyment and to promote an environmentally friendly form of transportation.

The area is also known for its beer. Anheuser Busch has a plant here, as do several award-winning microbreweries. Although beer tasting isn't exactly a family activity, you've got to eat somewhere, right? You'll find many Fort Collins restaurants and grills offer locally made lager and ale. (A brew labeled Fat Tire is our favorite.)

Fort Collins's neighbor city, Loveland, 12 miles to the south, has several parks, lakes, and reservoirs in its vicinity that make ideal picnic settings. Although they are not considered tourist destinations, both communities offer a high quality of life on the edge of the Rockies for residents and visitors alike.

RAFTING THE CACHE LA POUDRE RIVER

The Poudre comes tumbling out of the mountains northwest of Fort Collins, a young and boisterous river. Its full name is romantically French: *Cache la Poudre*, meaning a cache or hiding place for gunpowder. It was named by French trappers in the 1820s.

You can take a beautiful drive up twisting, turning Highway 14, which follows the free-flowing stream, which is classified as a

National Wild and Scenic River. But most kids don't enjoy car rides, no matter how scenic. Kids want to get out and do something. Like float down the river on a raft!

"River rafting is hot," says Pat Legel, owner of A Wanderlust Adventure rafting company, "and we're growing in popularity every year." The Poudre is famous for giving experienced rafters and kayakers some of the wildest runs in the state. Fortunately, there's a 3-mile section that's suitable for rookies. "A taste of white water," is what Pat calls this short but exciting trip geared toward families and beginners. It's popular—75 percent of his customers choose this introductory rafting experience.

"We take groups of older kids, Girl Scouts and Boy Scouts, ten and eleven years old, all the time. And we take kids as young as seven, as long as they have a parent or guardian along," Pat says. "Since the run is short, we do it twice. The second time down, most people enjoy it even more. Sometimes we stop at a swimming hole, if conditions are right."

Plan on about three hours, Legel says. Be sure to wear clothes that can get wet and still keep you warm. Windbreakers are recommended, worn over lightweight wool shirts. And don't forget a change of clothes for the ride home.

A Wanderlust Adventure is a member of the Colorado River Outfitters Association and has been in business since 1982. For a complete list of professional river outfitters in the area, contact the Fort Collins Chamber of Commerce at (970) 482-3746.

WHERE: A Wanderlust Adventure in La Porte, just northwest of Fort Collins on Highway 14; (800) 745-7238 or (970) 484-1219.

WHEN: Mid-May through the end of August, conditions permitting; reservations are recommended.

ACTIVITIES: River-rafting experiences of varying lengths for all abilities.

FACILITIES: Provides appropriately sized life jackets and helmets and all other equipment.

BE SURE TO BRING: Early in the season, wool or polypropylene gloves can protect hands against the icy water. Don't underdress—you're probably going to get splashed. And be sure to bring a change of clothes and a snack for the ride home.

CAUTIONS: Heavy rains or snowmelt can make rafting dangerous. To minimize your risks, check with the Forest Service on current river conditions and always raft with a professional outfitter. The Fort Collins Forest Service Ranger Station can be reached at (970) 444-6600.

POUDRE RIVER MULTI-USE TRAIL

This multi-use paved path begins northwest of town and winds through Fort Collins on its way to the plains. It's a good place for families to enjoy the Cache la Poudre River without leaving town. Here the river slows down after its tumultuous descent from the mountains, providing a somewhat safer and easier environment for hiking, biking, or riverbank exploring. Numerous woodlands and wetlands interspersed with residential and industrial areas make for good wildlife viewing. Observant naturalists might see red foxes, raccoons, muskrats, beavers, great blue herons, cormorants, great horned owls, and ospreys— all within the city limits.

The Poudre River Trail is over 8 miles long. Ambitious bikers can continue in a westerly direction, picking up the 5-mile Spring Creek Trail, which joins the Poudre River Trail near the southeast end at Prospect Road. Not far from the intersection of the trails is a cluster of fishing ponds, an interpretive boardwalk describing wetland habitat, and Colorado State University's Environmental Learning Center, which is open from dawn to dusk seven days a week. The Learning Center is also the home of Colorado State University's Raptor Rehabilitation program. In conjunction with the University's school of veterinary medicine, the raptor rehab program helps wounded birds of prey heal and readapt to the wild. If you're interested, you can take the volunteer training program and learn how to help care for these birds, or you can adopt your own raptor and contribute to its room, board, and medical treatment (but no, Artie, you can't take it home with you!).

WHERE: There are many places to access the trail; first-time users might park at the Lee Martinez Park (North College Avenue and Cherry Street) or at the Environmental Learning Center (Prospect Road and Sharp Point Drive, not far from I-25). For more information, contact Fort Collins Parks and Recreation, (970) 221-6640.

WHEN: Year-round.

ACTIVITIES: Walking, running, and biking; fishing, bird-watching, and other nature study.

FACILITIES: Wheelchair-accessible paved trail and fishing piers, picnic tables; restrooms and drinking water at various city parks along the trail; emergency telephone and air pump at northwest trailhead. Bicycles and in-line skates can be rented at several different locations, including Rock 'n Road Cyclery at 4206 South College, (970) 223-ROAD.

BE SURE TO BRING: Stop at any sporting goods store and ask for free maps of the Poudre River Trail and the city's entire bike trail system. You can also get maps at any of the city's recreation centers.

URBAN AND COUNTY PARKS

SPRING CREEK BMX PARK

A five-year-old in full racing gear was pushing his pint-size bicycle up a dirt mound with only a little help from his mother, who cheered him on as he rolled down the other side. Later, a group of middle-schoolers detoured off Spring Creek Trail for a run through the course. Just watching these kids made us wish we had dirt bikes too.

The BMX (bicycle motocross) park at Edora Park is small but ideal for children just starting out in the sport of off-road non-motorized racing. Bring your own bicycle, or rent one in town. Park here at Edora, or bike the Spring Creek Trail to reach the course.

WHERE: Edora Park at Prospect Road and Riverside Avenue. For more information, contact the Fort Collins City Parks Department at (970) 221-6660, or the nearby Edora Pool and Ice Center at (970) 221-6679.

WHEN: Year-round.

ACTIVITIES: BMX (bicycle motocross) course. Free to the public except when sanctioned races are being run.

FACILITIES: Free parking, restrooms, water fountain, picnic tables, access to bike path. Nearby Edora Pool and Ice Center has food concessions.

BE SURE TO BRING: A suitable bicycle and helmet.

CITY PARK

Sheldon Lake, on 85 acres of City Park in north Fort Collins, is a good place for locals and visitors to go for an afternoon of picnicking, golfing, Frisbee throwing, or just strolling around the lake watching the ducks and geese. Tots might like a ride on the miniature train (in the summer months; there is a small charge), and kids of all ages will enjoy the playground. Besides swings, slides, and jungle gyms, it has a full-size cannon to climb on. Teens might enjoy beating Mom, Dad, or Uncle Joe in a game of tennis or golf. During the summer you can rent a canoe or a paddleboat for an old-fashioned Sunday boat ride.

During the winter, City Park is an ideal place for ice skating or for beginners to learn to cross-country ski. There are no ski or skate rentals at the park, however; you'll have to bring your own or rent from a sporting shop such as Adventure Outfitters, 514 South College Avenue, (970) 244-2460.

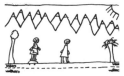

WHERE: 1500 West Mulberry, Fort Collins, (970) 221-6640 or 6600.

WHEN: Year-round from 6 A.M. to 11 P.M.

ACTIVITIES: In summer, miniature train for tots, paddleboat and canoe rentals, picnics, swimming, tennis, golf. In winter, cross-country skiing, ice skating (bring your own equipment).

FACILITIES: Restrooms, shaded picnic tables, playgrounds, ball fields, outdoor swimming pool, tennis courts, nine-hole junior golf course.

LEE MARTINEZ FARM AND PARK

"Old Martinez had a farm—ee-yi–ee-yi–oh." Little kids might like changing the words to the familiar nursery song on their way to the Lee Martinez Farm, next to the Lee Martinez Park in north Fort Collins. You can walk around the farm and look at the animals, or you can register for classes offered through the city's parks and recreation department. Here "city kids" can learn to milk cows, slop pigs, and perform other farm-related chores. Local youths can even sign up to feed and care for the animals on a regular basis.

Stimulating sights, sounds, and smells mingle here, making it a very exciting place for a small tot (like the smell of a clean barn and the touch of a horse's velvet nose).

WHERE: 600 North Sherwood, in Fort Collins. From north College Avenue, go west on Cherry, then north on Sherwood; (970) 221-6640.

WHEN: All year; seasonal programs.

ACTIVITIES: Animal-viewing, pony rides, farmyard demonstrations and organized learning activities for kids of all ages. Adjacent park for picnics, sports, and access to paved greenbelt.

FACILITIES: Restrooms, soda machine, nearby park and picnic facilities, maintained trail system.

BE SURE TO BRING: Picnic lunch or snack; change for soda pop machine and pony rides.

HORSETOOTH MOUNTAIN PARK

An old Arapaho legend says Horsetooth Rock is the heart of a great warrior god slain in a battle in the sky. His blood is said to have colored the rocks red. The legendary molar-shaped chunk of Precambrian granite standing 7,255 feet above sea level is the namesake of this county park, which features trails for hiking, biking, and horseback riding.

Although ambitious kids will want to tackle the steep trail up to Horsetooth Rock (a 1,500-foot climb in less than 2 miles), others will be more comfortable on the easier trail to Horsetooth Falls. This mile-and-a-half-long path leads to a small cascade without much overall change in elevation. But water levels change according to season, generally decreasing in volume as the summer wears on. By September, which is our favorite time of year in Colorado, the waterfall is usually a mere trickle. That's okay—the natural history and the views are worth it.

When you pay your user's fee at the self-pay station, pick up a trail map. Unless you have some experience mountain biking,

The gentle trail to Horsetooth Falls is a good one for younger children.

we suggest you hike, for the trails are a bit rocky and steep in places. Although the parks department has provided a few picnic tables near the parking lot, a roof is all that shelters you from the sun. Better to find a smooth rock in a shady nook to enjoy your picnic.

WHERE: 6 miles west of Fort Collins (and about 3 miles beyond the Horsetooth Reservoir) on County Road 38E. Contact the Larimer County Parks Department, (970) 679-4570.

WHEN: Open year-round and busiest on summer weekends. Early spring can be muddy, and midsummer is usually sunny and very hot—go on an overcast day or during the autumn months.

ACTIVITIES: 25 miles of hiking, mountain-biking, and horseback-riding trails.

FACILITIES: Parking, primitive restrooms, water, trail maps, several sheltered picnic tables and grills.

BE SURE TO BRING: Hiking shoes or boots with good tread, water bottles, sunscreen, hats, and a hearty lunch or snack. Binoculars are fun for older kids and adults, and a field guide to wildflowers, birds, insects, or rocks will be helpful.

SCULPTURE PARKS
SWETSVILLE ZOO

A metal zoo, we guess you'd call it, this fanciful collection of creatures fashioned by Bill Swets. It's one family's private streamside glen populated with a motley assortment of dinosaurs, dragons, spiders, birds, aliens, spaceships—and a "heavy metal" band. All sculptures are created from discarded farm machinery, engine parts, and other scraps that look like they came from the garbage bin of a machine shop. (Linda's favorite is a towering tyrannosaur whose open jaws hold a real bird's nest. It's amusing to watch the birds fly in and out between his metal teeth!)

Although there's a map that describes what each creature is, it's more fun to guess first, before looking. Creative kids can make their own books with snapshots or drawings to illustrate stories or fairy tales they make up about these characters.

If you're in Fort Collins, don't miss this unique private collection. It's a good impromptu activity that all ages will enjoy. You can breeze through in half an hour, or you can bring lunch and spend the afternoon here. The Swets have thoughtfully provided a shaded picnic table.

WHERE: 4801 East Harmony Road, Fort Collins, .25-mile east of I-25 (Exit 265); (970) 484-9509.

WHEN: Year-round, daylight hours.

ACTIVITIES: A private zoo featuring creatures fashioned from metal. Donations are accepted. There's also a miniature steam-powered train nearby; during the summer kids can ride for a small fee.

FACILITIES: Parking, picnic area, shade. No public restroom, so plan ahead; you'll find gas stations less than a mile away, just west of the interstate, or use the highway rest stop .25-mile north of Harmony Road.

BE SURE TO BRING: Imagination!

BENSON SCULPTURE GARDEN

Welcome to the children's sculpture garden, a sculpture garden within a sculpture garden, on the north side of Lake Loveland Park. Child-size statues such as turtles and alligators beg to be petted and climbed upon. The kids can explore a sand pile, a lily pond, a garden path, and a whole collection of artwork sculpted with kids in mind.

Adults, children—everybody enjoys this park. Even Bob, who initially pooh-poohed the plan. We walked around, discovering whimsical life-size figures and watching other people's kids romping, young mothers pushing baby strollers, and white-haired couples holding hands. It was like being part of an Impressionist painting—dappled with sunlight and laughter, sparkling water, bright flashes of flowers and glistening bronze.

Spring and summer days are perfect for a picnic at Benson's, but for a different experience stop by just after a snowstorm, when the sculptures are capped in white. You can add to the artwork by making a snowman. Or snow angels (do you remember how?).

WHERE: In Loveland, east side of Twenty-Ninth Street and Taft, just north of North Lake Park; (800) 551-1752 or (970) 663-2940 (Loveland High Plains Art Council). Or contact the Loveland Parks Department at (970) 962-2727.

WHEN: Daylight hours, year-round. The annual Sculpture in the Park show (juried) is held here in early August.

ACTIVITIES: Strolling, picnicking, photography, outdoor art appreciation.

FACILITIES: Nearby restrooms and playground at North Lake Park.

LAKES, RESERVOIRS, AND WATER PARKS

HORSETOOTH RESERVOIR

Horsetooth Reservoir is one of the most popular outdoor destinations in the Fort Collins vicinity. The reservoir itself is 6.5 miles long and covers over 1,800 acres; there's plenty of water for fishing, boating, and scuba diving. (If you're interested in scuba, check with a certified dive shop. In general, kids must be at least twelve years old. Linda's son Matt had "the best time of my life" during an introductory scuba lesson sponsored by Boulder's Scuba Joe. For more information on scuba, see Activity Resources in Appendix A.)

On the reservoir's south end is Stout, the remains of an old quarry town where you can buy bait, soft drinks, and beer. Traces of quarry activity can still be found on the north end of the reservoir. Horsetooth Reservoir is a good place to boat, dive, fish, camp, or just set up lawn chairs near the water and watch everybody else.

WHERE: On the west edge of Fort Collins. From I-25 north from Denver, turn west on Harmony Road, north onto Taft Hill Road, then west onto County Road 38E, follow 38E to the reservoir; (970) 226-4517 or 679-4570.

WHEN: Year-round; often crowded on warm-weather weekends.

ACTIVITIES: All water sports, fishing, camping, hiking, mountain biking.

FACILITIES: Full-service marina, boat and equipment rentals, food store, pay phone; 180 campsites with toilets, water, picnic tables, and fire grates. Open camping where access allows along shoreline. Off-road-vehicle-use area; hiking, biking, and equestrian trails.

NORTH LAKE PARK

This large lake and surrounding park is in the heart of Loveland. Its view of Longs Peak is magnificent. Sunbathing, swimming, and fishing from the piers are some of the simple pleasures you can indulge in. Several playgrounds, lots of shaded picnic tables and a seasonal miniature train are on North Lake's shores. Also an old one-room schoolhouse (reminding kids how lucky they are to be on vacation today).

If you don't feel like making sandwiches or bringing barbecue fixings, stop at one of the grocery stores or fast-food restaurants along Highway 34 and buy some deli sandwiches or a bucket of chicken.

WHERE: Loveland, 12 miles south of Fort Collins. On the north side of Lake Loveland, off Highway 34 at Taft; (970) 962-2727.

WHEN: Year-round; more activities during summer months.

ACTIVITIES: Swimming, fishing, boating, water skiing; seasonal miniature train.

FACILITIES: Playgrounds, ball fields, restrooms, picnic pavilions, summer snack concessions, swim beach, fishing piers, and plenty of grassy shade.

CRYSTAL RAPIDS WATER PARK

Loveland kids Luke and Adam Mader agree: Of all the things to do in town, they like going to Crystal Rapids Water Park best.

Besides slippery excitement like the Bonsai Bodyslide and the Zoom Flume, there's a wave pool, Adventure Golf, and a playground. Although not nearly as big as Denver's Water World, Crystal Rapids is neither as expensive nor as crowded. It's great fun for young tots and school-age children.

WHERE: In Loveland at 3601 East Eisenhower (Highway 34 1.3 miles west of I-25); (970) 663-1492.

WHEN: Daily from 10 A.M. to 7 P.M. Memorial Day through Labor Day.

ACTIVITIES: Swimming, sliding, water games, miniature golf.

FACILITIES: Restrooms, concessions, some shade (but not much).

BE SURE TO BRING: Waterproof sunscreen and long-sleeved shirts; money for concessions. No glass is allowed in the park.

***

CARTER LAKE

If you like your water on the brisk side, you'll love Carter Lake, nestled in the foothills overlooking the eastern plains. Windsurfing and fishing are popular here, and swimming is allowed in one area—at Dam #2. For sailors and boaters there's a marina where you can rent or moor a boat. Seven campgrounds have nearly 200 sites, issued on a first-come first-served basis. No fires are allowed on the west side of the lake.

WHERE: Southwest of Loveland on Highway 56. Follow the signs from the community of Berthoud; (970) 679-4570.

WHEN: Open year-round.

ACTIVITIES: All water sports, fishing, swim beach, camping.

FACILITIES: Restrooms, water, dump station, full-service marina, rentals.

HORSEBACK RIDING

There are several stables in the Fort Collins–Loveland area where you can rent horses or go on a guided trail ride.

ELLIS RANCH

Activities include horse rides, hay and sleigh rides, wildlife-viewing (elk sightings are guaranteed), petting and feeding farm animals. No overnight lodging. Full catering for on-site western-style parties; live country-western music featuring the Ellis family. Open daily from Memorial Day through Christmas. 2331 Waterdale Drive (west of Loveland off Highway 34); (970) 667-3964.

DOUBLE DIAMOND STABLES

Year-round activities including horseback riding, breakfast and dinner rides, hay and sleigh rides. Within Lory State Park, north of Fort Collins off Highway 287; (970) 224-4200.

ARCHERY RANGE

The Fort Collins Archery Range is on flat wetlands just west of Interstate 25 near the banks of the Cache la Poudre River. For the youngster who needs a challenge, archery is a sport that develops concentration and confidence and is an outdoor activity the family can participate in together. It's a particularly good recreation for older kids and adolescents who enjoy competition and need something more than a nature walk to keep them involved and interested in family activities.

WHERE: East Prospect Road and I-25 Frontage Road, follow the signs 1.5 miles; (970) 221-6640 (Fort Collins City Parks and Recreation).

WHEN: Open daily during daylight hours.

ACTIVITIES: Bow-and-arrow target practice, wildlife-viewing, picnicking.

FACILITIES: Barbecue grills, picnic shelters, restrooms, and river access.

BE SURE TO BRING: Bows and arrows! For instruction and equipment rental and sales, contact Arrow Dynamics Pro Shop, 2538 Midpoint Drive, Fort Collins, (970) 484-4900.

NEVER SUMMER NORDIC YURTS

Just what is a yurt? Linda wondered. A few weeks later she was sleeping in one—a big canvas dome built on a wooden deck. Used for centuries by Mongol nomads as portable homes, the Colorado versions are stationary shelters that can be reserved and rented—kind of like a backcountry Motel 6. (Actually, a Motel 6 might be a little cheaper, though not nearly so romantic.)

Although there are several hut systems in the state for wilderness touring, some are too remote for the average family. But Never Summer Nordic Yurts offers the opportunity to enjoy Colorado backcountry without getting too far off the beaten path. Built in the Colorado State Forest along trails with a very low avalanche risk, three shelters—Grass Creek, Ruby Jewel, and North Fork Canadian Yurt—are private, cozy, and well-maintained. We stayed in Ruby Jewel after a mere two-hour ski from the parking lot and spent a memorable evening making spaghetti, swilling Beaujolais, poking at the fire, and watching the sparks fly.

Grass Creek Yurt is ideal for novice adventurers and families with children: It's less than a mile from the nearest plowed road, with a 120-foot elevation change. All the yurts are popular, so make reservations well in advance. And plan carefully, taking plenty of warm clothing: Frostbite and hypothermia are very real threats. If your family doesn't have much experience cross-country skiing or you don't like camping out when there's two feet of snow on the ground, go in the summer, either by foot or mountain bike.

WHERE: About an hour's drive from Fort Collins, southeast of Walden in the Colorado State Forest; (970) 484-3903.

WHEN: Year-round.

ACTIVITIES: In winter, overnight cross-country skiing, snowshoeing. In summer and fall, mountain biking or hiking. Great wildlife-viewing opportunities all year—including moose near North Fork Canadian Yurt for the lucky! Fees are charged for entrance to Colorado State Forest and for the yurts.

FACILITIES: Private hut lodging with wood-burning stove, propane cookstove, lantern, padded bunks, kitchen, outhouse toilet.

BE SURE TO BRING: Colorado State Forest map, food, water, first-aid kit, and clothing appropriate for the season. In winter, bring extra hats, mittens, and socks for all. Don't forget the Beaujolais!

AREA STATE PARKS AND NATIONAL FORESTS
LORY STATE PARK

If you think state parks are becoming too much like theme parks, you'll like this one. Two thousand acres of forested foothills make Lory one of the best underdeveloped state parks in the region. But don't expect to enjoy it alone—it's a heavily visited area. Hiking and mountain biking are very popular here, as is horseback riding on the more than 25 miles of trails. In winter, these same trails are used for snowshoeing and cross-country skiing. Backcountry, primitive camping is allowed. From Fort Collins, take Highway 287 north through the community of Laporte. Follow signs from the Bellvue exit; (303) 493-1623.

BOYD LAKE STATE PARK

Sunrise over the eastern prairie and sunset behind Longs Peak make this park a beautiful setting for camping or picnicking. There are over 140 campsites and 95 individual picnic tables, some covered. The 1,750-acre lake makes water sports number one. Fishing, paddleboating, windsurfing, sailing, water skiing, jet skiing—you name it and you can do it or rent it at the marina. In the summer you can even buy your lunch (and a beer) at the marina restaurant. Gosh, it hardly sounds like camping! Kids and adults can ride bicycles around the lake and on connecting gravel roads north and south of the park. In the winter, these make good cross-country ski trails. This park is close to the conveniences of Loveland and only about an hour's drive from Denver. One mile east of Loveland, just west of I-25. Follow the signs from Highway 34; (303) 669-1739.

ROOSEVELT NATIONAL FOREST

There are over 200 campsites northwest of Fort Collins near the Poudre River corridor. Most are rather primitive and operate on a first-come, first-served arrangement. For a complete list, contact the U.S. Forest Service at (970) 482-3822, or stop by the Forest Information Center at 1311 South College Avenue in Fort Collins. Two campgrounds have piped water and pit toilets. The first is Mountain Park, 25 miles west of Fort Collins on Highway 14. There are forty-five sites; the Poudre River and a trailhead are its features. The second is Kelly Flats, 26 miles west of Fort Collins on Highway 14. There are twenty-three sites along the Poudre River.

Guest Ranches
Beaver Meadows Guest Ranch

This year-round ranch features cross-country skiing and sleigh rides in the winter, and horseback riding, carriage rides, mountain biking, and fishing during the warm months. There's a kid's fishing pond for young anglers. Cabins and condos with kitchens make this a good choice for those who don't mind doing their own cooking; there is a restaurant and lounge for those who do. Beaver Meadows is 55 miles northwest of Fort Collins. Follow the signs to Red Feather Lakes; (800) 462-5870 or (970) 482-1845.

Sylvan Dale Ranch

Features programs for kids ages five to twelve. Adults can play too, and if they get tired of riding, fishing, and overnight pack trips, they can swim in a heated pool or play tennis. This is one guest ranch that is close to civilization—a prime consideration for those families who have an urge to eat a fast-food taco or go to the mall. The ranch is 7 miles west of Loveland (15 miles south of Fort Collins) on Highway 287; (970) 667-3915.

Outdoor Fairs and Festivals
Larimer County Fair

Good old-fashioned entertainment, much of it free. Early to mid-August at the Larimer County Fairgrounds in Loveland. Follow signs from Highway 287; (970) 679-4512 or 669-6760.

New West Fest

A three-day-weekend outdoor celebration featuring a carnival, magic shows, live music, skateboarding and rollerblading exhibitions, and arts and crafts. Free bicycle parking and shuttle. Mid-August in downtown Fort Collins; (800) 274-3678.

IN CASE OF BAD WEATHER

DISCOVERY CENTER SCIENCE MUSEUM

An interactive learning and fun center for kids of all ages. Tuesday through Saturday from 10 A.M. to 5 P.M., Sunday from noon to 5 P.M. 703 East Prospect, Fort Collins; (970) 493-2182.

EDORA POOL AND ICE CENTER

An impressive indoor pool and ice rink complete with food concessions. One of Fort Collins's Parks and Recreation facilities, this is a great place for your budding hockey player, figure skater, or swimmer to learn more. 1801 Riverside, just south of Prospect Road; (970) 221-6679 or 6683

BOULDER AREA

For many generations the Southern Arapaho tribe wintered in the foothills we now call Boulder, protected by the mountains and the great tilted slabs of sandstone on the Rockies' east face. In 1859, prospectors found gold in the mountain streambeds just 11 miles west of today's city limits. They named the site Gold Hill, and a town sprang up nearby. Chief Niwot and the Arapaho were tolerant of the immigrants who came seeking gold and gave them no trouble. Entrepreneurs followed and built a town on the boulders at the base of the mountains to supply nearby mining operations. Farmers settled nearby, planted crops, and raised livestock.

Today Boulder is a picturesque town, home of the University of Colorado. It's an outdoor-loving, fitness-obsessed town, a place where serious runners, cyclists, and other athletes live and train, and where everyone, it seems, participates in some kind of sport. The multi-use paths and open space parks are filled year-round with cyclists, joggers, walkers, skaters, skiers. The Flatirons —the same sandstone slabs that once protected Niwot's people from winter winds—are now scaled daily by world-class rock climbers. Chief Niwot (or Left Hand, as he was called in English) left his name to the town of Niwot, now nearly engulfed by Boulder's northern edge, and to nearby Left Hand Canyon.

Boulder isn't usually thought of as a vacation spot, but many who call it home wouldn't dream of living anywhere else on earth.

CHAUTAUQUA PARK

Chautauqua Park has been a Boulder favorite since 1898, when an orchard in the foothills became part of the national Chautauqua movement—America's turn-of-the-century renaissance of community culture and education. Neighbors and friends turned out to hear lectures and concerts on summer evenings.

A century later the spirit lives on. During the summer the wooden auditorium hosts a concert series, a film festival, speakers, and various performers, and the old dining hall opens up to serve meals. You can rent a cottage or just walk the trails. Those impressive sandstone formations known as the Flatirons rise out of Chautauqua's backyard, where the meadows are full of prairie grasses, sunflowers, and purple thistles. You can walk for miles along numerous trails that start here. Be sure to stop at the Ranger Cottage for trail maps and advice.

McClintock Nature Trail is great for little people, as well as for big people like us who occasionally like to walk short trails. Pick it up behind the auditorium, or follow the fire road south from the parking lot. This trail is well marked, less than a mile long, and enhanced with interpretive signs.

When Linda's kids were teenagers and too busy for short nature walks with Mom, she'd often hike Chautauqua's trails alone. Once she came across a pack of boys about eight or nine years old who were climbing onto boulders and brandishing big sticks. By their conversation it sounded as if they had become pirates for the afternoon. Linda had a real urge to join them, forgetting for a moment that she was probably older than their mothers, who were undoubtedly having lunch on Chautauqua's veranda or lounging under the shade trees watching college boys throw Frisbees to leaping dogs.

WHERE: In Boulder, south side of Baseline and Ninth. Colorado Chautauqua Association, (303) 442-3282. Chautauqua Ranger Cottage, (303) 441-3408.

WHEN: Year-round; some activities seasonal.

ACTIVITIES: Summer activities include picnicking, concerts, lectures, films, and educational forums. The restaurant is open during the summer months. Year-round hiking, snowshoeing, or cross-country skiing.

FACILITIES: Restrooms, drinking fountain, seasonal restaurant, auditorium, and playground. The parking lot is often full: Street parking can usually be found on Ninth or Tenth Streets.

CAUTIONS: Beware of crossing Baseline Road; there are no crosswalks or traffic lights.

NATIONAL CENTER FOR ATMOSPHERIC RESEARCH (NCAR)

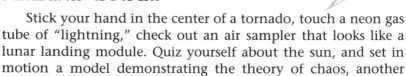

Stick your hand in the center of a tornado, touch a neon gas tube of "lightning," check out an air sampler that looks like a lunar landing module. Quiz yourself about the sun, and set in motion a model demonstrating the theory of chaos, another contributing factor in Colorado's crazy weather.

The National Center for Atmospheric Research is a world-renowned facility dedicated to the study of the atmosphere, climate, weather, and the sun. Scientists from around the globe use the center for research and collaboration. Much of what we know about the ozone layer, for example, comes from the work of researchers here at NCAR.

Besides looking at the learning exhibits, you and your young scientists can browse the library, eat lunch in the cafeteria with the professionals who work here, or take a walk out back along the Walter Orr Roberts Nature Trail. The building itself is an impressive sight; designed by architect I. M. Pei, it seems to rise out of the Flatiron formation as if it were fashioned from the sandstone, a part of the foothills.

NCAR provides an hour or two of indoor/outdoor activity for most families.

WHERE: In the foothills of south Boulder. From South Broadway, take Table Mesa Drive west, following the signs; (303) 497-8601.

WHEN: Year-round from 8 A.M. to 5 P.M. weekdays, 9 A.M. to 3 P.M. on weekends. Guided tours are Wednesdays at noon.

ACTIVITIES: Free tours of the atmosphere- and weather-related exhibits; hiking and picnicking on the nature trail.

FACILITIES: Parking, restrooms, drinking fountain, library, cafeteria; wheelchair- and stroller-accessible Walter Orr Roberts Nature Trail.

BOULDER CREEK PATH

A mountain stream much like any other, Boulder Creek meanders through the city on its way to the plain. But this particular stream is more than a sluice of water: Boulder Creek *is* Boulder, a cross-sectional view of its culture and natural history.

The paved 6-mile-long trail is shaded by old willows and huge cottonwoods too fat to wrap your arms around. A flotilla of teens floating in inner tubes down the creek might bob on by, shouting and squealing. Store clerks and college students sit on rocks, lift their skirts, and cool their feet in the creek. Ten-year-olds chase minnows, their faces streaked with mud. A mother warns, "Jeremy, put that stick down before you poke somebody's eye out!" Helmet-clad young bicyclists pedal by in a wobbling row, reminding one of a family of ducks. In-line skaters speed by in full gear. A mother raccoon and her babies move gracefully along the slippery bank. A shaggy man sleeps in the underbrush, unseen by most.

In addition to following the path, you can take your youngsters to the Kids Fishing Pond behind the Boulder County Justice Center, at the southeast corner of Sixth and Canyon. And from here it's a short walk west along the creek path to Eben G. Fine Park, where you'll find young families, college kids, and postmodern hippies enjoying the day. Follow the north fork in the path under Canyon Boulevard to "Settlers Park" for more picnic and hiking settings. Or follow the creek west up Boulder Canyon until you're tired (it goes for miles). On the east end of the path, behind the Harvest House off Twenty-Eighth Street, is an unusual exhibit that gives us a different perspective on the lives of cutthroat trout and other river creatures. By replacing part of the bank with plexiglass portholes, a sort of aquarium has been constructed. Here you can actually look inside the creek and see the river the way the fish do. (If you're fortunate you might even see some fish; a quarter will buy you a handful of approved food to increase your chances.)

Not just an activity to do once and check off, Boulder Creek is a place to continually discover, a Saturday tradition, a streamside adventure for city families and people of all ages. Teens love it too—though they might prefer to explore it on their own. In any case, Boulder Creek is free, it's fun, and it's Boulder.

WHERE: When school is not in session, you can park at Boulder High School on Arapahoe Road and pick up the path behind the school. Or park anytime at the municipal building on the south side of Canyon Boulevard, between Broadway and Ninth. As you explore the path you'll find your own favorite parking places. For more information, contact the City of Boulder Parks Department at (303) 441-3400.

WHEN: Year-round. Seasonal festivals and activities include the Boulder Creek Festival held late in May and featuring a rubber duck race, a kids' fishing derby, storytelling, a parade, and a community creek cleanup that precedes the annual event.

ACTIVITIES: Walking, biking, skating, fishing, people-watching.

FACILITIES: Restrooms at Eben G. Fine Park at the west end, at the Boulder Public Library, and near Scott Carpenter Park on the east end. Rent bicycles or in-line skates from one of many sporting shops: The Boulder Bikesmith in the Arapaho Village Shopping Center, (303) 443-1132, and University Bicycles Ltd. at 839 Pearl Street, (303) 444-4196, are two suggestions.

PEARL STREET MALL

You can't write about Boulder without writing about the Pearl Street Mall. It's definitely an adventure!

A pedestrian-only shopping district on Pearl Street, the mall is lined with clothing boutiques, art galleries, health food stores, restaurants, beer gardens, bookstores, New Age shops, and more. What makes it more than an outdoor shopping mall are the street performers—dozens of them during the warm months—who play harmonicas, steel drums, banjos, classical guitars, saxophones, mandolins—in hopes you'll toss some money in their hats. You'll see magicians, jugglers, sword swallowers, and mimes, too. Have a pocketful of change ready in case you like the act. Strolling the Pearl Street Mall can be a real social education. Minstrels, college kids, shoppers, tourists, and an entire social stratum of people who make their living asking for money all hang out here. To avoid having your kids beg you for money at every shop, visit on a summer evening after dinner when most of the stores are closed. The entertainers will still be out in full force.

WHERE: Pearl Street is a pedestrian mall running east from Broadway to Fifteenth Street. The easiest way to find it is to turn west on Pearl from Twenty-Eighth Street, the main business thoroughfare through Boulder.

WHEN: Most of the street performers will be found during the late afternoon and evening hours of the summer and autumn months, usually up until Christmas. (Avoid Halloween and University of Colorado football home-game days, when traffic and crowds will detract from the fun.)

ACTIVITIES: Enjoying magicians, musicians, and other street performers. You can also shop, eat, and people-watch.

FACILITIES: There are some public restrooms you can use in a pinch, but if you patronize any of the restaurants you'll have no worries.

BE SURE TO BRING: Layered clothing for the swings in temperature common here. Even if you're not shopping, a handful of change for the performers will be appreciated.

HIKES AND CLIMBS

With more than 100 miles of trails to be found within the city's Mountain Parks and Open Space System, Boulder is indeed a hiker's dream. Many paths are accessible by wheelchair, others are narrow, rocky, and require treaded hiking boots to negotiate safely. If you like to hike and you live in Boulder or are spending a few weeks here, buy the Boulder Open Space Parks and Trails Map, available at most sporting stores that sell guides. Or call the

Open Space Department at (303) 441-3440. If you enjoy ranger-led walks, the city offers them regularly during the summer months. These are great for school-age children and for curious adults who want to learn something while they're burning a few calories. For a schedule contact Open Space Ranger Services at (303) 441-4142.

If those great slabs of rock known as the Flatirons grab your imagination and you or someone in your family has a desire to climb them, you'll want to enroll in a climbing course to learn the necessary skills and safety measures. The Boulder Parks and Recreation Department sponsors classes for a reasonable fee and maintains an indoor practice rock wall at the East Boulder Community Center. This center also hosts an "Adventure Program" featuring rock-climbing, kayaking, skiing, and orienteering courses for teens and adults. For program and registration information, call the East Boulder Community Center at (303) 441-3412; for the indoor climbing wall, call (303) 441-4401.

MESA TRAIL SYSTEM

The Mesa Trail is a 6-mile path that wanders along the face of the foothills south from Chautauqua Park, intersecting with Towhee and Dowdy Draw Trails near Eldorado Springs. It's a great byway for enjoying the views of the mountains and plains, and for discovering the variety of nature found just outside Boulder. The smell of ponderosa pine needles in the sun, the sight of butterflies dancing on wildflowers, the sound of the breeze in the chokecherry thickets, the trickle of small streams over rocks—these are some of the sensory treasures you might find.

Most families won't want to walk the entire 6 miles of Mesa Trail, since that requires a 6-mile hike back (avoid this by having a vehicle waiting at the South Mesa Trailhead off Highway 170 just east of Eldorado Springs). What most of us do is take a shorter loop on one of the minor trails that connect to Mesa: Bluebell-Baird and the McClintock–Enchanted Mesa Trails may be reached at Chautauqua Park. Pick up a trail map and other helpful hints at the Chautauqua Ranger Cottage. From the west side of the station, follow the trail up through Chautauqua Meadow.

WHERE: Take Baseline Road west to Grant Place (one block west of Ninth Street). If the Chautauqua parking lot is full (on the south side of Baseline) you can park on one of the side streets. To access the south end of Mesa Trail, drive south on Broadway and take Colorado 170 toward Eldorado Springs—it's about 2 miles to the parking lot and trailhead.

WHEN: Summer, fall, and winter are best for hiking (it can get pretty muddy by spring). The trail is less crowded on weekdays.

ACTIVITIES: Hiking, mountain biking, snowshoeing.

FACILITIES: Easy to moderate unpaved trails; restrooms and water at trailheads.

BE SURE TO BRING: Water bottles, sun protection, and layered clothing.

CAUTIONS: Lightning is prevalent during the afternoons from late spring through late autumn. Watch the weather closely and hike early in the day to avoid problems.

MOUNT SANITAS TRAIL

Here's a steep 1.2-mile hike that provides an exhilarating hawk's-eye view of Boulder and the plains below. Don't neglect the wonders close at hand, however. If you hike during the midmorning or early afternoon you're likely to see raptors soaring above you. You might also see engineless gliders circling for lift, just like the hawks. If you listen closely you can hear their wings cutting through the air. Underfoot are sedimentary rocks—unlike the igneous varieties you'll find farther west. Deer are probably the most frequently seen wild animal in this area, although coyotes, rabbits, and snakes are not uncommon. Porcupines, wild turkeys—even mountain lions—have been spotted here, though very rarely.

If you're ambitious, get up early and watch the sun rise along the trail. You're in for a real treat, and the only company you'll have is the wildlife.

WHERE: West Mapleton Avenue, just past the hospital on the north side of the road. From here you can also reach Red Rocks Trail, on the south side of the road.

WHEN: Year-round. The trail is less crowded on autumn and winter weekdays.

ACTIVITIES: Hiking, snowshoeing.

FACILITIES: Restrooms at trailhead.

BE SURE TO BRING: Water and sun protection. Wear shoes or boots with good tread.

CAUTIONS: Watch out for slippery sections of trail and afternoon lightning.

MALLORY CAVE

This short, strenuous hike is for rugged kids who like a challenge, and for adults who can keep up. It's 1 mile round-trip from the Walter Orr Roberts and Mesa Trails, behind the NCAR buildings. Head south on Mesa Trail and watch for the Mallory Cave sign; the cave trail leads off to the west. This hike requires scrambling over boulders and scaling a short but sheer slope. We took our sons Adam and Matt when they were adolescents. Though we think they expected a bigger, darker, scarier cave, it was a cave nonetheless. They delighted in racing ahead of their poor struggling parents to get there first.

WHERE: In the Flatirons, the jagged sandstone formations just west of Boulder. Easiest access is from behind NCAR (National Center for Atmospheric Research) at the west end of Table Mesa Drive.

WHEN: Best hiked in summer or fall. Ice and mud in winter and spring could make for slippery footing.

ACTIVITIES: Hiking, about a mile round-trip from NCAR. There is a 700-foot elevation gain.

FACILITIES: Parking and restrooms at NCAR.

BE SURE TO BRING: A flashlight. Wear sturdy shoes or boots with good tread. Water and a small first-aid kit are important, even on short hikes such as this. And a snack, eaten at the cave, will be appreciated.

CAUTIONS: Afternoon lightning is always a danger when hiking in Colorado. Go in the morning, if possible.

FLAGSTAFF MOUNTAIN

Want to climb a mountain but don't think you're ready for a fourteener (what Coloradans call a 14,000-foot peak)? Flagstaff Mountain is a friendly peak that can be climbed and descended in a few hours with minimal preparation. This adventure is particularly suited for older children who don't want to do a boring walk but aren't ready to tackle Longs Peak.

Adolescents can be given directions and allowed to charge ahead. Make plans to meet at the American flag on top. Caution your children about the paved road that zigzags up the mountain and intersects the footpath four times. Follow the trail signs closely and watch out for summer afternoon lightning. Always have a contingency plan in case family members get separated.

If your family doesn't want to walk up Flagstaff, you can drive up, following Baseline Road. At the peak there's a park where you can cook out on a grill, visit the nature center, or enjoy one of the short trails that begin near the parking lot. The view up here is grand, but you won't have it all to yourself. This is a popular spot with visitors and locals alike; so popular that a parking fee has been put into effect for those who don't live in Boulder County. In spite of the heavy usage, we think the trip is worth it.

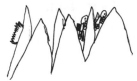

WHERE: Traveling west on Baseline Road in Boulder, cross the stone bridge, and turn off on the dirt road leading to Baird Park where Baseline becomes Flagstaff Road. The Flagstaff trailhead is just to the north.

WHEN: Year-round, but may be too slippery in winter and early spring. To avoid crowds, go on a weekday in the autumn or early winter.

ACTIVITIES: A steep hike about a mile and a half one way (and over 1,000 feet in elevation gain).

FACILITIES: Marked dirt trail to top; paved road for cars. Expect to pay for parking if you're not a Boulder County resident. Nature displays and seasonal programs at the Summit Center amphitheater, picnic tables, water, restrooms, and nature trails.

BE SURE TO BRING: Water bottles, sun protection, and hiking boots with good tread.

CAUTIONS: The trail is steep and slippery in spots, and afternoon lightning is a concern from spring through autumn. We don't recommend riding bicycles up Flagstaff Mountain. The footpath is too steep and the paved road is full of hairpin turns and is heavily traveled by motor vehicles.

Boulder County Parks and Open Space

In addition to the city's parks, Boulder County manages more than 9,000 acres of Open Space parks. Head in any direction from Boulder and you will discover these edge-of-the-city preserves (look for the brown Open Space signs). Consider taking part in one of the Discover Nature walks and lectures. There are also Saturday-morning activities, sunset, and fireside programs throughout the summer and early autumn. Many activities are designed especially for families with young children. For more information about any or all of Boulder's parks, contact the county parks office at (303) 441-3950.

Here are a few of our favorite Open Spaces. All are for day use only.

Wonderland Lake and Foothills Trail

"Hey lady, I just saw a turtle go in the water," said a little boy fishing on the banks of Wonderland Lake. He didn't seem to mind that he hadn't caught any fish. In fact, we're not sure he had any bait. But he was having a great adventure on that August afternoon.

Turtles aren't the only wildlife to be seen here. Ducks, geese, herons, and red-winged blackbirds are common, as are rabbits and deer. There's a 1.5-mile path around the lake, just long enough for a pleasant walk. A longer dirt trail takes off north with access to other biking and hiking routes. The trail is on the north edge of town at 4201 North Broadway (park at Foothills Nature Center).

Betasso Preserve

This beautiful park covering me than 700 acres of partly wooded land is 6 miles west of Boulder, where the town of Orodell once thrived. A general store, post office, and school served the neighboring miners, lumberjacks, and ranchers until the town was partially destroyed by a fire in 1883 and finished off by a flood in 1894. Although it was never rebuilt, you can still see traces of history rusting and rotting in the weeds.

Amateur geologists can examine good specimens of granodiorite, estimated to be 1.7 billion years old—far older than the slabs of sedimentary rock that makes up the Flatirons, a few miles east. This igneous rock is identified by its speckled pink, white, and black appearance. This is the same rock that held (and still holds) veins of gold and tungsten.

Ponderosa pines and Douglas firs are the predominant trees here. Pygmy nuthatches and woodpeckers can be seen or heard in the trees. Abert's squirrels and mule deer are common. Don't let the mountain-lion-warning signs ruin your picnic! Few people have actually seen these cats in the wild, so your chances of seeing one in Betasso Preserve are quite slim. But just to be on the safe side, don't let the kids wander off unattended. Remember—it's the mountain lions' backyard. To get there, go 5 miles west up Boulder Canyon (on Canyon Boulevard) to Sugarloaf Road, turn right, and continue 1.3 miles; turn right again at the water treatment plant sign. From here it's .4-mile to Betasso Preserve.

WALKER RANCH

At one time this park was one of the largest cattle ranches in the region. It was started in 1882 by Jim and Phoebe Walker, a homestead claim to 160 acres in a mountain meadow. By 1959 the Walkers' descendants had increased the size of the ranch to 6,000 acres. The ranch buildings are now being restored by the Boulder County Parks and Open Space Department. Picnicking, fishing, and hiking can be enjoyed at this park, but your best bet is to visit during one of the scheduled historical weekends. These are generally held in the early autumn at the old homestead site and feature demonstrations such as butter churning, blacksmithing, ploughing, old-time baseball games, and the like. A favorite of ours is the old-fashioned storytelling that takes place in the barn. Why not bring an old-fashioned picnic? (Be aware that glass containers are not allowed inside the park.) Drive west on Baseline Road, which becomes Flagstaff Road, to just past the 7-mile marker; watch for signs. The homestead is on the left side of the road. For more information and upcoming-event dates, call the county open space department at (303) 441-3950.

Pools, Springs, and Water Sports

Boulder has five municipal swimming pools to satisfy water lovers—three of these are indoor pools that are open year-round. Looking for something a little different? Try the Eldorado Artesian Springs Pool just south of town. And for those who need a little sand between their toes, there's the Boulder Reservoir, locally referred to as "the Res." With a little imagination, it's Boulder-by-the-Sea.

Boulder Reservoir

This is where our teenage daughter Sarah had her first sailing lesson. We should mention that Sarah's first lesson was also her last, at least for that year. She capsized her Sunfish sailboat countless times in the fickle breezes—nearly as many times as Linda capsized hers.

The reservoir is a great place to get wet, no matter how you do it. It's popular with families, especially those with adolescents. If you want to make your ninth-grader happy, offer to drive her and a carload of her friends to the Res for the afternoon. Or plan to celebrate someone's summer birthday there on the "beach." Bring food to cook on the grill, or money to buy hot dogs and soft drinks. Plan to swim, take a windsurfing or sailing lesson, play volleyball, or just bask in the sun and the sand.

Where: North on Colorado 119 (Diagonal Highway) to Fifty-First Street. Follow the signs north to the reservoir entrance; (303) 441-3468.

When: Memorial Day through Labor Day, day-use only.

Activities: Swimming, sailing, windsurfing, jet skiing, water skiing, fishing, volleyball, picnicking.

Facilities: Swim beach, picnic tables and grills, restrooms and showers, food concessions, marina, boat rentals, and sailing lessons.

BE SURE TO BRING: Folding chairs, swimsuits, towels, sunscreen; food and drinks, or money to buy them.

SCOTT CARPENTER POOL AND PARK

The main summer attraction at this park is the outdoor swimming pool. Right along the Boulder Creek Trail two blocks east of Twenty-Eighth Street, this pool is a favorite among Boulder residents. For a small fee the family can swim, splash, and slide—or shoot curls in the skateboard park. The year-round playground is free, it features rocketships and celestial bodies to climb on.

Bring a picnic and enjoy it in the shade. If you didn't bring a lunch, you can buy a snack at the concession stand or at one of the many grocery stores, cafés, and espresso bars nearby.

WHERE: Thirtieth Street and Arapahoe; (303) 441-3400 or 3427.

WHEN: Pool open Memorial Day through Labor Day with open-swim and adult lap hours (in general, open-swim hours are in the afternoon; call for specifics). Skateboard park is open daily in the afternoons.

ACTIVITIES: Swimming, sliding, picnicking, playing organized team sports, skateboarding. A fee is charged for use of the pool.

FACILITIES: 50-meter outdoor pool, wading pool, slides; large playground and park, shade, restrooms, summer snack bar, skateboard park; easy access to Boulder Creek Trail.

BE SURE TO BRING: Swimsuits and towels; food, or money for the seasonal concession stand.

Eldorado Artesian Springs Pool

In the early part of the 1900s, Eldorado Artesian Springs was a popular resort, drawing thousands of tourists each season to bathe, bask in the high-altitude sunshine, and watch daredevil Ivy Baldwin walk a tightrope 582 feet above the canyon floor. (Today you can watch rock climbers scale the sides of the canyon with just as much bravado.) Sometime during the thirties the hotel burned and a flood destroyed most of the pool. Fifty years later new owners have rejuvenated the facility.

Today the Eldorado Artesian Springs Pool is a great place for a family outing. You won't find too much eye-stinging chlorine in the water, nor will you find too many frivolities to spend your money on. You will find an abundance of shade, picnic tables, a quaint dirt street and stream to explore, and the Eldorado Canyon State Park a short distance away.

Don't expect the water to be toasty warm. These aren't hot springs, they're artesian springs. Their water flows from fountainlike wells deep within the earth.

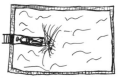

Where: 7 miles south of Boulder on Road 170; (303) 499-1316.

When: Memorial Day through Labor Day, 10 A.M. to 6 P.M. daily.

Activities: Swimming and playing in a 76-degree spring-fed pool. Nearby state park for hiking.

Facilities: Pool, food concessions, picnic facilities.

Be sure to bring: Suits and towels, sunscreen, money for concessions, or your own picnic lunch.

Skiing
North Boulder Park

The very gently sloping North Boulder Park is an excellent place to teach youngsters (or oldsters) the basics of ski touring, otherwise known as cross-country skiing. This is where Bob and Linda practiced our fledgling Nordic techniques—and tried out the brand new skinny skis we got each other for Christmas one year. This would also be an ideal place to snowshoe for the first time.

Mountain Sports is a nearby shop that rents and sells equipment of all sorts, including cross-country skis, and offers free Wednesday-evening clinics on topics ranging from avalanche safety to animal-tracking skills. It's located at 821 Pearl Street; (303) 443-6770.

WHERE: Ninth and Balsam, just west of Boulder Community Hospital. For more information, contact the Boulder Nordic Club at (303) 447-2780.

WHEN: After any good snowfall.

ACTIVITIES: Free cross-country skiing in urban park. Also skate skiing, snowshoeing, or just pulling young ones on sleds.

FACILITIES: Tracks set by Boulder Nordic Club and City of Boulder Parks Department. Parking, restrooms, play area.

BE SURE TO BRING: Your own equipment. Dress in layers, and don't forget a water bottle and a pocketful of snacks.

ELDORA MOUNTAIN RESORT

Eldora is close to many Front Range communities, is less expensive than many of the bigger resorts, and is usually not very crowded. It's a basic, nonpretentious ski area that's popular with Boulderites, Denverites, and other Front Range families. There are no overnight lodges at the base and no power shopping to be done here, just really good skiing when conditions are right, especially after a heavy snow hits the Front Range. Be sure to call about conditions before you set out.

Eldora's Nordic Center maintains 45 kilometers of trails, and its ski school is one of the finest in the state. For a family of experienced cross-country skiers, the Tennessee Mountain Cabin along the Tennessee Mountain Trail (rated difficult) can be reserved for overnight stays.

Although there aren't any fancy gourmet restaurants at the Eldora Mountain Ski Resort, in the afternoon tired parents can enjoy a snack at the Alpenhorn Bar and watch their twelve-year-olds ski until the lifts close. Skiing teenagers may want to go night skiing—generally on Thursday, Friday, and Saturday evenings during peak season.

WHERE: 21 miles west of Boulder via Canyon Boulevard (Highway 119). The resort is 1 mile west of Nederland. Follow the signs; (303) 440-8700.

WHEN: Depending on snowfall. Generally December through April.

ACTIVITIES: Downhill skiing, Nordic center and cross-country trails, snowboarding; night skiing Thursday through Saturday.

FACILITIES: Equipment rentals, instruction, and a designated learn-to-ski area; Nordic center and maintained trails for all abilities; children's center, restaurant, and bar. Half-pipe for snowboarding. Boulder RTD has bus service from Boulder.

HISTORIC GOLD MINING TOWNS

Boulder County has almost one hundred ghost towns and mining camps. Although all that remains of many are just a few overgrown foundations, others have been kept alive and restored. Some aren't ghost towns at all, but rather historic mining districts. If you're into exploring off-the-beaten-track ghost towns, your best bet is to get a guidebook, some good maps, and a four-wheel-drive vehicle. On the other hand, if you just want to get the feel of what a mining town was like in the 1860s, and maybe have lunch or dinner in a historic saloon or inn, take a drive west of Boulder to Gold Hill or Nederland. Summer and autumn are the best times. Don't forget to bring sweaters or jackets.

GOLD HILL

Gold was discovered here in 1859, the first found in this part of Colorado. A town sprang up but burned to the ground in 1860. It was rebuilt the following year, but in 1872 a new Gold Hill was built nearby, closer to the site of a tellurium deposit. Today Gold Hill retains much of its rugged charm. Mining is no longer of any importance, however. This is now a residential town with a few antique shops, a café and general store, and the Gold Hill Inn restaurant to keep it alive. Gold Hill is 11 miles northwest of Boulder, up Sunshine Canyon Drive.

NEDERLAND

Nederland began as a supply town for Caribou, a nearby silver camp. It boomed with the discovery of tungsten, but after its peak in the early part of the twentieth century, the population shrank. Nederland never gave up and died, however. Today it's a great destination drive just 16 miles west of Boulder. There's a lake for fishing east of town. In the small "downtown" strip you'll find several interesting shops and a sometimes-open museum. Be sure to stop at Nature's Own of Nederland, a kind of New Age rock shop. Here you can see (and of course buy) minerals, crystals, fossils, geodes, gemstone jewelry, and toys. There's also an impressive selection of natural history books and field guides. Top off your mining-town visit with a hamburger at one of Nederland's several simple but good restaurants. Nederland is 16 miles west of Boulder by way of Highway 119 (Boulder Creek Road).

IN NEARBY LONGMONT
ST. VRAIN GREENWAY

Here's a real find for families who think Boulder has grown too big and sophisticated: Longmont, just 15 miles north of Boulder, has a developing greenway trail system to rival Boulder's and Denver's—without the traffic! Huge cottonwoods line the paved path with willows and aspen, providing shade for humans and homes for squirrels and jays. Try visiting on a glorious October afternoon when the sun is warm, the air is cool, and those cottonwoods are the color of a bonfire. Or on a morning in late May or early June when the air is full of fluffy white cottonwood seeds drifting on the breeze. Bring a lunch and a fishing pole and tackle box—there are several ponds to fish in, or fish in the St. Vrain River itself.

This is an ideal outing for local families with very small or school-age children. You can spend an hour or all afternoon.

WHERE: 15 miles north of Boulder in Longmont. Take Highway 119 north from Boulder; access and parking off 119 at South Pratt Parkway, or on Hoover Road just north of Boulder County Fairgrounds.

WHEN: Year-round.

ACTIVITIES: Walking, wheeling, biking, skating, cross-country skiing, picnicking, fishing, and urban wildlife-viewing.

FACILITIES: Parking, restrooms, picnic and play areas, pond and stream fishing, wetlands. Near to grocery stores and restaurants.

ROCKY MOUNTAIN PUMPKIN PATCH

Linda is crazy over pumpkins. When she was a kid, pumpkins were a big October ritual at her house, with as much thought given to choosing one at Halloween as was given to picking the family Christmas tree. Linda and her sisters drew the faces and their dad cut them out. She remembers scooping out fistfuls of orange pulp and slippery, slimy seeds; the smell of charred pumpkin and the eerie glow at night from a sputtering candle inside the shell. She remembers eating salted pumpkin seeds and her mother's homemade pumpkin pies—absolutely the best in the world. (She also remembers pumpkin chucking. This sport is performed by high school students at night from moving automobiles and is definitely not a family activity.)

If you're crazy over pumpkins, as Linda is, take your kids to "the Ranch." Besides choosing a pumpkin, picking it off the vine, and hauling it in from the field in an old-fashioned red wagon, you can shop for Halloween costumes, paper skeletons and black cats, wander through Uncle Oscar's Hay Maze, pet compliant farm animals, sip hot cider, and enjoy the sunny Indian summer Colorado's Front Range is famous for.

WHERE: In Longmont, north of Boulder on Highway 66, 2 miles west of Highway 287; (303) 684-0087.

WHEN: Every day from the end of September through October. The exact days may vary with the weather.

ACTIVITIES: Pumpkin picking and other Halloween activities.

FACILITIES: Pumpkin field, wagons to haul the pumpkins in on, amusements, and refreshments to buy.

BE SURE TO BRING: Money for pumpkins and treats. And bring your camera—rosy cheeks, blue October skies, and orange pumpkins make for great pictures.

AREA STATE PARKS AND NATIONAL FORESTS

BARBOUR PONDS STATE RECREATION AREA

Fishing and camping are the main activities here. Swimming is prohibited, and only nonmotorized watercraft are allowed. The park is closed to vehicle traffic during bird-hunting season. This small park has sixty campsites with no electrical hookups. It is close to fast-food stores on Highway 119 but too close to the interstate for some of us. Barbour Ponds is 7 miles east of Longmont on Highway 119, the entrance is just 2 miles west of I-25; (303) 669-1739.

ELDORADO STATE PARK

Here's a place to hike steep trails and learn about wildlife. Experienced rock climbers flock to scale the pointed slabs. (If you're interested in learning more about this sport, stop in at the Eldorado Climbing Shop in Eldorado Springs.) Be sure to check out the visitor center—park rangers have compiled a notebook of trees, animals, and plants found in the park. Kids can look through a box of pinecones, bark, rocks, and bones. Black bears, mountain lions, and rattlesnakes are sometimes spotted, but don't let that scare you off. Learn what to do in case of an encounter, ask for a trail map, and venture forth. Unfortunately, no camping is allowed in this park. Head south out of Boulder on Broadway (Highway 93) to Eldorado Springs, then follow the signs a few miles west; (303) 494-3943.

ROOSEVELT NATIONAL FOREST

Just west of Boulder, the Roosevelt National Forest touches Rocky Mountain National Park and Indian Peaks Wilderness Area to the north and Arapaho National Forest to the south. Like all of Colorado's national forests, this valuable natural resource offers camping, hiking, and wildlife-viewing in remote terrain. Camping here is probably the best way for a family to really experience the great outdoors (it's always been Artie and Matt's favorite Colorado activity). Following are two campgrounds a short drive from Boulder. For a complete list of Roosevelt Forest campsites and information on hiking trails, contact the U.S. Forest Service Boulder Ranger District at (303) 444-6600 or 6601.

Kelly Dahl Campground: Forty-six sites for tents and campers with piped water and vault toilets. A beautiful area, convenient to the small town of Nederland. Open from mid-May to late October. Head 14 miles west of Boulder on Highway 14 to Nederland, then 3 miles south on Highway 119.

Pawnee Campground: On the Brainard Lake Recreation Area, this fifty-five-site campground has drinking water and picnic tables and features hiking, biking, fishing, and nonmotorized boating. Half the sites can be reserved, the others are first-come first-served. Services are reduced after mid-September. Drive 14 miles north of Nederland on Highway 72, then west 5 miles on Brainard Lake Road.

Guest Ranches

Peaceful Valley Lodge and Ranch Resort

This resort is a bit slick for those seeking a no-frills, authentic ranch experience. But if you're looking for organized fun with a family focus, this might be your ideal vacation. In addition to horseback riding, four-wheel-driving, and chuckwagon breakfasts, you'll find some not-so-rugged features like heated pools, spas, and saunas. For the devout, there's a chapel. Depending on your mood and your pocketbook, you can stay in a cabin, a lodge, or a chalet. Weeklong programs are available from April through November, bed & breakfast packages are offered during the off-season. Located about thirty-five minutes northwest of Boulder off Highway 72. 475 Peaceful Valley Road; (303) 747-2881 (Denver Metro number, (303) 440-9632).

Lazy H Guest Ranch

Besides the usual horseback riding, river rafting, fishing, camping, and cookouts, this resort offers country-western dancing and an archery range. Seven-night packages are available, and there is a three-night minimum stay. Choose from rooms or cabins. Children's programs are offered for ages four to twelve. About half an hour's drive northwest of Boulder, off Highway 7 near Allenspark; (303) 747-2532 or (800) 578-3598.

Outdoor Fairs and Festivals

Boulder County Fair

The oldest county fair in the state claims its beginnings in 1869. Activities include a kids' pedal-power tractor pull, rocket shoot, young farmers volleyball, dairy goat milking contest, and more. In early August at the Boulder County Fairgrounds in

Longmont (Nelson and Hover Roads, just north of Highway 119, the Diagonal Highway). (303) 772-7170.

Boulder Creek Festival

Sponsored by the Boulder Parks and Recreation Department, this event has a real family focus. A rubber duckie race down the creek, a kids' fishing contest, live music, free entertainment, and a community volunteer cleanup are traditional events you can take part in. The festival takes place on Memorial Day weekend, along Boulder Creek from Ninth to Eleventh Streets; (303) 441-4420 or 3400.

Colorado Shakespeare Festival

You haven't seen Shakespeare until you've experienced *Macbeth* or *A Midsummer Night's Dream* outdoors, under the stars, with the night wind blowing capes, gowns, and long tresses. Although children under five are not allowed, most adults, older children, and teenagers will enjoy the productions. (If you're not sure, choose a comedy.) Take a picnic dinner to eat on the lawn before the performance. No glass is allowed inside the theater. Performances generally run five nights a week from mid-June through mid-August at the University of Colorado's Mary Rippon Outdoor Theater; (303) 492-0554.

Louisville's Labor Day Festival

Here's real small-town entertainment that'll make you nostalgic for the good old days. Held in Memory Square Park, this festival features such entertainment as a hoops tournament, a street carnival, a country-western street dance, and the annual pet parade. On Labor Day weekend in the community of Louisville, just east of Boulder via South Boulder Road; (303) 673-0613.

In Case of Bad Weather

Boulder Public Library

This is one of the best places anyone can go on a rainy or snowy day in Boulder. Besides books, you'll find a tot's play area and puppet theater, aquariums of fish indigenous to Boulder Creek, a coffee shop, movie presentations, an art gallery, writing workshops for high school students, a library concert series, and more. The Rocky Mountain Storytellers' Guild presents Story Circles one Sunday afternoon a month. Here kids can enjoy the art of storytelling and even tell their own tales. On Arapahoe Road between Broadway and Ninth; (303) 441-3100.

UNIVERSITY OF COLORADO HENDERSON MUSEUM

Excellent natural history exhibits, including insects, dinosaur bones, and fossils. A hands-on corner has everyone touching and feeling—even parents! Free admission and limited free parking seven days a week. University of Colorado Boulder campus, Fifteenth and Broadway; (303) 492-5892.

FISKE PLANETARIUM AND SOMMERS-BAUSCH OBSERVATORY

Don't wait for rain to go to the planetarium—you won't see anything! Go on a clear Friday evening at 7:30 during a scheduled educational program. Afterwards you can go next door and look through the telescopes. Best for school-age kids, teens, and adults. There is a small fee. University of Colorado Boulder campus, Regent Drive; (303) 492-5001.

COLLAGE CHILDREN'S MUSEUM

Tucked away in this obscure spot is an award-winning learning and entertainment center to keep kids busy on a rainy or snowy Saturday. Although designed for preschool- through elementary-school-age kids, adults will find vicarious pleasures here. Linda's favorite toy is the giant soap-bubble maker. The museum is in a building to the east of Boulder's Target store, and north of Crossroads Mall, at 2065 Thirtieth Street; (303) 440-9894.

WILD BIRD CENTER

Here's a store that offers all the basics for wildlife-viewing—binoculars, bird feeders, books—and handfuls of free brochures and checklists. Browse the store and learn about bats and hummingbirds, songbirds and eagles. Sign up for a free bird walk, too.

1641 Twenty-Eighth Street, in the Buffalo Village Shopping Center; (303) 442-1322.

CELESTIAL SEASONINGS

You have to go here just to smell the herbs and teas. (We bet you'll never forget the mint room!) Kids must be at least five years old to go on the free tour. Free tea tasting in the gift shop; bring money and have a light lunch at the cafe. Northeast of Boulder, 4600 Sleepytime Drive (off of Jay Road); (303) 581-1202.

LONGMONT MUSEUM

For a small-town museum, this one is great—especially for kids. Besides looking at historical displays (including one on the space program), parents and kids can make crafts together in the Kid's Corner and play with simple educational toys. At 375 Kimbark in Longmont (between Third and Fourth Streets); (303) 851-8374.

DENVER METROPOLITAN AREA

Denver started out as a campground. In 1859 prospectors set up tents near a longtime Arapaho campsite at the convergence of Cherry Creek and the South Platte River. Surface gold had been discovered farther upstream, with hints of much more to be found in the mountains to the west. The mining camp grew to become an important supply town named after General James W. Denver, a Virginian who had served as governor of the Kansas Territory.

Today the Denver metropolitan area claims nearly two million people, and one of America's youngest populations. Denverites are by and large an active, outdoor-loving people. There are more than two hundred urban parks to play in. Spectator sports are big here too; four major professional sports teams call Denver home. And Denver has more sporting goods stores per resident than any other city in the world.

In Colorado's capital city you can combine sports and outdoor adventures with metropolitan culture. The Art Museum, Denver Center for the Performing Arts, and The Tattered Cover (one of the country's largest privately owned bookstores) are within biking distance of crosstown greenbelt trails. But if you tire of city life, if doesn't take very long to get away from tall buildings and traffic into tall mountains and rushing streams. Not all cities are so easily escaped.

A sort of gold fever lingers in this modern city that over the years has weathered booms and busts in gold, silver, railroads, petroleum, and high-tech industries. There's an optimism in Denver you can feel; a belief that anything can happen, anybody can make good, that no problem is too big to solve (including fixing Denver International Airport's baggage system!). And if you don't find your fortune here in the Mile-High City, you might find yourself.

DENVER'S PROFESSIONAL SPORTS

Denver is one of the few cities in the country with a team in each of the four major professional team sports, and many children follow one or more of them avidly. Taking your kids to see the Broncos, Rockies, Nuggets, or Avalanche is neither cheap nor culturally uplifting, but it's an experience most will enjoy, even if they don't watch the entire game.

A Colorado Rockies baseball game would be our first choice, especially for younger children. Tickets for almost every game are available if purchased a few days in advance (we usually get ours at a King Soopers grocery store) and are moderately priced. Families on a tight budget should consider seats in the center-field bleachers, the "Rockpile"; they're sold on game day only, and tickets for children cost only a dollar. The crowds at Coors Field are enthusiastic but seldom inebriated or obscene (those who are are quickly ejected). The ballpark itself is clean, well designed, and loaded with amenities. And if you get to the park early, there's a chance of talking to a player or getting an autograph or two during batting practice.

If your son or daughter is an avid fan, consider taking a tour of the field or signing up for the Rockies Rookies Kids Fan Club—

membership is only five dollars (in 1996) and includes invitations to a party at Coors Field and a baseball clinic given by members of the Rockies.

Unless your wife's cousin's niece happens to be Pat Bowlen's secretary, it's not easy to get tickets to see the Broncos, but if the opportunity arises, take your children to see them—you'll be a hero. Be aware, however, that the crowds tend to be extremely spirited at a Broncos game, the game itself can be quite intense, and the weather is sometimes unpleasant or worse, so the experience might not be much fun for a younger child.

The Broncos offer tours of their training facility during the season, generally on Tuesday and Friday afternoons. Call for reservations. Practices during the season are all business, so there's no chance to meet the players or get autographs; the best opportunity for this is at the Broncos' training camp in Greeley (see page 13).

If one of your outdoor winter experiences gets weathered out, a Nuggets or Avalanche game might be a fun alternative, especially since smoking was banned at McNichols Arena.

Colorado Rockies Baseball: general information,
     (303) 762-5437; tickets, (800) 388-7625
Denver Broncos Football: (303) 433-7466
Colorado Avalanche Hockey: (303) 893-6700
Denver Nuggets Basketball: (303) 893-6700

Amusement Parks Wet and Dry
Elitch Gardens and Amusement Park

Every Colorado kid we asked named Elitch's as their favorite outdoor activity in the state. Every single one!

After more than one hundred years of delivering family fun, Elitch Gardens outgrew its shady North Denver location. In 1995 it was moved to lower downtown along the Platte River Valley, on 72 acres near Coors Field and Mile High Stadium. We were among those who mourned the move. It'll be many years before the new gardens mature to be as luxurious and beautiful as the old ones were.

"Who cares about flowers?" say the kids, who certainly don't go to Elitch Gardens to smell the roses. They go to be whirled and tossed and plummeted and scared until they squeal and their faces turn green. They go to see and be seen, and to spend their entire allowances on arcade games, greasy pizza, and pink cotton candy.

Older kids and thrill-seeking adults will stand in line to get on more than twenty major rides, including the renowned Twister roller coaster and the Sky Coaster—the closest thing to real free fall we've seen. Clowns on stilts and other performers stroll the park, where new rides are mixed with old favorites. There are eight entertainment stages, and Kiddieland for the tots. All with a magnificent view of Denver's skyline to the east and lofty Mount Evans to the west.

If there's a drawback, it's cost. Call for current prices, but expect to pay about twenty bucks for an adult day ticket. To add insult to injury, no food or drink may be brought into the park. So much for the old-fashioned family picnic. You won't go hungry, however; there are six restaurants and more than twenty food stands and carts to patronize.

The good old days are gone, we guess. But at the new Elitch Gardens Amusement Park, nostalgic parents like us can still ride the same antique carousel that's been entertaining Denverites for years. Linda has dibs on the prancing black horse.

WHERE: Downtown Denver at I-25 and Speer Boulevard, go east about .25-mile; (303) 595-4386.

WHEN: Daily from Memorial Day through Labor Day. Open on weekends during late spring and early autumn.

ACTIVITIES: A major amusement park with fledgling gardens and ongoing entertainment. Special seasonal events, such as a harvest festival in October; call for more information.

FACILITIES: Parking, handicap-accessible restrooms, plenty of food and drinks to buy.

BE SURE TO BRING: More money. Food and drink may not be brought into the park.

HIGHLAND HILLS WATER WORLD

Forty acres of fantastic water rides—we've seen cattle ranches smaller than this! If the only water park you've ever experienced is a dinky little water slide with a turn or two, you're in for some surprises at Water World. Like Thunder Bay, a giant pool with 5-foot waves, and Screamin' Mimi, a water roller coaster. Our teenage son Matt's favorite is a contraption called Journey to the Center of the Earth, involving dark tunnels, speed—and lots of water.

Although school-age kids love Water World, tots may be intimidated by the sheer size and complexity of this amusement park. Parents will surely be intimidated by the cost.

WHERE: Eighty-Eighth and Pecos in the Federal Heights district of north Metro Denver; (303) 427-7873.

WHEN: Memorial Day through Labor Day from 10 A.M. to 7 P.M.

ACTIVITIES: 40 acres of elaborate water rides: huge slides, waves, sleds, chutes, rivers, pools, oceans of water.

FACILITIES: Restrooms and lockers, concessions, picnic pavilions, able to accommodate group parties.

BE SURE TO BRING: Lots of money for admission and snacks. Swim suits, towels, and long-sleeved shirts to wear in the water (they're even better than waterproof sunscreen). Leave alcohol and glass at home.

CAUTIONS: Water World is built on the highest hill in metropolitan Denver. If thunderstorms threaten, leave early.

THE BAY AT BROOMFIELD COMMUNITY PARK

If Water World is too big or too expensive for your tastes, take your little ones to Broomfield's Community Park. Not many community recreation centers boast an outdoor water park like this one. It's got chutes and slides in addition to swimming and wading areas. Best of all, you can't beat the low admission price. Unless you're a resident of Broomfield—and then it's even lower!

WHERE: East Third and Main in Broomfield (from Denver, take I-25 north to Highway 36, then west to Broomfield; (303) 469-5354 or 5351.

WHEN: Daily from Memorial Day through Labor Day.

ACTIVITIES: An outdoor aquatic park with three pools (including a wading pool) and water slides. Geared toward younger children—from infants to preteens.

FACILITIES: Outdoor and indoor pools, recreation center, restrooms, concession stand, lighted tennis courts, softball complex, amphitheater, and fitness trail.

BE SURE TO BRING: Long-sleeved shirts and sunscreen.

SOUTH SHORE WATER PARK

South Shore is South Denver's answer to Water World. Let's face it, most kids love water, slides, rides—and other kids. Throw in some concession stands and an arcade and you have preteen heaven. If you can put up with it for an afternoon—hauling wet towels, dripping coolers, and kids in the back of the car and spending lots of dollars on soft drinks and greasy burgers, think of the fun you'll have. If you live in the South Denver area, consider it for a special occasion: a summer birthday party, or a sixth-grade commencement celebration.

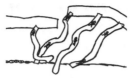

WHERE: Southeast Denver (Englewood), 10750 East Briarwood Avenue, 1 mile east of I-25 at Arapaho and Havana; (303) 649-9875.

WHEN: Memorial Day through Labor Day; after hours for private parties.

ACTIVITIES: Swimming and water rides and slides; volleyball courts.

FACILITIES: Parking, locker rooms, sandy "beaches," Kiddie Island, group shelters, arcade, catering for parties.

BE SURE TO BRING: Suits, towels, sun protection—and money.

LAKESIDE AMUSEMENT PARK

Elitch's disadvantaged cousin, Lakeside is built on the shore of an urban lake in North Denver. Although adolescents will undoubtedly prefer Elitch's, families with small children might choose Lakeside because the general admission is a fraction of Elitch's cost. Once inside, you must buy tickets for each ride. If you take tiny tots who tire quickly, you'll get by for less than ten dollars. Although Lakeside's rides are a bit tame by modern standards, the lines aren't usually long. And right across Sheridan Boulevard is shady Berkeley Park—a great place to watch Lakeside's Fourth of July fireworks.

WHERE: North Denver at 4601 Sheridan Boulevard (just south of I-70); (303) 477-1621.

WHEN: Generally Memorial Day through Labor Day; weekends only in May. Hours vary; call for current information.

ACTIVITIES: Amusement park rides, picnics, private parties.

FACILITIES: Restrooms, concessions, picnic pavilions.

BE SURE TO BRING: A picnic and a pocketful of dollar bills.

HERITAGE SQUARE

Frank climbed the tower with steady knees. Seventy feet below, his mother, Kim, trembled more than he. Would he do it? Would he jump?

The man said "Go," and with only a second's hesitation Frank went. We watched him leap into space, his legs running through thin air like a cartoon figure. Gravity won, Frank fell. It was all over in a heartbeat. The thick elastic bungee cord prevented his impact with the big air mattress beneath him and he bounced up and down like a puppet on a string. Frank had just made his first bungee jump at the ripe age of eleven!

The bungee tower is only one of several thrilling rides at Heritage Square. Also popular is the Alpine Slide—two side-by-side cement troughs that wiggle down the hillside. You take a ski lift up, then ride down the trough on a plastic sled on wheels. (As alpine slides go, this one is rather tame, but many parents and kids love it, including us and ours.) Kids under six can ride for free, but they must ride with a paying adult. Six-year-old Nathan, who was not big enough to bungee-jump (one must weigh at least 75 pounds), was big enough to make his first solo alpine descent.

After all this excitement, mother Kim had enough, but it was only two o'clock in the afternoon and there was still a water slide, a trampoline, bumper cars, and go-carts to play on. In our search for adrenaline we missed the afternoon performance of *The Wizard of Oz* at the Heritage Square Theater, but we found time to souvenir-shop at the Victorian Shopping Village. And time to enjoy our dripping ice cream cones.

WHERE: West of Denver near Golden on U.S. 40 between I-70 and Sixth Avenue; (303) 279-2789.

WHEN: In summer, daily from 10 A.M. to 9 P.M.; in other seasons, Monday through Saturday from 10 A.M. to 6 P.M., Sundays from 12 to 6 P.M.

ACTIVITIES: Bungee jump, alpine slide, water slide, paddle-boats, bumper cars, go-carts, and more. Also kiddie rides, games, hayrides, shopping, children's theater and melodrama productions, Lazy H chuck-wagon suppers, and western shows.

FACILITIES: Free parking, restrooms, restaurants, food concessions, souvenir stores.

BE SURE TO BRING: Money. Admission is free; you pay per ride or activity. Most rides are inexpensive. The bungee jump, however, costs plenty (forty dollars, when we went in 1996). "Bring as much money as you can," six-year-old Nathan advises. "Your kids are gonna need it."

RIVER RAFTING ON CLEAR CREEK

You've always wanted to try it, right? Float down a river like Huck Finn on a raft. If you live in Denver, Clear Creek is your closest river-rafting opportunity. But we wouldn't call it floating; it's more like bobbing, dunking, and splashing.

Clear Creek Rafting Company offers some very short runs to give kids a taste of the sport—before parents commit too much time and money. The Lickety Split trip (minimum age three) and the beginner run (minimum age six) are perfect for tykes. Longer intermediate and advanced trips are popular with teenagers and adults. You can even do an evening trip—a real plus for working parents in the Denver region.

On most excursions you usually have two choices of boat: paddleboats, in which all passengers help by rowing an oar, and oar boats, where all you do is hold on and enjoy the ride. If you're taking a young child, the second option might appeal to you, since you'll be using all your strength to hang onto your squirming child. You'll be glad for a professional to do important things, like steer the raft.

Older kids, teens, and adults will most likely want to be part of the paddling experience says John Rice of Clear Creek Rafting Company. "The effort of paddling together is a big part of it. It's a team thing, it's part of the fun."

Rafting's season is spring through fall, conditions permitting, but the best time for beginners is usually July, when the spring snowmelt has run off and the water is usually sufficiently high but manageable.

"We handle just about everything," says John. "But don't forget to bring dry clothes—including shoes and socks—for the ride home!"

WHERE: Clear Creek Rafting office at Heritage Square, 18301 West Colfax Avenue, Building U-3, Golden; (303) 277-9900.

WHEN: Generally from late May through early September. Season may be longer or shorter depending on water levels.

ACTIVITIES: Rafting on several of Colorado's rivers; experiences for all abilities.

FACILITIES: Appropriate-size life vests and helmets are provided. Clear Creek Rafting has much experience teaching kids to raft safely.

BE SURE TO BRING: Polypropylene or wool clothes will help keep you warm, even when wet. On a cloudy day, or a day early in the season, this could be important. In any case, bring dry clothes to change into for the ride home.

WILDLIFE-VIEWING
DENVER ZOO

Our nieces Elinor and Alanna liked the zebras the best. Until they saw the hyena. And then it was the lions. It's easy to be fickle at the zoo! On a weekday afternoon in early autumn it's an ideal place for a family outing.

We hadn't been in years—since our own kids were little—and we found quite a few changes. The Tropical Discovery exhibit was new to us. The humid 45-foot glass pyramid is filled with thousands of tropical plants and exotic animals—beautiful blue but poisonous frogs, beetles the size of small turtles, and neon green snakes (harmless, unless you're a tropical mouse). The Primate Panorama is a 5-acre natural habitat for everyone's favorites—monkeys, apes, and other shirttail relations.

Most important, we discovered that modern zoos don't just cage animals up and charge you money to look at them. Modern zoos work to save endangered species and habitats through education and research. The snow leopard, the Siberian tiger, the black rhino, the Siamese crocodile, and the Komodo dragon are all threatened species represented at the Denver Zoo.

The zoo offers free days to Denver residents several times a year. If you can afford to take your family to the zoo (kids under four are free) you should avoid free days because they're very crowded and parking is nearly impossible. Weekdays during the fall, winter, and spring are the least-crowded times. Be sure to rent a wagon by the main entrance if you have children under six. Even big four-year-olds eventually get tired of walking.

WHERE: 2300 Steele Street and Twenty-Third Avenue at City Park; (303) 331-4111.

WHEN: Open daily from 10 A.M. to 5 P.M.

ACTIVITIES: The Denver Zoo hosts many educational programs as well as pure entertainment—summer outdoor concerts featuring local and nationally recognized performers, and a winter holiday lights display. Call for current information.

FACILITIES: Handicap-accessible restrooms, wheelchairs and wagons for rent; picnic tables, pavilions for parties, food concessions.

BE SURE TO BRING: Extra money for snacks, drinks, and souvenirs. Wear comfortable walking shoes and dress in layers.

BUTTERFLY PAVILION AND INSECT CENTER

Imagine walking into a lush tropical garden with hundreds of butterflies all around you. Some are easy to see. Big and brilliantly colored, they land on your shirt and your hair, thinking you're a flower. Others are tiny or are camouflaged under leaves, and it takes a curious child stooping down to find them.

A stroll through the butterfly pavilion would be worth the price of admission alone. But wait—there's more. An insect room houses live specimens of some of the world's largest and strangest bugs. When we visited, a volunteer let willing onlookers hold a tarantula. Most kids were eager to do this. After making sure everyone else in the room had their chance, Linda gingerly held out her own hand. This spider (like most tarantulas, she learned) was docile toward human beings. It sat quietly in Linda's palm, its furry legs soft against her fingers. In fact, it felt much like holding a kitten.

Outside the pavilion is a large garden featuring indigenous wildflowers. This part of the facility was still being developed when we visited, with a short nature trail in progress. If you go in the summer or early autumn you'll be able to enjoy not only the wildflowers but Colorado's own butterflies and other insects who live in the gardens.

The gift shop has a variety of interesting souvenirs for all pocketbooks, from butterfly feeders to plastic scorpions. The book section is particularly good; Linda couldn't resist the *Handbook for Butterfly Watchers* by Robert Michael Pyle. There are dozens of children's books, coloring books, and serious field guides covering just about the entire Arthropoda phylum!

Our teenage son Matt had this to say about the pavilion: "Girls seem to love it; it's a great place to go on a date." Make a date with your family—it's something everyone will enjoy.

WHERE: 6252 West 104th Avenue (Highway 36 and 104th Avenue); (303) 469-5441.

WHEN: Tuesday through Sunday, 9 A.M. to 5 P.M.

ACTIVITIES: See (and sometimes feel!) live butterflies and insects. A fee is charged. Special programs and presentations by entomologists and other experts at no additional cost. (Examples are Butterfly Gardening With Children and Colorado Spiders.) Call for a schedule.

FACILITIES: Walk-through butterfly habitat, picnic area, gift and book store, restrooms, snack concession. A nature walk is being developed.

ROCKY MOUNTAIN ARSENAL NATIONAL WILDLIFE REFUGE

East of Denver there's a piece of land 27 square miles in size that was once the site of a chemical weapons facility and later a pesticide-manufacturing plant. Over the last decade it's been cleaned up and reclaimed and is now, once again, home to mule deer, coyotes, jackrabbits, reintroduced bald eagles, and hundreds of other indigenous species. (So far there have been no reports of two-headed animals.) If you want to see the wonders of reclaiming a chemical waste dump, sign up for one of the weekend tours on a double-decker bus. However, don't count on seeing too many animals at close range. Bring binoculars, a pen and notepad to record what you see and learn, and plan on spending between one and two hours. This activity is best for -

schoolchidren and adults with a reasonable attention span—and a strong interest in reclaiming the environment.

WHERE: Quebec and Seventy-Second Avenue near Commerce City; (303) 289-0232.

WHEN: Weekends, year-round; Saturday morning and Sunday afternoon, usually. Reservations are required.

ACTIVITIES: Free guided bus tours and special events such as full-moon hikes, nature films, eagle-viewing. Call for upcoming activities, and to reserve your spot.

FACILITIES: 27 square miles of cleaned-up chemical dumping grounds—an encouraging experiment in environmental reclamation. Nature center, eagle observation point, double-decker buses.

BE SURE TO BRING: Binoculars and a notebook—and a few Snickers bars in the pocket.

PLAINS CONSERVATION CENTER

Pronghorn antelope, badgers, coyotes, and swift foxes are some of the mammals you might see—if you're lucky—on a trip to this unique conservation center. Even the unlucky will surely see black-tailed prairie dogs, thirteen-lined ground squirrels, or at least a western harvest mouse. (Did you even know there were such important-sounding rodents living in east Aurora?)

Wagon rides and full-moon walks are regular events here, featuring bonfires, marshmallow roasts, and informative talks. Also fun are Haunted Prairie—an outdoor Halloween party for nature lovers—Pioneer Christmas, and other seasonal happenings.

Local scout troops are highly involved with the Plains Conservation Center, but many activities are open to the public by reservation. If you live in Denver, you might want to join this nonprofit organization and take advantage of reduced prices for all activities and receive a newsletter of upcoming events. It's a great way to get the family involved in conservation and have some outdoor fun.

WHERE: 21901 East Hampden Avenue in Aurora; (303) 693-3621.

WHEN: Year-round for special events. No drop-in visitors; call to register for upcoming activities.

ACTIVITIES: An opportunity to learn about the wildlife of the eastern Colorado grasslands through guided tours and educational programs.

FACILITIES: 1,900 acres of prairie on the edge of town, visitor center, restrooms.

BE SURE TO BRING: Sun protection for daytime activities, an extra sweater for moonlight walks.

LOOKOUT MOUNTAIN NATURE CENTER

Did you know that the flowers of the yucca plant open at night and can only be pollinated by the pronuba moth? Just as we were pondering the improbability of this, we saw a speckled fawn and a doe walking through the pines just ahead of us. As many times as we've seen deer, we're still surprised by their delicate grace and their awareness. We stood still for minutes while they grazed and nibbled, stopping frequently to look around. Voices farther up the trail caused them to run, or should we say "spring" away. Three leaps and they were gone.

If you're not fortunate enough to see deer, you'll likely see Abert's squirrels, chipmunks, cottontails, Steller's jays, magpies, nuthatches, and hummingbirds. And if you go during the warm months you'll learn to identify grasses and wildflowers. Purple gayfeathers, Oregon grapes, parsley and pasqueflowers, junegrass and larkspur. If you live nearby, go every season and watch the wildlife change.

WHERE: West of Denver and Golden; 910 Colorow Road on Lookout Mountain. Take I-70 west to Exit 256; follow signs to the nature center. For an interesting drive, on your way back continue down the Lookout Mountain Road and you will end up in Golden at Sixth Avenue and Nineteenth Street; (303) 526-0594.

WHEN: Nature center open Tuesday through Sunday from 10 A.M. to 4 P.M.; trails are open every day. Call to find out about after-school activities for children ages five to ten and guided weekend nature walks and programs.

ACTIVITIES: Educational nature displays, independent or guided wildlife-viewing, interpretive nature trail, scheduled programs. Donations are appreciated.

FACILITIES: Visitor center, restrooms, picnic area, interpretive trail; handicap-accessible, but trails exceed minimum grade.

BE SURE TO BRING: A picnic lunch and a light jacket—even in July it can get chilly up here when the sun goes behind a cloud. Plan enough time to make several unscheduled stops on Lookout Mountain to watch hang gliders and slope soarers who catch warm updrafts and circle like colorful hawks.

DENVER BOTANIC GARDENS

If you're a new parent or grandparent looking for a beautiful place to push a baby carriage, this is it. If you have older children who are interested in planting seeds and making crafts, check out the ongoing Saturday activity programs. These drop-in half-day events are called Kidding Around and feature family projects like making planters, birdhouses, kites, and the like. I recommend getting involved with these structured activities rather than just walking through looking at flowers. First of all, if you come in the winter or early spring, you'll likely be disappointed. Except for the greenhouse of tropical plants, about all you'll see in bloom then are the alpine tundra plants. (When we went in May there still weren't many blossoms—Denver had been knee-deep in a spring snowstorm two weeks before.) High-spirited, rambunctious tykes won't appreciate being forced to march on walkways and just look.

WHERE: Central Denver at 1005 York Street; (303) 331-4000.

WHEN: Daily, year-round; special evening entertainment, events, and educational programs. Call for current schedule.

ACTIVITIES: The Kidding Around program featuring gardening and make-it-and-take-it craft projects. Strolling, picnicking, and summer evening outdoor concerts.

FACILITIES: Outdoor and indoor handicap-accessible gardens (including a Japanese tea garden), restrooms, classrooms, library, gift shop, picnic areas, and pavilions; the Chatfield Arboretum at 9201 South Carr Street in Littleton.

DINOSAURS! A VISIT TO DINOSAUR RIDGE

Dinosaur Ridge is a spine of sedimentary rock about 3.5 miles long between I-70 and the town of Morrison to the south. Important discoveries have been made on this ridge, beginning in 1877 when Arthur Lakes first found bones from what would prove to be an apatosaurus. In 1937, when Alameda Parkway was being built, iguanodon and some ostrichlike tracks were discovered, then in 1992 more tracks were found. In 1989 the Friends of Dinosaur Ridge formed—a nonprofit group to protect the ridge and further develop it as an educational park.

Before going to see the dinosaur bones and tracks, stop at the Morrison Natural History Museum to brush up on your geologic time scales and such (501 Highway 8, on the south edge of Morrison; (303) 697-1873). Be sure to check out the very interesting dinosaur egg exhibit. Watch a video previewing the history of Dinosaur Ridge, then watch your little ones dig in a sand pit and "discover" real fossils. Or try your hand at the tedious job of removing a dinosaur bone from the rock its been embedded in for the last fifty million years or so. By the way, volunteers are always needed, not only to chip away at rock but also to help with exhibits and educational programs. What a great way for the family to learn more about the dinosaurs that once roamed the area around Interstate 70.

If you have an extra hour, stop at the nearby "point of geologic interest" at the junction of I-70 and Highway 26. This road cut provides a half-mile interpretive trail on which you can learn to appreciate the different layers of rock—and discover life-forms that lived during that period. It kind of makes your head spin to know that in half an hour you've just walked through twenty million years of earth history! It's the closest thing we've got to a time machine.

The best way to see and understand the tracks, bones, and microfossils along Dinosaur Ridge is to visit on one of the Open Ridge Days. One Saturday a month from April through October Alameda Parkway is closed to traffic and guided tours are given. This activity is free if you walk the 2-mile round-trip trail, or you can pay a small fee to walk halfway and ride the bus back. Either way, it's a much safer way to view the ridge because the road shoulders are very narrow and there are few safe places to pull off.

WHERE: West of Denver on Alameda Parkway (Highway 26) just north of Morrison and directly east of the Red Rocks Park entrance; (303) 697-DINO.

WHEN: Self-guided trail open year-round, or take part in a guided tour during Open Ridge Days—one Saturday a month from April through October.

Activities: Viewing fossils, dinosaur tracks, and points of geologic interest. The iguanodon tracks are the most spectacular and can be viewed from the road.

Facilities: Parking, interpretive signs, restrooms.

Be sure to bring: A book on dinosaurs appropriate for your child's age.

Red Rocks Park and Amphitheater

If your idea of outdoor adventure is to listen to Ozzie Osborn under the stars with the lights of Denver spread like a constellation at your feet, you'll be in heavy metal heaven at Red Rocks. If Ozzie's tunes aren't to your liking, you can also hear the likes of the Moody Blues, Bonnie Raitt, Herbie Hancock, Willie Nelson, or the Denver Symphony Orchestra at this famous natural amphitheater. This is one outdoor activity most teenagers can really appreciate; the hard part will be convincing them to let you come along!

Drawbacks to Red Rocks performances include the high cost of tickets, additional parking fees, waiting in line for what seems to be as long as the concert itself, and sometimes witnessing folks who have abused one sort of chemical substance or another (although if you go to see the Denver Symphony this is much less likely). For these reasons an outdoor concert at Red Rocks may not be your idea of a family activity, but it can be an adventure, of sorts. The challenges include deciding on an entertainer both you and your kids enjoy—and finding your vehicle after the concert is over.

Where: West of Denver near Morrison. From I-70, take Exit 259 south toward Morrison and follow signs to park entrance; (303) 575-2637.

When: Open year-round for hiking and picnicking; seasonal amphitheater performances and Easter sunrise service.

ACTIVITIES: Best known for outdoor musical performances in the spectacular amphitheater. Free day use includes picnicking, biking, and hiking on several trails. Camping and climbing on rocks are prohibited.

FACILITIES: Amphitheater, restrooms, and concession stands open before and during scheduled performances. Trails, picnic facilities, and restrooms for day use.

BE SURE TO BRING: For concerts, bring a picnic dinner, nonalcoholic drinks in plastic containers, a cushion or old pillow to make the stone benches a little more comfortable, and extra sweatshirts or jackets.

DRAG RACING AT BANDEMIER SPEEDWAY

Linda spent one Memorial Day weekend sunburned and hoarse, cheering her seventeen-year-old daughter, Mindy, as she raced her '68 Chevelle in Bandemier's yearly High School Drags. Before you recoil in horror let us assure you, it's safer than cruising around town. Helmets and seatbelts are required, as is a safety inspection of the vehicle. Best of all, the drivers have the road to themselves.

The young contestants put a lot of work into their cars and their time trials. You'll groan out loud when one of them "red lights" or jumps the gun. And you'll cheer a smooth-running classic car that makes a good run—especially when that competitor is your own teenage daughter!

Spectators can buy a seat in the grandstand or pay extra to get into the pits to check out the cars a little more closely.

WHERE: Near Morrson off Highway C-470 between Alameda and Morrison Road; (303) 697-4870 or 6001.

WHEN: Scheduled weekend and some weekday events from late spring through fall; call for a schedule.

ACTIVITIES: Watching or participating in drag racing, professional and amateur. The annual High School Drags are on Memorial Day weekend.

FACILITIES: Open bleachers, restrooms, food concessions, souvenirs.

BE SURE TO BRING: Sun protection—hats, sunscreen, long-sleeved shirts. Ear protection is advised. And unless you want to spend a fortune on drinks, bring plastic water bottles.

THE PHOENIX MINE

If you have school-age youngsters who are rock collectors or get As in earth science class, they'll probably enjoy a tour of the Phoenix Mine. Not a museum or a trumped-up Hollywood set, Phoenix is a real gold mine still in operation in west Idaho Springs. A professional gives the tour: Ours was led by a female miner.

Although the hour-long tour may exceed the attention spans of some, it's never boring. You're inside a mountain and you get to wear a hard hat and even wield a pick, hammer, or chisel if you want to. You can touch cool, damp veins of ore (they aren't pure gold, but they contain gold), and after the tour you can try your luck at gold-panning in a real stream—not in a tub of sand the way some places do it. You can even keep what you find, but we must warn you—the only gold we saw was in the aspen leaves. However, there were enough of them to make us all a little richer.

WHERE: 30 miles west of Denver and 1 mile west of Idaho Springs, on the south side of I-70 at Exit 239; (303) 567-0422.

WHEN: Daily from 10 A.M. to 5 P.M. You might want to catch gold fever and visit the mine during Gold Rush Days, an Idaho Springs celebration held one weekend a year, usually in mid-July.

ACTIVITIES: Tour of a working underground gold and silver mine, panning for gold in a mountain stream.

FACILITIES: Parking, restrooms, picnic tables, gift shop.

BE SURE TO BRING: Jackets or sweaters for the cool underground temperatures. Wear hard shoes, not open-toe sandals (you might trip on a rock in the dark). Bring mittens to warm up small hands after panning for gold in the mountain stream. Don't forget something to eat, or treat the family to lunch at a café in Idaho Springs.

GEORGETOWN NARROW-GAUGE RAILROAD

Even if you're not a railroad buff, a ride on the Georgetown is an adventure. The most exciting part is crossing Devil's Gate Bridge 100 feet above Clear Creek. Parents will hold their little ones a little tighter and everyone will breathe a little faster. The bridge is a replica of the original built in the 1880s, an engineering marvel for its time.

During the nineteenth century narrow-gauge railroads were commonly used in the steep mountainous areas of Colorado. Since the builders had to use more ties laid closer together to accommodate the steep grade, material costs were controlled by making the tracks narrower; therefore, each tie could be significantly shorter. You can learn this, and lots more, on the ride.

There are several historic narrow-gauge trains in the state, but Georgetown's is the closest to Denver. For many families it's the best experience because of its short length. At just over an hour, the round-trip ride is not long enough for anyone to get fidgety or bored. In one direction the conductor gives a running commentary as he points out old mine sites, bridges, and other highlights. You can learn quite a bit about local history, geography, geology—even economics—by paying attention. Halfway through, the train stops at one of its two depots for about ten minutes to move the engine to face the other direction. At this point you can get off and use the restroom, or you can watch as the engine is turned around. On the return trip the engineer rests his voice and you're left to enjoy the sights and sounds.

At a little over an hour, a round-trip ride on the Georgetown Narrow-Gauge Railroad doesn't allow much room for boredom.

In mid-September, when we rode, the aspens and sumacs were putting on a colorful show. The air was crisp enough in the open cars to make Linda wish she'd brought a warm cap in addition to her light jacket.

A class of middle-schoolers seemed to be having as much fun as two toddlers riding with their mothers. An elderly man was captivated; he recorded everything on a camcorder and questioned the engineer about fuel consumption, horsepower, and other technical stuff. What we most enjoyed was the sensory experience—the rattling, rolling, puffing, and creaking, the singing wheels and shrill whistle blasts, the smell of diesel and pine needles, the cold air and warm sunshine. Our only regret was not bringing any kids along.

If your family really enjoys the Georgetown–Silver Plume Railroad, consider one of Colorado's longer historic train rides. For more information, see Railroads in Appendix A.

WHERE: Georgetown Station Headquarters. Take Exit 228 off I-70, go south on Fifteenth Street to 1106 Rose Street; (303) 569-2403 or 670-1686 in the Denver area. When you purchase your ticket you will get directions to the nearby boarding area 2. Or purchase your ticket and get on at the Silver Plume Station (boarding area 1). It's 2 miles west on I-70, off Exit 226.

WHEN: Daily from late May through early October. Generally six round-trips a day, rain or shine.

ACTIVITIES: An hour-and-ten-minute train ride in open cars. One covered car is available.

FACILITIES: Wheelchair accessible. Also gift shops, restrooms, and drinking fountains at both terminal depots, and a café at the Georgetown Depot. Three runs a day serve food for an additional charge.

BE SURE TO BRING: Extra sweaters, at least. Close-fitting caps and even mittens might be appreciated due to the altitude (over 9,000 feet at the highest point). The ride isn't long, but a snack is fun to eat along the way. Or sign up for the breakfast, brunch, or afternoon-tea runs.

YEAR-ROUND SKIING AT KIDSLOPE

Put away the snowsuits and put on the shorts. Your kids can learn to ski on a gentle slope in the heart of Denver—on a warm day in July! KidSlope, a PSIA (Professional Ski Instructors of America) certified ski school, is the only year-round artificially surfaced ski hill in the country. Skills are taught based on PSIA guidelines, and instructors are experts with children. Just imagine, you don't have to bundle up the family, drive into the mountains, spend a lot of money, and maybe find out little Katie hates snow and would far prefer to be inside reading a book. If, on the other hand, she discovers she loves to ski, your next visit to a snowy mountain resort will probably be a lot more fun because she'll be confident she has mastered the basics of skiing.

WHERE: Downtown Denver at the Children's Museum; take Exit 211 (Twenty-Third Avenue) off I-25 and follow the signs; (303) 433-7444.

WHEN: Year-round, days and hours vary.

ACTIVITIES: Ski lessons for children age four and older on a slope covered with artificial snow. (It's plastic!) Reservations are required. A special program for disabled kids is also offered.

FACILITIES: Artificial ski slope, equipment, and certified instructors. Packages available that include KidSlope lessons and discount lift tickets at various Colorado ski resorts.

BE SURE TO: Call well in advance for reservations.

ICE SKATING

Outdoor ice skating is an old-fashioned form of winter fun your kids may have seen on Currier and Ives Christmas cards or read about in *Hans Brinker*. In the heart of winter, if temperatures have stayed below freezing long enough, you can sometimes find good outdoor skating near Denver. Here are two places you can go.

EVERGREEN LAKE

As soon as it freezes over—often by Christmas—this mountain lake is open every afternoon and evening, weather permitting. There's a snack bar, and skates to rent for a small fee. Go west on I-70 to the El Rancho exit, then 8 miles southwest on Highway 74, following the signs to Evergreen Lake; (303) 674-2677.

CHATFIELD STATE RECREATION AREA

Winter is a great time of year to have fun at this state park in southwest Denver; you'll miss the crowds. There aren't any rentals, though, so bring your own ice skates, hockey sticks, and other equipment. (Don't forget a thermos of hot chocolate.) Drive 15 miles southwest of Denver on Wadsworth, then south on Colorado 121, following the signs; (303) 791-7275.

METRO DENVER'S GREENWAYS AND URBAN PARKS

Dozens of parks dot Denver's map. Big, small, medium-size, some with lakes and some just a scrap of grass and a playground. All are designed for day use only, and most have restroom facilities, drinking fountains, and a paved path for wheeling, jogging, biking, or in-line skating. After a heavy snowfall these same parks are perfect places for city folks to try out their snowshoes and cross-country skis or to gather the neighborhood kids, build snow forts, and have snowball battles. If you live in Denver your favorite park is likely the one closest to your own backyard. Here are our favorites.

WASHINGTON PARK

Known as Wash Park among the locals, this central park is a popular place to jog, skate, picnic, and play volleyball. It's also a fine place to fish or watch ducks on the lake. At 701 South Franklin; (303) 964-2500.

SLOAN LAKE

People come to Sloan to fish, water-ski, play soccer, and walk or jog around the path. On summer weekends big family picnics are popular. The lake is formed from a natural artesian well. If you didn't bring a picnic you'll find grocery stores and fast-food restaurants just across Sheridan Boulevard between Twenty-Third Avenue and West Seventeenth. The park is just north of St. Anthony Central Hospital; (303) 964-2500.

DEL MAR PARK

A recreation center and swimming pool are the main draws, but there are enough grassy acres here to throw Frisbees and balls as hard as you can. Or just let the kids run wild. A wheelchair-friendly playground is another one of this park's notable features. In Aurora at Sixth and Peoria; (303) 695-7200.

MATTHEWS PARK

A Jefferson County Open Space Park, Matthews is less than a twenty-minute drive from downtown Denver. Its location in the foothills makes it a great getaway for city dwellers. Hiking and mountain-biking trails, a stream for creekside picnicking, and the remains of a townsite add interest to this park. Other nearby interests include the I-70 road cut and Dinosaur Ridge. West of Denver at I-70 and Highway 26, just south of the interstate; (303) 271-5925.

PLATTE RIVER GREENWAY

More than 20 miles of paved path, and still in progress. On the greenway in downtown Denver you'll cruise by Mile High Stadium, Elitch Gardens, Coors Field, and enjoy views of the Denver skyline and majestic Mount Evans. Be sure to stop at Confluence Park, where the South Platte and Cherry Creek meet, because this is where Denver began. What once was an Arapaho camp became a prospector's tent city, followed by a settlement. Today outdoor summer concerts are performed in the small park. And there's a kayak course on the South Platte beginning just above the actual confluence. In the spring and early summer it's fun to watch the experts compete. Or sign up for lessons at Rapid Adventures Kayak School, 1537 Platte Street, a block away; (303) 433-3676.

As you bisect Denver on this multi-use path, don't be surprised to see homeless people setting up camp under viaducts and trees. Be prepared for questions from your youngsters; it's a good opportunity for a family discussion on social issues. The greenway goes from Chatfield Reservoir to Confluence Park, and is in the process of being extended farther north. First-time users may want to begin walking at the Children's Museum near Confluence Park, I-25 and Fifteenth Street; (303) 698-1322.

CLEAR CREEK GREENWAY

This trail is one of Denver's best-kept secrets. Just ask Linda's kids, who spent many days during their adolescences exploring it. You might see muskrats, raccoons, beavers, and foxes. Wetland birds are frequently spotted, and songbirds are plentiful. It's a good place to cruise along on a bike or throw a stick for your dog to chase. This greenway follows Clear Creek through the community of Wheat Ridge from Kipling to Wadsworth; eventually it will connect with Platte River Greenway. There are parking, restrooms, and playgrounds at the Albert E. Anderson Park in Wheat Ridge, by the Recreation Center on Forty-Fourth Avenue, between Wadsworth and Kipling. You can also begin from Johnson Park on the west side of Wadsworth just south of I-70; (303) 235-2877.

AREA STATE PARKS AND NATIONAL FORESTS
GOLDEN GATE CANYON STATE PARK

There are over 160 campsites here on more than 10,000 acres of forests and meadows, much of it designated backcountry. You'll find excellent geology and ecology exhibits at the visitor center to supplement your excursion. This is a quiet park, without the whining of outboard engines, jet skis, and model airplanes that fill the air of some state parks. The 60 miles of hiking trails and 30 miles of biking trails make Golden Gate one of the best places to explore backcountry near the Denver area. The park is 30 miles east of Denver, near Golden; follow the signs from Highway 93; (303) 592-1502.

BARR LAKE STATE PARK

People come to this reservoir and wildlife sanctuary primarily to fish and observe birds. The nature center hosts regular programs, many designed just for kids. A 9-mile trail goes around the lake—a good bike ride or an ambitious walk in the spring or fall, or a tour on skis after a big snow. No swimming or motorized boats are allowed on the lake, which maintains a quiet environment for the bird sanctuary. Birds are the big attraction at Barr: Geese, herons, cormorants, owls, and bald eagles are frequently seen. Be sure to bring sun protection any time of year and insect repellent during the warm months. Day use only. Barr Lake is 25 miles from Denver; from I-25 take I-76 northeast; (303) 659-6005.

CHATFIELD RESERVOIR STATE RECREATION AREA

This is an immensely popular park that offers something for everyone. You can swim, fish, boat, and participate in any water sport you can think of here with the facilities of a full-service marina. Camping is available from April 15 to October 15 at over 150 sites. Walking, bicycling, mountain biking, and horseback riding on more than 25 miles of trails should keep any family busy for more than one visit. You can rent horses during the warm months from B & B Livery, a park concession. Opportunities to study nature are plentiful with guided nature walks and evening programs when staffing permits. The heronry here is of interest to bird-watchers, but no humans allowed during nesting season! Winter fun includes cross-country skiing, ice skating, and ice fishing, but bring your own equipment. If you don't like all that nature stuff, check out the model airplane runway or rent a jet ski. The area is 15 miles southwest of Denver. Take Wadsworth Boulevard to Colorado 121 south; (303) 791-7275.

CHERRY CREEK RESERVOIR STATE RECREATION AREA

This popular park features water sports and has a full-service marina. Swimming is permitted at the artificial beach. Fishing access and picnic areas designed to accommodate wheelchairs are thoughtfully provided here. There are 10 miles of riding trails and a year-round stable to provide the horses. For naturalists there's the obligatory nature trail—this one is 1.5 miles long. More unusual is the prairie dog observation area, the rifle range and trap area, and a model airplane field. Over one hundred campsites are available from late spring through early autumn.

For winter-sport lovers there's ice skating and ice fishing on the frozen Cherry Creek Reservoir. Take I-225 to Parker Road, then go south about 1.5 miles to the east entrance; the west entrance is off South Yosemite Street; (303) 699-3860.

ROXBOROUGH STATE PARK

A day-use-only park, Roxborough showcases nature. The striking sandstone rock formations that typify the region are interesting to rockhounds and photographers alike. The wildlife to be encountered here is diverse, since both prairie and foothills ecologic zones are represented. Watch for prairie falcons, golden eagles, kestrels, and other birds of prey. And look down at your feet for bull snakes, hognose snakes, garter snakes—and possibly rattlesnakes. There's an interesting visitor center that hosts nature programs, most geared toward families with young children. The park is 15 miles southwest of Denver via Highway 85; (303) 973-3959.

CASTLEWOOD CANYON STATE PARK

Another day-use-only park, this one is ideal for picnicking, hiking, boulder climbing, or cross-country skiing after a heavy snow. There are over 800 acres of piñon- and juniper-studded canyon country. A visitor center with educational displays is open year-round and features guided hikes during warm-weather months. No off-road bicycling is permitted. Castlewood is 30 miles south of Denver on Highway 83; (303) 688-5242.

PIKE NATIONAL FOREST

Several good Forest Service campgrounds can be found in the Devil's Thumb region near Sedalia, 10 miles south of Littleton on Highway 85. If you live in Denver, this is a convenient place to go weekend camping. For more information, call the regional Forest Service office at (303) 236-7386.

FLAT ROCKS

From Sedalia, drive 10 miles west on Highway 67 and 4.8 miles south on Forest Service Road 300. There are twenty-two sites here for tents and small motor homes, with piped water and pit toilets.

DEVIL'S HEAD

Continue past Flat Rocks about 4.3 miles, then head .4-mile southeast on Forest Service Road 3008C. Here are another twenty-two sites for tents and small motor homes, with piped water and pit toilets. A big rock formation called Devil's Head is a short but steep hike away. You can also hike to the only staffed fire lookout station in Colorado.

☀OUTDOOR FAIRS AND FESTIVALS

ADAMS COUNTY FAIR AND RODEO

Billed as Colorado's largest county fair, this one features free admission and a special Kid's Day. There's a small fee for parking, and an opportunity to spend lots of money once you are admitted. In early August at the fairgrounds on 124th Avenue and Highway 85; (303) 659-3666.

THE PEOPLE'S FAIR

Arts, crafts, free entertainment, and activities for children. Pay to park, and expect crowds. Bring strollers for young children, water bottles, and money for extras. Wear comfortable walking shoes and bring jackets—it's probably going to be a long walk back to the car. In early June in Civic Center Park. Follow the signs from Speer Boulevard and Colfax; (303) 830-1651.

A TASTE OF COLORADO

Blocks of free outdoor entertainment of all kinds, much of it specifically for kids. There's a catch—the food is not free. You buy tickets and then use the tickets to sample food from dozens of Colorado chefs. Pay to park, and expect crowds. Bring strollers for young children, water bottles, jackets, and money for food. It's delicious! On Labor Day weekend in Civic Center Park. Follow the signs from Speer Boulevard and Colfax; (303) 534-6161.

CINCO DE MAYO

Six blocks of Santa Fe Drive become one big outdoor Mexican heritage celebration. It's very colorful—great food and music. Bring money for parking and for treats. Don't forget sunscreen, hats, and jackets. A May day in Colorado can start out warm and end up snowing! The first weekend nearest May 5. Hasta luego! (303) 534-8342.

GOLD RUSH DAYS

A mid-July weekend of rodeos, a parade, mining demonstrations, and children's games. Most events are free. West of Denver, in Idaho Springs; (303) 567-2079.

HIWAN HOMESTEAD'S MOUNTAIN RENDEZVOUS

A free August festival commemorating the days of fur trapping and trading. Donations are appreciated. For more information, contact Hiwan Homestead Museum just west of Denver in Evergreen; (303) 674-6262.

CIDER DAYS HARVEST FESTIVAL

An October weekend of entertainment, kids activities, and demonstrations at Lakewood's historical Belmar Village, 797 South Wadsworth Boulevard; (303) 987-7850. Donations are appreciated.

IN CASE OF BAD WEATHER

In a city the size of Denver it isn't hard to find indoor activities. Here are a few of our favorites.

DENVER MUSEUM OF NATURAL HISTORY

The excellent exhibits include lifelike ecological dioramas, rocks, minerals, and fossils. Dinosaurs are featured in a $7.7-million walk-through exhibit (complete with sound and light effects) called Prehistoric Journey. You needn't wait for a rainy day to visit this museum! The IMAX Theater and Gates Planetarium are located here too. Open daily from 9 A.M. to 5 P.M., except December 25. A fee is charged. All three venues can be crowded on weekends and school holidays. At 2001 Colorado Boulevard; (303) 322-7009.

DENVER ART MUSEUM

Free family workshops are offered every first and third Saturday. Besides a guided tour of some of the exhibits, your kids can make their own works of art, inspired by what they've seen. Alternate Saturdays feature backpacks to be checked out: The packs are full of games, guides, and activities to enhance your visit. A section called the Kids Corner is always open with all the materials and instructions to make something—a mask, a hat, a plate. In downtown Denver at Fourteenth Avenue and Bannock Street; (303) 640-4433 or 839-4812.

CHILDREN'S MUSEUM

Centrally located near Mile High Stadium and along the Platte River Greenway, this huge learning-made-fun complex is fun for adults too. ("Come on Bob, we have to go—they're locking the doors on us!") Little kids will also enjoy a short ride on the Platte River Trolley that runs a short distance along the Platte River and Trail in the museum's backyard. Park in the same place for both activities. At 2121 Crescent Drive. Take the Twenty-Third Street exit from I-25 and look for the small sign; (303) 433-7444.

FORNEY TRANSPORTATION MUSEUM

Here's an unusual collection of cars and trains in a dusty old warehouse. As fun to explore as Uncle Albert's barn. Free parking. At 1416 Platte Street, take Exit 211 from I-25 just northeast of the Children's Museum; (303) 433-3643.

YOUNG AMERICANS BANK

Here your kids can tour a bank, look inside the safe, start their very own checking and savings accounts—even apply for a loan! The bank's innovative summer program, Young Ameri-Towne, features a week-long day camp where kids run an entire "town" on the second floor. At 311 Steele Street, Cherry Creek; (303) 394-4357.

COLORADO SCHOOL OF MINES GEOLOGY MUSEUM

This free museum should be a priority for any family of rock and mineral collectors or paleontology buffs. There's also a good exhibit about gold mining. In Golden at Sixteenth and Maple; (303) 273-3815.

CASA BONITA

There's no redeeming educational value here at all—it's just outrageous entertainment in a restaurant setting. Practically a Denver landmark, Casa Bonita and its food has gotten better over the years. But you don't really go there for the food. You go there to watch the melodramatic stage shows, to listen to the strolling mariachi band sing "Aye-yi-yi-yi" at your table, surrounded by delightfully fake palm trees. And where else in Colorado can you watch high divers plunge more than a story into a tiny pool of water—while you sit there eating a tostada? If this isn't enough to put the kids into sensory overload, then turn them loose in the arcade room while you enjoy a cold cerveza. At 6715 West Colfax Avenue (look for the pink tower in a small shopping center); (303) 232-5115.

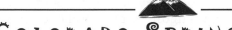

COLORADO SPRINGS AREA

Drive to Colorado Springs from nearly any direction and the first thing you see is Pikes Peak. On a clear day you can see it from Denver, 70 miles north. Colorado Springs grew up in the protective shadow of this 14,110-foot mountain that once was an anticipated landmark for wagon trains traveling across the plains.

The Ute knew the mountain's lower slopes intimately, but the Peak was named for Lieutenant Zebulon Pike, a military explorer who, in 1806, failed to reach its summit (and voiced his doubt that it could be done by anyone). But where there's a will there's a way, as the saying goes. In the decades to follow a number of men climbed it, and in 1858 Julia Holmes became the first woman to reach the summit. In 1895 Katherine Lee Bates, an English professor, was inspired to write a poem while riding to the top of Pikes Peak along the new carriage road. Soon after, it was set to the music of Samuel Ward and titled "America the Beautiful." Today you can drive to the parking lot at the top of Pikes Peak in your own car, for a fee. You can also ride to the top in a train, or you can bike or hike your way up the side. So much for Zebulon Pike's prediction.

Sprawling at the base of Pikes Peak, Colorado Springs was designed by railroad magnate William Jackson Palmer in the 1870s as a retreat for the wealthy. In 1918 the famous Broadmoor Hotel was built there, and by the early twentieth century Colorado Springs had become the richest city in the United States.

During World War II the character of the city changed when it became a center for military operations with the building of Fort Carson, Peterson Air Force Base, and, later, the North American Aerospace Defense Command (NORAD). In the midfifties Colorado Springs was chosen as the site for the United States Air Force Academy, and more recently as site for the Consolidated Space Operations Center.

The military isn't the only game in town; tourism brings in a lot of money as well. From the spectacular to the contrived, there is plenty to spend your vacation money on in and around Colorado Springs. You can find an attraction for just about any interest you can imagine: obscure coins, giant South American insects, costumes of famous figure skaters, saddles cowboys have known and loved, mining picks and pans, dead presidents, prefab ghost towns, relocated ruins, waterfalls with elevators, and outdoor light shows on canyon walls. There's everything here but WallyWorld, it seems.

On the other hand, if you're looking to discover some simple outdoor fun in and around Colorado Springs, don't despair. Beyond the commercialization, there's a bit of unspoiled nature left in the shadow of Pikes Peak.

GARDEN OF THE GODS

This is our favorite place in Colorado Springs, and we are not alone in our admiration. Go there on any summer afternoon and you'll see busloads of tourists from all over the world, come to enjoy the views. Twisted, sculpted blocks and spires of sandstone—red, pink, and orange-and-brown—resemble the work of some gargantuan imaginative artist. Geologists tell us the rock was formed 300 million years ago, eroded by the elements over the eons, and is still in the process of change. The sculptures are not yet finished.

To drive through the park is breathtaking. But don't settle for just a drive. The first thing your kids will want to do, of course, is climb the rocks. Sorry, you are not allowed—unless you are an experienced climber and get permission from the visitor center. If someone in the family is seriously inspired, check into a rock-climbing course through the Colorado Springs Parks and Recreation Department, or a school in your own hometown.

But you don't need a permit to walk the nature trails, bike the paved roads, or have a picnic out of the back of your car. You can also explore the park on horseback—nearby Academy Stables offers guided trail rides. Whether you walk, bike, or ride, be sure to stop at the visitor center for trail maps and to see some good displays, like samples of rocks you can pick up and examine. We liked the road sign out front that said the Atlantic Ocean lies 1,774 miles to the east. We felt like we could practically see it, the air was so clear and dry.

If you have kids ages six to eleven who like a structured challenge, ask for the Junior Explorer Activity Guide. It's a seek-and-find quiz designed to be completed with Mom, Dad, or Uncle Bob on an afternoon's visit. It involves watching a short video and taking an interpretive walk, keeping eyes open for answers to questions in the guide. Upon its successful completion, junior explorers are awarded certificates and badges in a small ceremony at the visitor's center.

The park can be very crowded during summer afternoons with see-America tour groups and motor homes the size of army tanks. Beat the noise and exhaust fumes by going in the late fall, when the juniper berries are ripe, the air is brisk, and the scrub oak turns the color of wine. Or better yet, go in midwinter, when the strange rocks look like decorated gingerbread men dusted with powdered snow.

WHERE: In northwest Colorado Springs; exit on Garden of the Gods Road from I-25 or from Highway 24 and follow the signs to the park; (719) 634-6666.

WHEN: Daily, year-round, from 5 A.M. to 11 P.M. The park is usually most crowded during weekends in warm weather. It is seldom crowded at sunset, and even less crowded at sunrise.

ACTIVITIES: Sight-seeing, hiking, horseback riding, picnicking. There is a nearby living history museum, the White House Ranch Historical Site, at Thirtieth Street, the east entrance to the park; (719) 578-6777. Entrance to the park is free; a fee is charged for the museum.

FACILITIES: Free parking, picnic areas, restrooms, visitor center, museum, educational programs, short nature trails, gift shop, and seasonal café. No camping in the park, but Garden of the Gods Campground is not far away.

BE SURE TO BRING: Sturdy shoes for walking, lunch, or money to buy it at the Trading Post Cafe, open from May to September.

UNITED STATES AIR FORCE ACADEMY AND HIKING TRAILS

The U.S. Air Force Academy, a training center for future officers, is one of Colorado's most visited attractions. Even if you don't have a cousin, niece, or nephew who's a cadet, a visit to this breathtaking 18,000-acre campus might be an activity your family would appreciate.

Call in advance to find out about upcoming events that are open to the public. These include daily guided tours of the facility, parades, drills and dress reviews, monthly planetarium programs, and occasional military aircraft and skydiving demonstrations. All activities are free of charge.

If you want to enjoy the outdoors, one of the best things you can do is take a hike on one of several trails that cross Academy land. The Falcon Trail, a 12-mile loop, is maintained by Boy Scout Troop 78. Stanley Canyon Trail begins near the parking area west of the Air Force Hospital. It's a steep and in some places rocky 2-mile climb with a 1,200-foot elevation gain. The New Santa Fe Regional Trail runs 14 miles between Palmer Lake in the town of Monument to the southern border of the Air Force Academy. This path is fairly level and is excellent for mountain bikers. You can get printed information and maps for all these trails by asking at the visitor center.

WHERE: From I-25, take Exit 156B and follow the signs to the visitor center; (719) 472-2555.

WHEN: The visitor center is open daily from 9 A.M. to 5 P.M. Hiking trails are open for use from dawn to dusk. Other activities as scheduled. For more information, call (719) 472-2555. For planetarium schedule call (719) 472-2778.

ACTIVITIES: Sight-seeing, flight and skydiving demonstrations, educational programs, hiking, and biking.

FACILITIES: Visitor center, museum, gift shop, snack bar, chapel, maintained trails, restrooms, picnic units.

BE SURE TO BRING: If exploring the trails, get a map from the visitor center. Don't forget good hiking shoes or boots, water, a snack, sun protection, and a small first-aid kit (and bike repair kit, if you will be pedaling). Be aware of the dangers of lightning, and know what to do to avoid it.

UNITED STATES OLYMPIC COMPLEX

"Quitters never win—and winners never quit." That's the thought-provoking maxim our guide left us with after an inspiring tour of the complex, home of the U.S. Olympic Committee and training center for Olympics-bound amateur athletes. Besides first-rate gymnasiums, courts, and coaches, participants can take advantage of the newest advances and technologies in training methods, sports physiology, psychology, and medicine.

The free tour lasts about an hour, not counting the exhilarating twenty-minute video shown beforehand. We all kept our eyes open for Olympians but saw few. Unfortunately for us, no competitions were scheduled for the day we visited, just after the 1996 Summer Olympics. If you want to see athletes in action, call ahead for a schedule of upcoming competitions and plan your visit accordingly.

The kids in our group seemed interested throughout the entire tour. As a memento, our guide took pictures of them individually, in front of the Olympic Rings, with a gold medal around their necks.

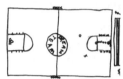

WHERE: Northwest corner of Boulder and Union. Follow the signs from I-25; (719) 578-4618. Tour hotline: (719) 578-4644.

WHEN: Daily tours, Monday through Saturday from 9 A.M. to 4 P.M., Sunday from 12 to 4 P.M. Open until 5 P.M. during the summer months. Tours begin every hour.

ACTIVITIES: A video presentation followed by a one-hour tour of the training center. Selected competitions are open to spectators. Activities are free, but donations are appreciated.

FACILITIES: Visitor center, spectator areas, restrooms, gift shop.

BE SURE TO BRING: Good walking shoes, sun protection, and layered clothing. The tour involves a good bit of walking and standing, indoors and out.

URBAN PARKS AND GREENWAYS
RAMPART PARK AND BMX COURSE

Rampart Park, with its truly spectacular view of Pikes Peak, is a small residential park best known for its ball fields and its excellent BMX track. BMX, bicycle motocross, might be described as off-road racing on nonmotorized vehicles. If you're old enough to ride a bike (or still young enough to), you can participate. Use of the course is open to the public at no charge except during scheduled races, when visitors are welcome to watch. Races are sponsored by Pikes Peak BMX, a nonprofit organization run by local parents for participating kids and adults.

WHERE: Northeast Colorado Springs at Lexington and Research Parkway; (719) 578-6640 (city parks and recreation).

WHEN: Park open year-round during daylight hours. The racing season is May through October, and races are generally scheduled on weekends.

ACTIVITIES: Bicycle motocross races sanctioned by the American Bicycle Association. Otherwise open to public for practice.

FACILITIES: Track with starting gate; also nearby restrooms, water fountain, and playground.

BE SURE TO BRING: Your own bike and required helmet. Also, there's not much shade, so bring sunscreen. Spectators, don't forget sunglasses and hats!

MEMORIAL PARK

A picnic at this city park goes hand in hand with a visit to the nearby Olympic Complex. Budding gymnasts can practice their cartwheels in the grass. In the summertime kids can work on their synchronized swim routine at Prospect Lake. You can walk, jog, or wheel around the perimeter path or just kick back and enjoy a lazy afternoon with a beautiful view of Pikes Peak.

WHERE: Pikes Peak Avenue and Union Boulevard. Take the Bijou exit east from I-25, follow the signs to the park; (719) 578-6640 (city parks department).

WHEN: Daily from 5 A.M. to 9 P.M., and until 11 P.M. May through November.

ACTIVITIES: Strolling, picnicking, in-line skating, tennis, swimming, boating, fishing, playing.

FACILITIES: Indoor/outdoor recreation center with restrooms, playground, and fishing docks (all are handicap accessible), picnic tables, tennis courts, paved trail, swim beach, boat rental, and a nearby velodrome for Olympic cyclists and skaters with grandstand seats for the public.

MONUMENT VALLEY TRAIL

This trail and park system runs north and south near I-25 along Monument Creek. We had fun just walking a section of trail near Bijou Street watching people pushing strollers and baby joggers and kids on bicycles breezing by in the warm afternoon. We left the path to explore the creek and saw two boys digging in the trickle of water. Maybe they were looking for crystals of selenite (a transparent form of gypsum), found in the streambeds of Fountain and Monument Creeks.

WHERE: Follows Monument Creek through the city; eventually to extend from Rampart Reservoir (north) to North Cheyenne Canyon (south). First-time users should take I-25 Exit 142 or 143 (Bijou or Uintah Streets) and go east to Cascade, where you'll find a grassy park with trail access; (719) 578-6640 (parks department).

WHEN: Year-round, dawn till dusk.

ACTIVITIES: Walking, jogging, biking, picnicking; cross-country skiing after heavy snowfall.

FACILITIES: Maintained trail that is part pavement, part gravel. Restrooms, water, playground, pool, and tennis courts at Monument Valley Park.

BEAR CREEK NATURE CENTER

A gurgling brook, the melodies of songbirds, the rustling of leaves—it sounds like a New Age relaxation tape. But the sounds were real enough, and on that peaceful Monday in September Linda had the Nature Center all to herself.

This park and nature center on the outskirts of the city is a delightful place to spend an afternoon outdoors. A short songbird trail that easily accommodates wheelchairs and strollers is a perfect beginning. Yarrow, camomile, and purple asters grow alongside the path in profusion. Bird feeders along the way entice the likes of rufous-sided towhees, whose call, according to the interpretive sign, sounds like *"drink, drink, drink your tea."*

Other trails are the Mountain Scrub Loop and the Creek Bottom Loop; both are less than a mile long. Coyote Gulch is slightly longer, at 1.2 miles. An energetic family can do them all in one afternoon. Look for the box that holds the trail maps, and return them when you're finished.

Besides songbirds, you might see mule deer, raccoons, weasels, coyotes—possibly even a black bear! Look for box turtles and toads near the creek. Snakes such as garter, hognose, and bull often seek out the warmth of a sunny rock unless it's hot, then they will more likely be in the shade of tall grasses.

Inside the nature center's education building you can learn more about the animals you've seen. Ask the naturalist on duty any questions you might have when you're browsing the exhibits. Bird-watchers, pick up a checklist before you begin your walk.

The nature center is part of Bear Creek Canyon Regional Park, covering more than 1,200 acres of foothills. There's also an equestrian center for those who have their own mounts, an archery range, and a fitness course. If you're visiting Colorado Springs, take a picnic lunch and spend the day. If you live in the area, consider it your backyard.

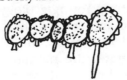

WHERE: Just south of Gold Camp Road and Twenty-First Street. Follow signs from Highway 24 west; (719) 471-5437 or 520-6387.

WHEN: Park and trails open year-round during daylight hours. The Educational building is open Tuesday through Saturday from 9 A.M. to 4 P.M.

ACTIVITIES: Guided or on-your-own nature walks, picnics, wildlife-watching. Nearby tennis, archery, horseback-riding facilities.

FACILITIES: Restrooms, water, and telephones at the educational building. Access to a larger park system, including nearby playgrounds, riding arena, tennis courts, archery range. Day use only.

BE SURE TO BRING: A picnic lunch and binoculars, a pen and notepad to record observations and impressions, dry socks and shoes in case someone "accidentally" steps in the stream.

NORTH CHEYENNE CANON PARK

The air cools noticeably as you drive up into the southeast foothills of Pikes Peak. On a hot summer day in Colorado Springs it's a welcome relief to put on a sweater before getting out of the car.

North Cheyenne Canon Park is a perfect place for an impromptu picnic; you'll find lots of creekside sites just off the winding mountain road. With a little more planning you can take a hike on one of several trails from 1 to 5 miles in length. Stop at the Starsmore Discovery Center at the junction of North and South Cheyenne Canon Roads for trail maps.

Plan to spend some time looking at the exhibits at this nature center. A hummingbird garden, a bird-watching station with binoculars, and an indoor climbing wall for kids make this facility particularly interesting. Young geology buffs will find a large selection of rocks and minerals with magnifying glasses and guidebooks to aid in identification. An exhibit entitled Anatomy of a Canyon demonstrates the natural forces at work here in Cheyenne Canon. Pun lovers will appreciate headings such as

"Whose fault is it?" and "Don't take it for granite." You might want to bring money to buy a book—there's a great selection of field guides, books about Colorado's history, natural history, and indigenous peoples for sale at Starsmore Discovery Center.

If you live in the area or are spending a few weeks here, make reservations to take part in one of many nature programs, guided hikes, and other activities designed with families in mind. The Colorado Springs Parks and Recreation Department has a real winner here!

WHERE: 2120 South Cheyenne Canon Road (just south of the junction of North and South Cheyenne Canon Roads); (719) 578-6146 (Starsmore Discovery Center) or 578-6640 (parks department).

WHEN: Starsmore Discovery Center open Sunday from 12 to 4 P.M., Monday through Wednesday from 10 A.M. to 4 P.M. The park is open during daylight hours year-round.

ACTIVITIES: Picnicking, hiking, and educational family activities. Some trails are off-limits to bicyclists, and those that aren't are best for skilled riders.

FACILITIES: Visitor centers at either end of the park have restrooms, telephones, and drinking fountains. There are several maintained trails and picnic facilities throughout the park.

BE SURE TO BRING: Warm clothes to wear in a layered fashion, water bottles, sturdy shoes with good tread for hiking. Don't forget snacks or a picnic lunch.

PIKES PEAK BY BIKE

You'd have to be in pretty good shape to bicycle to the top of a 14,000-foot mountain like Pikes Peak. It's not exactly an activity for your average family. But any kid age ten or older who can ride a bike might enjoy the long ride down the mountain. Challenge Unlimited offers a Pikes Peak downhill biking tour twice a day during the summer. Although moderately expensive by our standards, the company provides practically everything you need: transportation to the top, your picture at the summit, a guided tour down—and FOOD (which you'll consume ravenously in the cold thin air). If you drive your own vehicle up the mountain you have to pay a significant toll, not to mention gas—all in all, Challenge Unlimited's deal is pretty reasonable. And you won't have to worry about your car overheating or burning out the brakes on the way down.

Consider signing up for a morning run. Although you have to get up awfully early (your adventure starts at 6 A.M.!), the chance of your tour being canceled due to afternoon thunderstorms is far less likely. The morning tour costs about twenty dollars more than the afternoon tour, but it includes a full breakfast and lunch, instead of a snack.

WHERE: Challenge Unlimited is located at 204 South Twenty-Fourth Street; (800) 798-5954 or (719) 633-6399.

WHEN: Tours twice daily from June through August, weather permitting. In May, September, and October there is one tour a day, weather permitting. Reservations are a must, because this is a popular tour. June is generally the best month to participate.

ACTIVITIES: A 9-mile guided bike tour down Pikes Peak—a 14,110-foot mountain. (The operative word here is "down.") Kids must be at least ten years old. Other, shorter tours in the Colorado Springs area can also be arranged.

FACILITIES: All equipment, food and beverages, transportation, photos on the summit, walkie-talkies, and rain gear are provided; videos of your ride can be arranged.

BE SURE TO BRING: Your own water bottle, sunscreen, gloves, hat, and layers of clothes. Although the guides provide some of these items in case you come unprepared, it's smart to have your own. A pocketful of candy bars is also a good idea.

PIKES PEAK COG RAILWAY

Another way to see Pikes Peak is by rail—on the highest railroad in the United States. Powered by steam, the first train made it to the top of the mountain in 1891. Today diesel engines pull covered cars up and back in about three hours, including a short stop on top. Trains depart four times a day during the summer months and operate from May through October. Reservations are necessary.

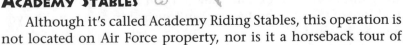

WHERE: 515 Ruxton Avenue in Manitou Springs, just west of Colorado Springs via Highway 24; (719) 685-5401.

WHEN: Daily from May through October. Four departures a day during the summer. During May and early June, however, snow may keep the train from reaching the summit.

ACTIVITIES: A three-hour round-trip train ride up Pikes Peak.

FACILITIES: Restrooms, gift and food concessions at the depot and at the summit.

BE SURE TO BRING: Warm clothes for the summit—even in July!

HORSEBACK RIDING
ACADEMY STABLES

Although it's called Academy Riding Stables, this operation is not located on Air Force property, nor is it a horseback tour of the Air Force Academy. Academy Riding Stables leads guided trail rides through the Garden of the Gods park. It's a fun way to see expansive views of the city and plains and to follow trails that wind through strange-shaped groups of rocks with imaginative names like Siamese Twins, Toad and Toadstools, and Weeping Indian. This is a good ride for inexperienced equestrians at least eight years old who don't mind riding single file while listening to a cowboy talk about local natural history and lore.

WHERE: 4 El Paso Boulevard, just north of Highway 24 near Garden of the Gods park; (719) 633-5667.

WHEN: Year-round, weather permitting. Reservations are required.

ACTIVITIES: Guided one-, two- or three-hour leisurely trail rides. One person per horse, must be at least eight years old and weigh less than 250 pounds. Families with members too young or too heavy to ride might inquire about the seasonal stagecoach and wagon rides.

FACILITIES: Uses Garden of the Gods park trails and facilities.

THE BROADMOOR STABLES

Chocolate, Sticks, and Tony Two-Feathers—those are the names of the ponies and the guide who took our nieces for a ride at the Broadmoor Stables when they were just knee-high to a horse. Although Elinor and Alanna were only five and three years old, they had a wonderful time.

"It was the highlight of their visit to the Broadmoor," says their mother. "The horses and ponies are well taken care of, and the guides were wonderful. They tell you a lot about the history and lore of the area, and we weren't rushed in and out, like you are at a lot of stables."

Adults and older kids will want to go on a longer trail ride up the mountain. Here the family might want to split up: Kids too young for the trail ride can have their own guide take them on a customized pony ride around the stables and paddock. Then there's a tepee to check out and farm animals to see.

Although Broadmoor Hotel guests frequent these stables, you don't have to be staying at the elegant hotel to ride here. (However, if you can afford to, we would highly recommend it. It's one of only eight American resorts to be awarded a Mobil five-star rating, combining elegance and atmosphere with excellent service.)

The stables are just a short drive west of the Broadmoor resort up the side of Cheyenne Mountain, where the air is crisp and the views spectacular. Our favorite time of year for a trail ride is late autumn, when the annoying horseflies are gone and it's almost cold enough to see your breath. But any time of year is fine, says the owner—unless it's so cold and blustery that the horses don't want to leave their warm barn.

WHERE: West of the Broadmoor resort on Cheyenne Mountain Zoo Road (just past the zoo); (719) 577-5792.

WHEN: Year-round, weather permitting; call for reservations.

ACTIVITIES: Guided one- or two-hour trail rides, pony rides, lessons, private carriage rides, group hayrides. Trail-riders must be at least seven years old (children under seven can ride ponies on lead lines in the arena). No riders over 250 pounds.

FACILITIES: Restrooms and nearby picnic areas; the stables are just a few minutes' drive from the amenities of the Broadmoor resort.

BE SURE TO BRING: Long trousers and hard-soled shoes or riding boots.

CHEYENNE MOUNTAIN ZOO

Way up on the side of Cheyenne Mountain, overlooking all of Colorado Springs and the prairie beyond, is America's only mountain zoo. Here you can see rare Mexican wolves, orangutans, ocelots, snow leopards, and many other endangered species in a somewhat naturalized environment.

During the warm months a seasonal "contact area" is open, and you can touch and feed domestic animals like goats and sheep. Petting zoos are usually a highlight of a small child's trip—never mind those giraffes and bears. Actually, they're most popular with the parents of little kids, who have their camcorders perched on their shoulders ready to capture the action!

In the past, we have avoided zoos. It's depressing to watch those caged cats pace and pant. But modern zoos serve a greater purpose in educating the public, in protecting vanishing species, in promoting legislation to save disappearing habitats. And of all the zoos we've ever been to, this high-altitude park has the wildest of habitats. The mountainous landscape makes you feel like you're visiting some of these animals in their own environments.

Besides educational and aesthetic wildlife displays, the park has other enjoyable features. At the far end of the zoo, beyond the elephants and giraffes, you'll find a quarter-mile nature loop, a shaded picnic area and playground, and a summertime carousel where, for a couple of quarters, your child can ride a wild animal. With all this activity you might find yourself a little breathless in the thin mountain air. Someone has thoughtfully provided benches throughout the park for us old folks to rest on.

WHERE: Southwest Colorado Springs. From I-25, take Exit 138 and go west on Lake Avenue. At the Broadmoor Hotel, follow signs on Miranda Road to 4250 Cheyenne Mountain Zoo Road; (719) 633-9925.

WHEN: Daily from 9 A.M. to 5 P.M., in the summer months from 9 A.M. to 6 P.M.

ACTIVITIES: Wild animal–viewing, many in open-habitat en-closures. (It's still a cage but is larger and more natural and eases our consciences.)

FACILITIES: Restrooms with diaper-changing tables, drinking fountains, first-aid station, shaded picnic tables, snack shops, and gift store. Wagons, strollers, and wheelchairs for rent; during the summer months you can ride the tram all day for a dollar.

BE SURE TO BRING: At least a sweater, even in July. At an alti-tude of 6,800 feet you'll probably need it sooner or later. Pack a lunch or buy something to eat at the snack shop.

SANTA'S WORKSHOP AT THE NORTH POLE

Don't bother taking your sophisticated fifteen-year-old to this theme park, but your four-year-old will love it. (Actually, your fifteen-year-old might secretly love it too. And if the word "Christmas" doesn't peg your stress meter, your inner child will enjoy it most of all.)

Even though this is an amusement park featuring performing elves, free magic shows, and rides like the Ferris wheel, the Pep-permint Slide, and Santa's Train, the quaint little North Pole vil-lage is also filled with gift shops. Be advised of the opportunity to spend money on toys, holiday decorations, and treats. Though the admission price includes unlimited rides and entertainment, it doesn't include the extra goodies or gifts you're sure to want.

The park might be most appreciated in early December, when Christmas and signs of snow are in the air and you're in the holiday spirit.

WHERE: 10 miles west of Colorado Springs on Highway 24, at the base of Pikes Peak; (719) 684-9432.

WHEN: June through August, open daily 9:30 A.M. to 6:00 P.M. From September through Christmas Eve the park is open Friday through Tuesday from 10 A.M. to 5 P.M.

ACTIVITIES: Amusements and rides for children; entertainment featuring elves, magic shows, music, Christmas shopping—and the Jolly Man himself.

FACILITIES: Restrooms, telephone, first-aid, food concessions, souvenir and gift shops, post office.

BE SURE TO BRING: Extra sweaters, hats, and mittens on all but the warmest of days. If you've got your Christmas cards ready, bring them to mail from the North Pole post office!

FLORISSANT FOSSIL BEDS NATIONAL MONUMENT

Florissant is North America's premier insect-fossil site. In fact, paleoentomologists rate it third in the world. Be sure to begin with the excellent displays inside the visitor center. One of the most amazing to us is the enlarged photographs of fossilized insects so perfectly preserved you can see the individual hairs on a bug's leg!

Florissant means "flowering," and if you drive up during the summer you'll understand the connection. This area is a mountain meadow filled with wildflowers—well, at least in this geologic epoch it is. Thirty-five million years ago, however, there were no flowering plants here. At that time it was a region of fiery volcanoes. It was the lava, mud, and ash that preserved the insects, plants, and other fossils so well.

The highlight of the visit is following a 1-mile interpretive path that leads to various fossilized remains, the most impressive being fifteen petrified sequoia stumps. The largest of these is thirteen feet in diameter—bigger than any found at Petrified Forest National Park in Arizona! There's also an outcropping of fossil-bearing shale along the way, which gives you an idea of what to look for when you're fossil-hunting in your own backyard. Of course, no fossil collecting is allowed here, but you can buy a fossil at one of the nearby rock shops in Florissant, 2.5 miles north. Better yet, for five dollars you can find your own at the Florissant Fossil Quarry. Watch for the signs as you drive through the small town.

For a different sort of experience, take cross-country skis or snowshoes and go in the winter after a snowfall. There are several fairly easy trails in the vicinity. Stop at the visitor center for trail maps and advice.

WHERE: 35 miles west of Colorado Springs on Highway 24 to Florissant. Turn south toward Cripple Creek on Teller County Road 1 and continue 2.5 miles to the visitor center; (719) 748-3253.

WHEN: Daily from 8:00 A.M. to 4:30 P.M. Longer hours during the summer. Closed Thanksgiving, Christmas, and New Year's Days.

ACTIVITIES: Seeing and learning about the fossils found in this area. Easy self-guided walks where you can see petrified stumps and outcroppings of fossil-bearing shale. In summer, guided tours and wildflower walks are given periodically. In winter you can explore the same trails on cross-country skis or snowshoes. A fee is charged.

FACILITIES: Nature center with good educational displays (and restrooms), interpretive trails. Nearby Forest Service campground and private campgrounds.

BE SURE TO BRING: A picnic is nice; you can pick up quick food at one of the convenience stores in nearby Divide or Florissant.

CRIPPLE CREEK NARROW-GAUGE RAILROAD

Here's a fun way for the whole family to enjoy fabulous mountain scenery, spot the remains of old mines, mining camps, and ghost towns, and get a history lesson to boot. Take a ride on the Cripple Creek Railroad, formerly called the Midland. The train is fully restored and pulled by a 15-ton locomotive typical of the steam engines of the late nineteenth century. Railroad and history buffs will want to spend time in the museum at the depot. And who can resist the gift shop filled with train-related souvenirs?

WHERE: 45 miles southwest of Colorado Springs in Cripple Creek. Bennet Avenue, at the Cripple Creek Museum; (719) 689-2640.

WHEN: Daily every forty-five minutes from the end of May through early October.

ACTIVITIES: 4-mile round-trip historic tours on a restored narrow-gauge railroad.

FACILITIES: Restrooms, snacks, and gifts at the depot. Nearby restaurants and other conveniences in Cripple Creek.

BE SURE TO BRING: Photographers, bring your cameras; the train makes several stops at points of interest. Bring an extra sweater or jacket for everyone.

THE ROYAL GORGE

What's the best way for kids to experience the Royal Gorge—a spectacular granite chasm spanned by the world's highest suspension bridge 1,053 feet above the Arkansas River? Some have their pictures taken with a stranger dressed in a chipmunk costume. Some feed fat tame deer, buy souvenir t-shirts at one of six gift shops, and eat ice cream cones at the snack bar built on the edge of the canyon. Some ride the incline railway down into the gorge. (Some adults jump off the bridge with parachutes or attached to bungee cords—an illegal stunt. Rafting the Royal Gorge is legal but can be very risky at certain times of the year.)

Frankly, we don't recommend any of these activities. Here's how Linda did it.

When Linda's eldest son, Artie, was young, he and she took off one weekend from Denver with a full tank of gas, a grocery sack of food, two sleeping bags, and less than twenty dollars in cash. Their destination—the Royal Gorge. They stopped in the town of Divide, west of Colorado Springs, for cold drinks, directions, and camping information.

"Watch out for cougars, young lady," the old man selling sodas warned. "There's plenty of 'em running around the back side of Pikes Peak."

Linda didn't sleep a wink that night in her makeshift campsite along a dirt road in Phantom Canyon. She could swear she heard growling noises. In the middle of the night she put her sleeping kid in the car's back seat and continued on, hoping she wouldn't get a flat tire on that dark and lonely road. She drove through Canon City as Orion was setting, stopping at an all-night coffee shop for caffeine and a short stack. Sunrise found her on the side of the road, just before the north rim tollgate. Shivering in the dawn breeze, Linda and Artie got out of the car and ran to the edge. There, more than 1,000 feet below them, was the magnificent chasm, pink in the early morning light. They could hear the roaring river far below, but from where they were standing it sounded like a whisper. At that early hour the theme park was closed, there was no one in sight, and the Royal Gorge was all theirs.

WHERE: About an hour's drive from Colorado Springs and 8 miles west of Canon City by Highway 50; (719) 275-7507. An alternate route, the road less traveled, is to go south on First Street at the west end of Canon City to the Temple Canyon Picnic Ground. Drive through this park and turn right when the road intersects a paved road; the south rim of the Royal Gorge is a short distance ahead.

WHEN: Open daily, weather permitting, although some attractions are seasonal. Park may sometimes be temporarily closed for maintenance.

ACTIVITIES: Is this a scenic natural wonder or a theme park? It's both, which in our eyes detracts from and ridicules the wonder of the Gorge. But that's only our opinion. Kids, and many adults, seem to love it; everything from the rides to the multimedia audiovisual presentation. A fee is charged to cross the bridge.

FACILITIES: Everything you could want or need, from souvenir shops to a pizza and beer garden. Nearby camping at KOA and other private campgrounds. A few nearby rock shops might be of interest to amateur geologists.

CAUTION: It's easy to miss the Royal Gorge itself in all the commercialism.

BUCKSKIN JOE'S PARK AND RAILWAY

There's not one but two theme parks on the edge of the Royal Gorge—practically side by side. Don't worry about driving past them—if you're driving to the Gorge on Highway 50, you can't miss either one.

One of Colorado's top commercial tourist attractions, Buckskin Joe's is a reconstructed Old West town with enough authenticity to be used as a movie set for numerous Hollywood westerns (such as *Lightning Jack*, starring Paul Hogan). In fact, many of the old buildings are actual buildings from old ghost towns that have been relocated and rebuilt. At this park you can experience everything you'd expect from an Old West theme park: daily gunfights, gold-panning in a tub, saloons tended by costumed barkeeps, stagecoach rides, and the ever-present gift shop. A bit contrived, but everyone seems to enjoy it.

WHERE: 8 miles west of Canon City, by Royal Gorge park. About an hour's drive south of Colorado Springs; (719) 275-5149.

WHEN: Daily, Memorial Day through Labor Day from 9:00 A.M. to 7:30 P.M.

ACTIVITIES: Reproduction Old West town featuring live entertainment such as gunfights, gold-panning, a canyon-rim train ride, horse-drawn wagon rides, magic shows, shopping, eating, and drinking.

FACILITIES: Museum buildings, seasonal restaurant (sells buffalo burgers), saloon, ice cream parlor, multiple gift and souvenir shops, restrooms.

BE SURE TO BRING: Sunscreen and money.

AREA STATE PARKS AND NATIONAL FORESTS

MUELLER STATE PARK

Protecting 11,000 acres of designated backcountry, this is the park for families looking for a piece of Colorado wilderness to explore. Camping and hiking are the main attractions. There are ninety campsites, ranging from primitive to modern, and 85 miles of trails to keep you busy for many visits. There's also 24 miles of mountain-biking trails. Pets aren't allowed on the backcountry trails, even on a leash. This is a fine place to see wildlife, maybe even elk and bighorn sheep. Twenty-five miles west of Colorado Springs on Highway 24 to Divide, then 3.5 miles south on Highway 67; (719) 687-2366.

PIKE NATIONAL FOREST

Pike National Forest borders Colorado Springs to the west, offering a good selection of Forest Service campsites. The Crags Campground, with seventeen sites for tents and small motor homes, piped water, and pit toilets, is one. Nearby attractions are the Florissant Fossil Beds and a trail to The Crags—a 750-foot climb to a rocky overlook. From the town of Divide (west of Colorado Springs on Highway 24) drive 4.5 miles south on Highway 67 and 3.5 miles east on Forest Service Road 1094. For more information, contact the regional Forest Service office at (719) 636-1602.

Outdoor Fairs and Festivals

Renaissance Festival

Step back in time to merry old England, to a time of lords, ladies, and knights in shining armor. A significant entrance fee allows you to participate in this make-believe world highlighted with lots of period entertainment. Some of the highlights include jousting tournaments, strolling minstrels, and costumed entertainers who engage the public in practical jokes and other shenanigans. Puke and Snot skits are extremely popular (you gotta see one to appreciate it), as are ax throwing, face painting, nonmotorized rides—and of course the ever-present opportunity to part with your farthings. The Renaissance Festival has been a favorite of our whole family year after year—in spite of the increasing crowds and commercialism. Weekends from mid-June through July. North of Colorado Springs in Larkspur. Follow the signs from I-25; (303) 688-6010.

Pikes Peak Auto Hill Climb

This automobile race up Pikes Peak began in 1916 when Spencer Penrose, builder of the Broadmoor Hotel, turned the old carriage road into the present-day highway and held an international racing event like none other. Over the years world renowned racers like Mario Andretti and Parnelli Jones have competed here. Held every year on July Fourth. Admission is charged; (719) 685-4400.

El Paso County Fair

Rodeos, 4-H exhibits, horticulture displays, draft-horse pull, dances—in other words, real country enjoyment. A week in late July at the Calhan Fairgrounds, about 30 miles northeast of Colorado Springs by Highway 24; (719) 575-8690.

Pikes Peak or Bust Rodeo

The state's largest outdoor rodeo features professional cowboys and cowgirls. Part of the fun includes a free pancake breakfast and a parade put on by the city. Held early in August at the Penrose Stadium, 1045 West Rio Grande Street. Contact the visitors bureau at (719) 635-1632, or the rodeo office at (719) 635-3547.

ANNUAL BALLOON CLASSIC

Three days of 7 A.M. balloon launches, afternoon skydiving and other aerial demonstrations, and evening activities. Labor Day weekend (Saturday through Monday) at Memorial Park; (719) 471-4833.

IN CASE OF BAD WEATHER

There's no shortage of museums, halls of fame, gift shops, and other indoor tourist attractions in this city. Here are some of our favorites. Some of them are a little offbeat and not to be found in other guidebooks.

COLORADO SPRINGS FINE ARTS CENTER

A good collection of Hispanic, Native American, and Western American art. A fee is charged. Tuesday through Friday from 9 A.M. to 5 P.M., Saturday from 10 A.M. to 5 P.M., Sunday from 1 to 5 P.M.; 30 West Dale Street; (719) 634-5581.

HALL OF THE PRESIDENTS LIVING WAX STUDIO

If your school-age kids have never been to a wax museum, spend a rainy afternoon reviewing history as the presidents of the United States seem to come alive before your very eyes. Open daily from 9 A.M. to 9 P.M. during the summer, from 10 A.M. to 5 P.M. the rest of the year. A fee is charged. 1050 South Twenty-First Street; (719) 635-3553.

IRON SPRINGS MELODRAMA DINNER THEATER

Kids and adults both love an old-fashioned melodrama where audience participation is encouraged. Boo the bad guy, cheer the good guy—it's all in fun. A family-style dinner is served before the show. Call for a current schedule of performances. A fee is charged. 444 Ruxton Avenue in Manitou Springs; (719) 685-5104 or 5527.

ROCKY MOUNTAIN MOTORCYCLE MUSEUM
AND HALL OF FAME

This small museum, free of charge, is associated with a motorcycle shop. Monday through Saturday from 10 A.M. to 7 P.M. 308 East Arvada Street, just west of I-25; (719) 633-6329.

MAY NATURAL HISTORY MUSEUM OF THE TROPICS

See three of the world's largest beetles and thousands of other insects and arachnids. There's also an RV campground. 710 Rock Creek Canyon, southwest Colorado Springs; (800) 666-3841 or (719) 576-0450.

SPACE DISCOVERY ADVENTURE
MUSEUM AND GIFT SHOP

Here's one indoor adventure the kids will love—it's located in a shopping mall! Exhibits include astronaut Irwin's space suit (it's interactive now—push a button and it talks!), space station mock-ups, and displays of space technology adapted for use in medicine. This small museum is connected with a unique gift shop that sells space-related toys, models, games, clothing, books, coloring books, and more. Who can resist? Open during mall hours. In Chapel Hills Mall, 1710 Briargate Boulevard; (719) 528-5190.

S🌞UTHEASTERN PLAINS

major highway once passed across the sparsely populated
plains of southeast Colorado. Not Interstate 70, but the
Santa Fe Trail, the historic nineteenth-century route that
connected the new state of Missouri with the Mexican provincial
capital of Santa Fe.

Over the centuries this seemingly desolate land has been
claimed by the Apache, Comanche, and Kiowa, the Spanish,
French, Mexicans, and Anglo-Americans. All found it desirable
because of its buffalo and other wildlife, and because of the life-
giving Arkansas River that flowed through it. Bent's Fort was an
important stop along the trail and a trading center for all nations.

Today a family with an interest in history could easily spend
a week exploring this corner of the state. For others, a weekend
is more to their liking. A Saturday or Sunday spent driving the
scenic byway that parallels the mountain route of the Santa Fe
Trail is an adventure to see what it might have been like to be a
Comanche on a buffalo hunt, or an entrepreneur at Bent's Fort,
trading manufactured goods from St. Louis for pelts and silver.
Pick up a map of the area highlighting the Santa Fe Trail at the
visitor center in Pueblo just west of I-25 and Highway 50.

PUEBLO AREA

If you're looking for inexpensive family fun, take another
look at Pueblo and its environs. True, you won't find any destination winter resorts called "Ski Pueblo." Nor will you find any
world-renowned amusement parks or lofty 14,000-foot peaks to

climb. What you will find is a small city 112 miles south of Denver that has an interesting history, a high quality of life, and a low cost of living—perks for the vacationer as well as the locals.

Not everything here is small, however. Lake Pueblo State Recreation Area, one of the biggest and most popular parks in Colorado, is just a few miles west. This city is also the home of the Colorado State Fair, one of the oldest and biggest state fairs in the United States.

But if you want to escape crowds, skip the state park and the fair and spend an afternoon at the peaceful Pueblo Greenway and Nature Center, along the banks of the Arkansas. In our opinion, this riverside haven is one of southern Colorado's best-kept secrets.

Nature Centers and Wildlife-Viewing
Pueblo Greenway and Nature Center

There's no better place to spend a pleasant afternoon than the Pueblo Greenway, a paved multi-use trail along the cottonwood-lined banks of the Arkansas River. On foot or by bike you can cruise from downtown Pueblo clear out to the state park, stopping at City Park, the Raptor Center, the Nature Center, or Cafe del Rio for some refreshment.

The Nature Center itself is not elaborate. A small building houses a few exhibits and nature-related gifts. This is as good a place as any to park your car while you're enjoying the greenway. Be sure to ask about upcoming events such as the annual Bluegrass Festival, the Halloween Spook Trail, and the Rolling River Raft Race. Little tots will like swinging, sliding, and climbing on the jungle gym. Kids of all ages will surely want to get their shoes wet on the riverbank or scramble up the rocky hill overlooking the trail. Fishermen might want to cast a line into the Arkansas from the fishing pier. Bicycles can be rented right here at the Nature Center for those who want to follow the trail.

But lazy adults (as we've been known to be on one or two occasions) will find it hard to get past Cafe del Rio, adjacent to the Nature Center. While the kids are playing nearby, you can relax at a shady outdoor table sipping your favorite beverage, listening to the gurgling of the river, and watching the bikers, skaters, and joggers go by.

The Pueblo Greenway, kids, and bikes are a winning combination.

WHERE: Along the Arkansas River from Pueblo State Recreation Area west of the city to its intersection with Fountain Creek, east of I-25. First-time users should begin at the Nature Center (just west of Pueblo Boulevard on Nature Center Road) or at City Park (Pueblo Boulevard, east at Goodnight); (719) 545-9114.

WHEN: Year-round.

ACTIVITIES: Biking, hiking, wheeling, skating, and fishing along the Arkansas River and Fountain Creek.

FACILITIES: Parking, restrooms, drinking water, playgrounds, picnic tables, organized activities, restaurant, bike rentals.

BE SURE TO BRING: Money to buy refreshments at the creek-side restaurant.

PUEBLO ZOO AND CITY PARK

Did you know the kick of an emu is strong enough to break a human thigh? Lots of zoological trivia can be learned at this charming zoo—a clean, green, and intimate biologic park. Every afternoon, usually about three o'clock, you can watch penguins eat mackerels out of the hands of the zookeeper lecturing on the ways of penguins while she carefully watches her fingers. The penguins (and their feeder) are behind glass, affording visitors a cross-sectional view of their habitat, which is mostly ice and water. Kids stand with their noses pressed to the glass to watch the birds gulp their lunch whole then dive in the icy water and swim around.

Bob liked the penguins the best. Linda liked the ringed-tail lemurs, whose only restraint was a moat of water around their island. We both enjoyed the remarkable collection of deceased bugs in the Tropical Discovery building; some are the size of a Frisbee.

For a small zoo, there's a lot here to see and do, including the feed-and-pet-the-farm-critters section. And when you tire of looking at animals you can go next door to the park. Here big people can lounge under the trees while little people run around like Tasmanian devils. In the summer you can swim in the public pool or ride the merry-go-round for a small fee.

WHERE: From I-25, take Highway 50 west, go south on Pueblo Boulevard to Goodnight. Look for a small sign as you go east at Goodnight to 3455 Nuckolls Avenue, through City Park; (719) 561-9664.

WHEN: Daily, from 9 A.M. to 4 P.M., year-round. On a weekday in spring or fall you'll practically have the park to yourself! Feeding time is usually in the afternoons (3 P.M. when we were there) and is fun to watch.

ACTIVITIES: Animals and other nature exhibits; picnicking at City Park; seasonal swimming and carousel rides.

FACILITIES: Restrooms, drinking fountains, first-aid, seasonal concession stand; wagons, strollers, and wheelchairs for rent. City Park has a swimming pool, tennis courts, and access to the multi-use trail.

BE SURE TO BRING: Pocket change to buy farm-animal food, or human food. And a cooler full of goodies, lawn chairs, or an old blanket for your picnic in the park.

THE RAPTOR CENTER OF PUEBLO

The Raptor Center is a rehabilitation facility, a sort of nursing home for birds, where you can see eagles, hawks, merlins, kites, kestrels, and other injured birds of prey in various stages of healing. If all goes well, the raptors are released in a suitable location and observed for adaptation. But if their injuries are too crippling to allow them to fend for themselves, they remain under the protection of the Raptor Center and are used to educate humans—who all too often are the cause of their injuries in the first place.

This is a good half-hour activity the whole family will find interesting, educational, and thought-provoking. Combine it with a walk along the Pueblo Greenway, a stone's throw away, where you may be fortunate enough to catch a glimpse of a healthy raptor soaring above.

WHERE: 5200 Nature Center Road, a mile west of Pueblo Boulevard and just east of the Nature Center; (719) 545-7117.

WHEN: From 11 A.M. to 4 P.M., Tuesday through Sunday.

ACTIVITIES: See and learn about birds of prey in a facility that rehabilitates injured raptors and releases them back to the wild when possible.

FACILITIES: Part of the Pueblo Greenway and Nature Center; nearby restrooms, picnic areas, food concessions.

BE SURE TO BRING: Cash donations are appreciated. So is bird food for the patients. Not seeds and suet but meat—in the form of frozen wild game!

ROCK CANYON SWIM AREA

Paddleboats, bumper boats, and a water slide—for most kids, this is the best part of Lake Pueblo State Park. If so, you'll want to head directly to the beach after paying your entrance fee.

WHERE: Just below the dam at the east end of Pueblo State Park. Accessible from park headquarters or from Pueblo Greenway, a paved hiking/biking trail that follows the Arkansas River (see page 128); (719) 561-9320.

WHEN: Memorial Day through Labor Day, daily from 11 A.M. to 7 P.M.

ACTIVITIES: Swimming, small-boating, and fishing, also picnicking and camping.

FACILITIES: Beach and lifeguards, restrooms, showers, picnic tables and grills. Nearby camping and a half-mile nature trail are handicap accessible.

BE SURE TO BRING: Swimsuits, towels, sunscreen, and sweatshirts for when lips turn blue. Food and drinks, or money for snacks from the concession stand.

Pueblo Airport and the Fred E. Weisbrod Museum

What's so interesting about a couple of acres of antiquated airplanes guarded by pigeons who nest in the fuselages? If you like grand old DC-3s, once state-of-the-art bombers; flying research laboratories; and experimental jet-propelled trains (another government boondoggle, says Bob), you and the kids'll enjoy spending half an hour poking around this unusual outdoor museum. When the kids get fidgety, take them over to the terminal for a better view of the planes taking off and landing. If you brought a picnic you can find a patch of shade (there's a single tree on the north side of the museum). Be prepared to share with the rabbits, who also seem to like hanging out at the airport.

This is a simple activity that doesn't take much planning or preparation. You can go on a whim, but in midsummer go early in the day or late in the afternoon to avoid the heat.

Where: 6 miles east of Pueblo on Highway 50. Follow the signs to the airport. On the southeast end of Bryan Circle; (719) 948-9219.

When: Daily, during daylight hours.

Activities: Watching airplanes take off and land and checking out vintage aircraft in the free outdoor museum.

Facilities: Restrooms and pop machines in terminal.

Area State Parks and National Forests

Lake Pueblo State Recreation Area

Welcome to one of the biggest and most popular state parks in Colorado! Boating, fishing, and camping are the primary activities in this 9,000-acre area, 4,000 acres of which is reservoir.

All water sports can be pursued here, but swimming can only be done at one designated beach. A full-service marina rents boats. Even with four hundred campsites the park often fills during summer weekends and holidays, and reservations are recommended. Mountain biking is permitted on 18 miles of trails through prickly pear cactus, piñon and juniper, cottonwoods and willows. The trails here connect with the paved Arkansas River Greenway, so you'll have plenty to explore. There's a fish hatchery, of interest to anglers and children who wonder how big a baby fish is. And for those who seek open spaces in which to make high-pitched whining noises, there's a model-airplane strip. Whatever you do, make your first stop the visitor center— you'll find some worthwhile nature displays and helpful advice on what to see and where to go. From I-25, go west on Highway 50 4 miles, then south on Pueblo Boulevard 4 miles, then west on Thatcher Avenue 6 miles; (719) 561-9320.

LATHROP STATE PARK

If picnicking in the same park as hundreds of other families is not your idea of fun, you'll probably prefer Lathrop to Pueblo, even though it's farther south. Just outside the small town of Walsenburg, two small lakes provide a place to fish, swim, windsurf, or water-ski—if you bring your own toys. One of the lakes, Horseshoe, is for wakeless activities only. Although there are boat ramps, there's no marina and no concession stand. This is just a good old-fashioned state park—well, except for the nine-hole golf course! Two campgrounds can accommodate ninety-eight tents or trailers any time of year. Ice skating is permitted when the water is sufficiently frozen; bring your own blades. The state's first buffalo herd (in modern times) grazes here. They are interesting to observe, but keep your distance. This isn't a zoo— these animals are wild. Go 49 miles south of Pueblo on I-25 to Walsenburg, then 3 miles west of Walsenburg on Highway 160; (719) 738-2376.

Outdoor Fairs and Festivals
Colorado State Fair

Bob remembers years ago, when, as part of a demonstration team, he parachuted into the Pueblo State Fair. Bands played, crowds cheered, and Bob missed his intended landing area, plopping down instead where the roller-skating elephant was about to perform. Both the elephant and Bob walked away unscathed.

There's always some kind of excitement at the Colorado State Fair, one of the oldest and largest state fairs in the United States. This is big-city entertainment in a cowboy hat. It's the biggest outdoor event of its kind in the Rocky Mountain West. You can see big-stakes professional rodeo, hear big-name bands, ride big-time amusement rides. There are scads of displays and exhibits and entertainment just for kids. Teens prefer the laser shows, the high-tech motion simulators, the bands. But everybody gets a kick out of watching world-famous Robinson's Racing Pigs.

Expect heavy traffic on the interstate. Expect crowds. If you're staying overnight (which we advise if you live more than 50 miles away) make your lodging reservations well in advance. You can buy tickets ahead of time, too, to avoid another long line. The fair runs a Found Kids Center you should check out first thing. Many activities are free, but of course the kids will want to do the ones that aren't. Bring water bottles. Bring sunscreen and hats. Bring more money! At the Pueblo State Fairgrounds. Follow the signs from I-25 to Prairie and Arroyo Avenues. Two weeks in late August, (800) 444-FAIR.

Weekend Festivals at the Pueblo Greenway and Nature Center

At least one weekend a month there's a special outdoor event hosted by the Nature Center on the banks of the Arkansas River. Some festivities are advertised as twenty-one-and-older events, since alcohol is sold. Many celebrations, however, are designed for family fun, such as the annual Halloween Spook Trail. For a list of upcoming festivals contact the Nature Center at (719) 545-9114. See page 129 for directions.

In Case of Bad Weather
Pueblo Plaza Indoor Ice Arena

This city-owned year-round rink offers public skating, lessons, and ice hockey. Inexpensive admission and rentals. Call for hours, which may vary seasonally. 100 North Grand; (719) 542-8784.

El Pueblo Museum

Historical displays depicting Native American life and the era of western exploration, railroads, ranching, and commercial development. Some items are touchable and interesting to kids. 324 West First Street; (719) 583-0453.

Children's Museum at the Sangre de Cristo Arts Center

Here's side-by-side indoor activity—art appreciation and creative play for kids. (Don't be surprised if you enjoy the Children's Museum as much as your children do.) 210 North Santa Fe Avenue; (719) 543-0130.

La Junta Area

If you're driving to La Junta, it seems like a long ride from just about anywhere. The road is straight; the scenery is flat and monotonous.

But La Junta is only 60 miles east of Pueblo by Highway 50. In the summer and early fall, roll down your window and see if you can smell onions in the air. Along with cantaloupe and watermelon, they're a big crop in the Rocky Ford area, between Pueblo and La Junta. Keep your eyes open for fields of yellow sunflowers and other commercially grown flowers. On your drive through southeast Colorado take the time to stop once in a while. Get out of the car and look closely; you'll find some interesting sites. Like Bent's Old Fort, for example. And ancient petroglyphs in the Comanche Grasslands just south of La Junta.

BENT'S OLD FORT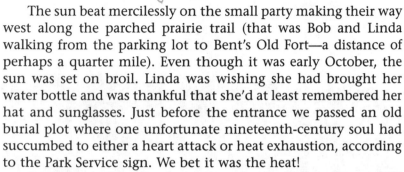

The sun beat mercilessly on the small party making their way west along the parched prairie trail (that was Bob and Linda walking from the parking lot to Bent's Old Fort—a distance of perhaps a quarter mile). Even though it was early October, the sun was set on broil. Linda was wishing she had brought her water bottle and was thankful that she'd at least remembered her hat and sunglasses. Just before the entrance we passed an old burial plot where one unfortunate nineteenth-century soul had succumbed to either a heart attack or heat exhaustion, according to the Park Service sign. We bet it was the heat!

Reconstructed on the site of the original structure, Bent's Old Fort was Colorado's official bicentennial project in 1976. Historical sketches, diaries, and letters were used, and intensive on-site archaeological work was carried out. The results are impressive. Instead of a commercialized rip-off, Bent's Old Fort is an outdoor museum, yet more interesting. Being here is like stepping back in time to 1835. And in spite of the temperature, it's worth the long drive from anywhere—unless you don't give a hoot about history.

Never designed as a military stronghold, Bent's Fort was a bastion of American capitalism and diplomacy built by William and Charles Bent and their associate Ceran St. Vrain on the border of what once was Mexico (but smack dab in the middle of Southern Cheyenne hunting grounds). For over a decade fortunes were made within these adobe walls; goods commonly sold for a profit of several hundred percent! For a few years everyone seemed to benefit: the traders, the trappers, the Mexican merchants, the Native tribes. It was the brief golden age of trade in the American West.

We learned all this and more from Karl, a guide dressed in buckskin whom we met in the carpenter's shop. Karl was building what we thought was a coffin but that turned out to be a "Mexican pantry"—a wooden bin for storing food. When not conducting tours or answering questions, Park Service employees make furnishings in much the same manner as frontiersmen of the last century would have.

As we wandered around the various rooms we discovered interesting details such as old letters, journals, and ledgers on desks,

Bent's Old Fort, with its careful reconstruction and emphasis on living history, is sure to please history enthusiasts of any age.

all open for reading. By studying the props and furnishings, observant visitors can figure out what different rooms were used for. Of course, you can always cheat and take the guided tour, or read about it first on your interpretive map. Watching the twenty-minute introductory video is definitely recommended.

For history buffs of all ages, Bent's Old Fort is a worthwhile destination. And for kids whose idea of history is anything that happened before their last birthday, it's a great place to spark an appreciation for the subject. Here at this adobe fortress you really get a feel for what life was like on the Colorado grasslands more than a century ago.

WHERE: 70 miles east of Pueblo via Highways 50 and 194. Follow the signs from La Junta; (719) 384-2596.

WHEN: Summer hours, from 8:00 A.M. to 5:30 P.M. daily, Memorial Day through Labor Day. Winter hours, from 9 A.M. to 4:00 P.M. daily, closed Thanksgiving, Christmas, and New Year's Days. Special events include Independence Day celebration, Kid's Quarters in August, when kids learn a craft or trade typical of the era, and Christmas activities in early December.

ACTIVITIES: Self- or guided tours of the reconstructed fort, including an excellent twenty-minute video; special events throughout the year.

FACILITIES: Restrooms, water fountain, bookstore. There are a few picnic tables out by the main road. Partially wheelchair accessible: The top level of fort can only be reached by climbing stairs. No refreshments on site. Transportation available for those who need assistance from the parking lot. Gas, lodging, public swimming pool, and a KOA campground in nearby La Junta.

BE SURE TO BRING: Sunscreen, hats, water bottles (so you won't have to run to the water fountain every five minutes, as Linda did). And everyone will appreciate a cooler full of refreshments back at the car.

COMANCHE NATIONAL GRASSLANDS

Ancient rock art, dinosaur tracks, and endangered prairie chickens. Those are three amazing things you can find in the Comanche National Grasslands—if you're willing to spend some time.

First, stop at the ranger station on the east end of La Junta (1420 East Third Street) for necessary maps and other current information. Then make a stop at a grocery or convenience store for food and drinks. Buy a gallon or more of water in plastic jugs.

Driving south out of town on Highway 109, you'll swear it's all a hoax. There can't be anything out there worth seeing, you'll think. All you can see is a dizzying stretch of flat earth and blue sky, and maybe some cows. Trust us, there's more.

Press on. About 13 miles south of La Junta turn right, or west, following the small signs to Vogel Canyon Picnic Area. Make sure you bring a picnic with you—there is no MacDonalds out here. Nor is a reliable source of drinking water to be found anywhere in the grasslands. This is a real adventure!

At the picnic area there's a few shaded tables. Out of the summer sun, the temperature is pleasant enough for you to enjoy your lunch. Make time to take a short hike along one of four trails. We walked Canyon Trail, a round-trip loop just under 2 miles. The hike really opened our eyes to some of the secrets of the grasslands.

Following the trail down into a small canyon, we walked through piñons, junipers, cholla and prickly pear cactus until we reached a wetland where lush grass and cattails grew. We found a spring and watched a number of frogs leap for cover under the water. Doves, swallows, and kingfishers flew out of the cliffs. Using our trail map, we found a rock panel of petroglyphs, though some of them had been vandalized. And here we caught a glimpse of a lesser prairie chicken—a native bird trying hard to make a comeback in eastern Colorado.

By this time we were wishing we had brought more food, more water—and our sleeping bags to spend the night. There was so much here to be discovered. But instead we pressed on in our car another 10 miles or so to the edge of Picket Wire Canyonlands in hopes of seeing thirteen hundred dinosaur footprints fossilized in stone!

The longest known set of prehistoric prints in the world, the Picket Wire tracks extend a quarter of a mile along the banks of the Purgatoire River. They are thought to have been made by creatures in the Sauropod and Theropoda suborders, brontosaurus and allosaurus being two familiar members.

But we didn't see any prints that afternoon. It was too late in the day to safely make the hike—a more than 10-mile trek in what are essentially desert conditions. We didn't have enough water with us and were unprepared should a thunderstorm have occurred. We continued on our journey but vowed to come back someday.

The Picket Wire Canyonlands, which encompasses the dinosaur tracks, is completely undeveloped at this time. In order to protect this priceless record in stone, visitors must be respectful of the fossil prints and of the land and wildlife that surrounds them. Visitors must also use good judgement and take responsibility for their own safety in this unforgiving land.

The best and safest way for most of us to see the tracks is to sign up for one of the Saturday tours given by the Forest Service during the autumn months. These guided trips are becoming increasingly popular, filling up months in advance. If you're interested, call in January to find out about the autumn schedule.

WHERE: The Comanche National Grasslands consists of two separate units covering 419,000 acres. The Timpas Unit, southwest of La Junta, is managed by the Forest Service rangers headquartered at 1420 East Third Street in La Junta; (719) 384-2181. The Carrizo Unit is located in the extreme southeast corner of the state and is managed by the Springfield Ranger Station at 27162 Highway 287; (719) 523-6591.

WHEN: Open year-round. Each season has its charms and curses. September through November may be the best months for most activities.

ACTIVITIES: Picnicking, hiking, wildlife-viewing, sight-seeing; petroglyphs and dinosaur tracks are of particular interest. In 1996, no fee is charged for use of the grasslands, although that could change if further development takes place.

FACILITIES: Vogel Canyon Picnic Area has covered picnic tables with grills, a vault toilet, and four hiking trails. No drinking water is available and no campfires are permitted. Picket Wire Canyonlands has portable toilets only.

BE SURE TO BRING: Pick up a map and current information from the ranger station. Don't forget hats, sunscreen, food, plenty of water, first-aid kit, and sturdy hiking shoes for everyone.

CAUTION: The weather here can be even more unpredictable and extreme than elsewhere in Colorado. Intense heat, lightning, flash floods, and blizzards present potential dangers throughout the year.

AREA STATE PARKS AND NATIONAL FORESTS
QUEENS STATE WILDLIFE AREA

Five natural lake beds provide a habitat for wetland creatures, a source of water for prairie animals, irrigation water and recreation for humans. Fishing, camping, and seasonal hunting are the main activities here. Wildlife-watching opportunities are excellent, but there is little shade from the intense summer sun. There is no charge for open camping in designated areas; fee-for-use improved campsites are also available. Take Highway 287 north of Lamar, at least an hour's drive from La Junta; (719) 438-5810.

OUTDOOR FAIRS AND FESTIVALS
ARKANSAS VALLEY FAIR

Hey, the state fair isn't the only fair around these parts. If you like your outdoor entertainment on a smaller scale, head out to Rocky Ford, along the banks of the Arkansas River. A carnival, a rodeo, a Mexican fiesta to honor the community's Hispanic culture all typify this mid-August celebration. And where else can you get a free watermelon? Every year 30,000 pounds of watermelons are given away to fairgoers, provided by local businesses and the Rocky Ford Rotary Club. After all, it's melons that have put Rocky Ford on the map. So when your child asks that dreaded question: "Mommy, where do melons come from?" you can take her to the Arkansas Valley Fair to see for herself. Fifty miles east of Pueblo on Highway 50; (719) 254-7483.

LA JUNTA KIDS RODEO

Calf roping, goat-tail tying, pole and barrel races and more for contestants aged 6 to 16. For a small fee you can watch the excitement every August; (719) 384-7411.

ROCKY FORD BALLOON FESTIVAL

A free event featuring early-morning balloon launches, evening balloon demonstrations, booths and concessions. Held in November, generally missing the extreme temperatures of summer and winter on the plains; (719) 254-7483.

In Case of Bad Weather
Koshare Indian Kiva Museum

Don't wait for bad weather; an hour spent at this museum will enrich your journey in the La Junta area. See an impressive collection of Native American art and artifacts and watch the Koshare Dancers, who perform June through August. The museum is open daily from 10 A.M. to 5 P.M. 115 West Eighteenth Street, La Junta; (719) 384-4411.

Rocky Ford Museum

Memorabilia of local interest is housed here. Combined with a day spent at one of the town's outdoor festivals, a half-hour of browsing and talking to the curator will give you a greater understanding of this farming and railroad community. Tuesday through Saturday from 11 A.M. to 4 P.M., mid-May through September. Winter hours by appointment. 1005 Sycamore; (719) 254-7483.

THE NORTH-CENTRAL MOUNTAINS

Mention Colorado and most people picture big mountains and lots of snow. Even though Colorado as a whole gets less snow than New Jersey does, we wager more people come to the Rocky Mountains for ski vacations than go to Hackensack.

In the north-central mountains, less than two hours from Denver, are six major ski resorts. And though many families come to Colorado in winter for the snow, these reports are open year-round. Warm-weather activities include mountain biking, hiking, horseback riding, boating, fishing, wildlife-viewing, and outdoor weekend festivals of all sorts. Another well-kept secret is the low cost of resort lodging during the "off" season.

The other big attraction in this part of the state is Rocky Mountain National Park. Nearly three million people visit the park each year, and most come during the summer months. But the park is open year-round. Skiing, snowshoeing, wildlife-viewing, and camping can be enjoyed during the winter months (when everyone else is at the ski resorts!).

To avoid the crowds but still enjoy the beauty in this most visited part of Colorado, consider coming to the ski resorts during the summer or autumn and visiting Rocky Mountain Park when everybody else thinks it's too cold.

ROCKY MOUNTAIN NATIONAL PARK

During her visit to what was to be Rocky Mountain National Park, Isabella Bird wrote, "I have found far more than I ever dared to hope for." With the help of packhorses and a trapper named Mountain Jim, this adventurous forty-one-year-old Englishwoman soon reached the top of Longs Peak in 1873.

"From the summit were seen in unrivalled combination all the views which had rejoiced our eyes during the ascent," she wrote in her memoirs, *A Lady's Life in the Rocky Mountains*. "It was something at last to stand upon the storm-rent crown of this lonely sentinel of the Rocky Range, on one of the mightiest of the vertebrae of the backbone of the North American continent, and to see the waters start for both oceans."

In 1915, President Woodrow Wilson signed the bill creating Rocky Mountain National Park. This was the end result of growing public concern for conservation of wild lands, spearheaded in part by Enos Mills, a resident naturalist, mountain guide, and writer. (Make time to visit his unrestored cabin, 8 miles south of Estes Park on Highway 7. Natural history exhibits and an interpretive trail are featured free of charge.)

Today Rocky Mountain National Park is Colorado's largest and most visited park. It encompasses 265,193 acres of mountainous land, one-third of it above tree line. Seventy-six of its peaks are above 12,000 feet, and nineteen mountaintops measure over 13,000 feet. Longs Peak is the highest point in Rocky Mountain National Park, towering 14,255 feet above sea level. More than 7,000 people climb it each year! (Surprisingly perhaps, Longs Peak is not the highest point in Colorado. Mount Elbert, south of Leadville, claims that distinction at 14, 495 feet.)

The park is divided east from west by a ridge of mountains that form part of the Continental Divide. Trail Ridge Road, one of the highest roads in the country, connects both sides. During the summer it's possible to drive from the east entrance near

Estes Park to the west entrance by Grand Lake—a total of about 50 miles. Trail Ridge Road closes in the winter because of snow, usually from mid-October until Memorial Day. But the park remains open year-round and is accessible from either entrance.

Rocky Mountain National Park makes a lasting impression on every visitor. Linda remembers her Uncle Jack, who was born and raised in Baltimore, trying to describe the wonder he felt standing not only above the tree line, but above the clouds themselves. Her kids remember the time she pulled their sputtering, wheezing, altitude-sick car into a parking area near the Continental Divide. They all raced up to the top of a windy knoll, following an alpine trail. (What impressed Linda most was leaving all the jackets in the car!)

Everyone who has visited the park has his or her own special recollection—that one vivid image that remains clear in the mind's eye. (We hope it's not the license plate of a Winnebago slowly pulling a trailer of jet skis up the pass in front of you . . .) Whatever image you're in search of, don't try to see the whole park in one day. It doesn't matter that you didn't personally view each and every mountain; instead choose one mountain and its diverse life zones to observe and explore. Park the car and walk— half a mile, or a mile and a half. Make a snowball from a patch of snow, or stick your fingers in an icy September stream. Be patient and you might see mule deer, bighorn sheep, or a herd of elk. By not trying to see the whole park, you'll see much more of it (and spend far less time in line behind a caravan of creeping tour buses, RVs, and minivans crawling up the passes).

In this section we've included a sampling of activities for families in and around Rocky Mountain National Park—keeping in mind that it's always more fun to do something than just to look at something. Beware the gateway towns of Estes Park and Grand Lake: Although they offer many activities and amenities like food and lodging, a whole slew of souvenir shops can soon rob you of your valuable time as well as your money. Whether you have just an afternoon or a whole week to spend, an unlimited budget or nearly empty pockets, you'll find a rewarding experience at Rocky Mountain National Park.

WHERE: The east entrance is 70 miles northwest of Denver by Highway 34/36. Park headquarters, (970) 586-1399.

WHEN: Open year-round. The biggest crowds can be found during the summer. Although Trail Ridge Road connecting the east side with the west side is closed usually from mid-October through May, the park is open all year.

ACTIVITIES: In general, wildlife-viewing, hiking, camping, fishing, and horseback riding. During the winter months cross-country skiing and snowshoeing can be enjoyed. Snowmobiling is restricted to the west side, on three defined trails. A check-in with a ranger is required. A ski lift once operated at Hidden Valley, which is now an area for sledding and tubing. Three campgrounds are open all year. Specific activities follow below.

FACILITIES: Five developed campgrounds, fee charged. Handicamp is a backcountry site designed to accommodate wheelchairs. There is no lodging within park boundaries. Five visitor centers on the east side and two on the west provide ranger-led educational activities, nature exhibits, maps, guidebooks, and gifts.

BE SURE TO BRING: Warm clothes and raingear any time of year. Dress in layers, and don't forget hats, sunscreen, and water bottles. Bring a cooler full of food and drinks.

RANGER PROGRAMS

Your first stop when entering the park from either direction should be at one of the visitor centers to see what's going on and where. Activities are planned throughout the year and daily during the summer months. Make the time to take part and we guarantee you'll discover something new—a wildflower you've

Ranger-led activities at Rocky Mountain National Park will enthrall every-one in the family.

never seen, a bit of Indian lore, an animal you wouldn't have no-ticed on your own.

Coffee with a Ranger and Campfire Talks are popular ongo-ing campground programs. Take advantage of these opportuni-ties to ask questions and chat with the rangers one-on-one. Some activities involve a walk or hike, like Bird Walks, Tracking a Glac-ier, Shoreline Stroll, and Tundra Nature Walk. Rocky After Dark and Full Moon Walks are two night adventures offered year-round. In the winter months you can even snowshoe with a ranger. Most programs are from thirty minutes to two hours long, and some require reservations.

SHORT NATURE WALKS AND HIKES

More than 350 miles of hiking trails wind through the park, from wilderness paths to wheelchair-accessible pavements. Find the trailheads on the official map and guide you'll receive when you pay your fee at the entrance gate. If you're interested in backcountry hiking, ask a ranger for some ideas. Here are a few trails ideal for short legs, or for families short on time.

Sprague Lake Nature Trail

An easy, level paved trail with picnic area and restrooms. Close to park headquarters on the east side, this nature trail can be crowded during the summer, but it's a good destination if you only have a few hours to spend in the park. The trail is .5-mile round-trip at 8,700 feet.

Bear Lake Nature Trail

This is another easy short walk around a subalpine lake formed by glaciers during the last ice age. The Bear Lake area is heavily used during the summer. Longer, less-frequented trails have their beginnings at Bear Lake too. The trail is .5-mile at an elevation of 9,475 feet. Access is from the east side of the park. Follow the signs to Bear Lake.

Moraine Park Nature Trail

This is another short, easy interpretive walk beginning at the Moraine Park Museum, which remains open throughout the year. September or October are great months to enjoy this area. The museum is a good place to warm up after your walk while you learn more about the park's ecology. Only .25-mile round-trip, at 8,000 feet. Follow the sign to Moraine Park Museum, not far from the east entrance.

Tundra Nature Trail

Here's an outdoor experience you'll have mostly to yourself because those other wimps will be inside their cars, out of the frigid wind. This short, moderate, high-altitude hike can be rigorous because of the thin air at 12,310 feet. But what better way to see the fragile plants, insects, and other animals that inhabit the tundra? Not to mention the view! We recommend you bundle up and brave the cold thin air—unless storm clouds are building and lightning seems likely. The trail is .5-mile each way, beginning at 12,310 feet. It begins about midway through the park on Trail Ridge Road, east of the Alpine Visitor Center. (Trail Ridge Road is generally open June through September, depending on snow conditions.)

NEVER SUMMER RANCH

On this picturesque, easy, west-side walk you can see the remains of a ranch and a few old homestead cabins in the river valley. It's a beautiful picnic spot and is often less windy than many places on the east side. If you're fortunate, you might spy a moose along the creek. It begins about 7 miles from the west entrance. The trail is 1 mile, fairly level, and at 9,000 feet.

COLORADO RIVER TRAIL

This easy to moderate hike is our favorite. Following the North Fork of the Colorado River, you can walk just long enough to stretch your legs, or you can make a day of it. Hike 7 miles up to Lulu City, an old silver-mining town named for Lulu Brunett, the daughter of the town's surveyor. Here you can see a few remains of building foundations and let your imagination run wild. Although the trail isn't difficult, it's long and rocky in places. The hikes are of variable length starting at about 9,000 feet. The Colorado River Trailhead is marked with a sign about 10 miles from the west entrance.

WILDLIFE-VIEWING

Okay, enough of the rabbits, squirrels, and birds, you say. We came here to see something big. Preferably something with hoofs, horns, or claws. Something wild and magnificent that you can't see in Boston or Baton Rouge.

The park is full of wild animals, but it takes patience and luck to see them. Remind the family that you're visiting someone else's home—that of the wild animals and plants. Never harass, bother, or try to feed wildlife. To do so could be dangerous and will certainly affect the animals' ability to find food on their own. When it's possible and safe, turn your car headlights off or down and keep noise to a minimum.

Take advantage of one of the many interpretive displays or ranger-led activities to further your knowledge and enjoyment of the wildlife here in the park. Stop at the headquarters or at one of the visitor centers to find out more about the park's wildlife and where to see it. And though the elk, bighorn sheep, and moose are exciting, the smaller mammals, rodents, reptiles, and birds can be equally fascinating. Perhaps your kids will want to keep a wildlife checklist, available at any visitor center, where you can also purchase excellent field guides.

Here are some guidelines for the best chances of spotting big animals.

Elk. Look in the morning or late afternoon along the edges of clearings. Kawuneeche Valley, Horseshoe and Moraine Parks, Upper Beaver Meadows, and Fall River Valley provide likely viewing opportunities. Perhaps more exciting than seeing these majestic creatures is to hear them bugle. These chilling calls can be heard during the fall mating season when the males are challenging one another.

Moose. Can be seen almost any time of day in willow bottoms, beaver ponds, and streambeds. They are seen most often on the west side of the park between the Kawuneeche Visitor Center and the Timber Creek Campgrounds. Usually seen alone or in pairs. Keep in mind that moose can be extremely dangerous if approached or threatened. Appreciate them from afar, perhaps through binoculars or a telephoto lens.

Bighorn Sheep. During late spring and summer the sheep come down into the meadows of Horseshoe Park on the east side, around Sheep Lakes. To get to the food and water they must cross Highway 34. Please drive slowly through this area and pull off if sheep are present. In case you want to know how to tell male and female sheep apart, the boys have the curved horns and the girls have the straight, pointed horns.

WINTER ACTIVITIES

Winter is a good time to visit Rocky Mountain National Park—if you'd rather deal with snow than flurries of other tourists. Although many miles of park roads are closed during the off-season, including most of Trail Ridge Road, there's plenty of access to do some exploring on foot—or on snowshoes or skis! Check with a ranger about current conditions before you go, paying special attention to avalanche warnings.

Two of the visitor centers stay open all year and offer ranger-led winter activities and learning programs. On the east side, the Headquarters Visitor Center on Highway 36 is open daily from 8 A.M. to 5 P.M. On the west side, the Kawuneeche Visitor Center is open daily from 8:00 A.M. to 4:30 P.M. For more information, call park headquarters at (970) 586-1206.

You can slide down hills on sleds and inner tubes at the Hidden Valley Sledding Area, and at Bear Lake. Call a visitor center for further regulations, and bring your own sleds. Sledding is restricted to approved areas.

Many of the walking trails can be snowshoe or ski adventures after a heavy snowfall. Valley bottoms and streambeds generally have more snow cover than the trails and can be traveled with caution. Kawuneeche Valley near Timber Creek Campground on the west side, and the Bear Lake trails on the east side are two recommended areas for novices.

On weekend days through the winter you can snowshoe with rangers—a great introduction to this winter sport that's growing in popularity. January and February are generally the best months for skiing or snowshoeing (spring snows can be heavy and wet). Be sure to call first and ask about conditions, and stop at a visitor center for a map. If you don't have your own equipment you can rent it in Grand Lake or Estes Park. (For instance, Outdoor World at 156 East Elkhorn in Estes Park; (970) 586-2114. This store is open daily and has skis and snowshoes to fit children.)

Grand Lake Touring Center, outside the park but near its west entrance, offers 30 kilometers of groomed trails, rentals, and a restaurant and lounge, all in an avalanche-free zone. It's located on County Road 48, off Highway 34; (970) 627-8008.

Not far from the park's west entrance you can ice skate for free at Grand Lake's outdoor rink any time, as long as it's frozen. For a very small price you can rent skates just down the street at the Grand Mercantile. In Grand Lake Village; (970) 627-3402.

CAMPING AND LODGING

Broomfield resident Phil Haas takes his Colorado kids camping in Rocky Mountain National Park as often as he can get away. "The kids like to help me set up the camp," he says. "Christopher has been carrying the firewood since he was old enough to walk. Haley carries the sleeping bags and sets them up inside the tent. They love having their own special job to do."

The park's five campgrounds are fee-for-use facilities.

MORAINE PARK

This is the park's largest campground, with 247 sites for tents and RVs. It's only 7 miles from Estes Park on Highway 36 and is a good choice for families with kids of the sociable age who like to make friends with other young campers. Open all year; seven-day limit. Reservations are required: (800) 365-2267.

GLACIER BASIN

A good choice for those who want a smaller campground than Moraine Park that is not too far from the comforts of Estes Park. With 150 sites for tents and RVs. Open early June to early September; seven-day limit. The campground is 9 miles southwest of Estes Park on Bear Lake Road. Reservations are required: (800) 365-2267.

ASPENGLEN

Set near the beautiful Fall River, you'll find good hiking and wildlife-viewing opportunities at this smaller campground. (On a short hike near here we came across a huge herd of elk.) There are fifty-four sites for tents and RVs that operate on a first-come first-served basis. (Get there early.) Open late May to mid-September; seven-day limit. From Estes Park it's only 5 miles west on Highway 34.

LONGS PEAK

If you don't like motor homes and their generators, this is the park for you. There are twenty-six sites for tents only. Open all year, with limited winter facilities. First-come first-served;

three-day limit. From Estes Park, 11 miles south on Highway 7, then 1 mile west.

HANDICAMP

A backcountry camping area at Sprague Lake designed for people who use wheelchairs. Can accommodate up to five wheelchairs, and ten campers total. Call (970) 586-4459 for reservations.

TIMBER CREEK

You'll find this west-side campground along the North Fork of the Colorado River near some good hiking trails. This is our favorite part of the park, especially in the early fall when the aspens are changing. Open all year with limited winter facilities; one hundred sites for tents and RVs. First-come first-served, seven-day limit. From Grand Lake, 10 miles north on Highway 34.

If you don't want to camp inside the park, there are dozens of campgrounds, many of them privately owned, in and around the gateway towns of Estes Park and Grand Lake. Although you may get lucky and find a vacant site just by dropping in, reservations are recommended from Memorial Day through Labor Day.

WINDING RIVER RESORT

You can pitch a tent, park a trailer, or rent a cabin on this 160-acre private ranch on the edge of Rocky Mountain National Park and along the North Fork of the Colorado River. The resort's entrance is actually inside the park's west entrance. For an additional fee you can go on a hayride, a horseback ride, or rent a mountain bike from the ranch. You can also just hang out at camp and play volleyball, basketball, horseshoes, or a wacky game called Frisbee golf, with other campers (no extra fee for these activities).

"We're really very family-oriented here," says Wes House who, together with his wife Sue, own and operate the campground. "We have ice cream socials several nights a week, a playground and farm animals for the kids to enjoy, in addition to all the horse rides and hay rides." Open mid-May through mid-October and also the month of December. Reservations are recommended. The resort is 1.5 miles north of the park entrance on Highway 34 (across from the Kawuneeche Visitor Center), then west on County Road 491 for 1.5 miles. Call (970) 627-3215; (303) 623-1121 in the Denver area.

ARAPAHO NATIONAL RECREATION AREA

Four campgrounds and five lakes and reservoirs make up this huge national forest recreation area adjacent to Rocky Mountain National Park's southwest boundary. More than 450 fee-for-use campsites are on the banks of these bodies of water; open camping is allowed around the more remote Meadow Creek Reservoir on undeveloped sites. This is a good choice for families who want to combine a visit to Rocky Mountain National Park with activities such as fishing, windsurfing, or sailing. In Arapaho National Forest, between Granby and Grand Lake; (970) 887-3301.

YMCA OF THE ROCKIES

More than two hundred cabins and over 450 lodge rooms can accommodate individuals, families, and organizations looking for a retreatlike environment on the edge of Rocky Mountain National Park. Although this is a Young Men's Christian Association camp, all denominations (and nondenominations) are welcome. The prices are reasonable, and there are lots of activities to keep you busy: hiking, swimming, horseback riding, volleyball, basketball, tennis, sledding, ice skating, and cross-country skiing, to name a few. Most activities are included in the fee, and you can rent needed equipment at an on-site shop.

If you tire of the great outdoors, you can seek solace in the chapel, the library, or the museum. Conveniences include a restaurant, grocery store, and gift shop. The YMCA is a good deal for the money, and an ideal place for families who like a little structure. Be sure to call well in advance for reservations. The original facility is 5 miles southwest of Estes Park on Highway 66; (970) 586-3341. A separate facility, Summer Mountain Ranch, is located 14 miles from Winter Park.

North-Central Mountain Ski Areas: Winter, Spring, Summer, Fall

Colorado is perhaps best known today for its ski resorts, where many families spend winter vacations on snow-covered slopes. In recent years these resorts have expanded, extending their seasons to become year-round playgrounds, promoting activities like hiking, mountain biking, horseback riding, golfing, and outdoor festivals. With so many ski resorts to choose from, how do you decide where to go?

Who hasn't heard of Aspen and Telluride, playgrounds of the wealthy and famous? And Vail, perennially at the top of every survey of America's ski resorts. Without a doubt, Vail provides some of the best downhill skiing on the continent, but unless yours is a family of Olympians (or Vanderbilts) you have to ask yourself: Do we really need 5,000 acres of world-class terrain?

In this section we've selected the ski areas in central Colorado we consider to be the best places to take your kids based on value, family atmosphere and services, and the availability of outdoor activities in addition to skiing.

Winter Park and Fraser Valley

Now known primarily for its skiing and mountain biking, the Fraser Valley was once hunting grounds for the Ute and Arapaho, then ranch land for settlers. In the early part of the twentieth century the Moffat Tunnel brought the railroad over the Continental Divide, connecting it with Denver. If you're interested in the area's history, spend some time at the Cozens Ranch House Museum along Highway 40 on the south edge of Fraser. Here, for a small fee, you can see a restored 1876 ranch house, stage stop, and post office; (970) 726-5488.

Winter Park Resort

Winter Park has slopes for everyone. The thrill seekers will head for Mary Jane Mountain while less-aggressive skiers will stick to the well-groomed slopes of Winter Park Mountain and Vasquez Ridge. Although it's an easy trip from Denver, on the way home you'll be tired and wishing you could've stayed the night, or at least taken the Rio Grande Ski Train that departs from Denver's Union Station on weekends from late December through early April.

Winter Park, like most destination resorts, offers a menu of packages you can choose from: Lodging, airfare, lessons, and even activities like sleigh rides, dogsledding, or snowmobiling can be combined in a money-saving package. Prices vary from year to year, so it's best to call for current deals.

When the snow melts and the days last longer, out come the mountain bikes, thundering along the hundreds of miles of old jeep trails that meander through these mountains. This is a sport whose time has come; in fact, Winter Park and the Fraser River Valley have officially copped the trademark Mountain Bike Capital, U.S.A.

Before you start, pick up a free map from any bike shop or from the area chambers of commerce. With 600 miles of interconnecting trails, there's a lot to choose from. If you didn't bring your own, you can rent bikes at the base of the ski lift and pay for a lift ticket to take you and your bike up the slopes, but novices should stick to the flatter trails until they are confident. For family touring, the best place to start is with the Fraser River Trail, which begins by the river in Old Town Winter Park, a little north of the main entrance to the resort. This fairly flat trail parallels Highway 40 for several miles, connecting the towns of Winter Park and Fraser. It's a good, easy trail to warm up on and get used to the altitude.

For those who can't seem to go fast enough on bikes, take a ride on the alpine slide, Colorado's longest such ride. This one's a real thrill; even the most daredevil adolescents should get a stiff dose of adrenaline with this one. (There is some risk involved, so caution your kids to obey the few safety rules; accidents can happen.)

WHERE: 67 miles northwest of Denver on Highway 40; (970) 726-4118.

ACTIVITIES: Downhill and cross-country skiing, snowboarding. Warm-weather activities include mountain biking, hiking, golfing, and riding the alpine slide. Good family outdoor festivals include the Kids Winter Ski Karnival, the Family Hike and Bike Festival, and the Winter Park Jazz Festival (in summer). Call (970) 726-5514 for details.

FACILITIES: Lodging and package plans that include a variety of activities. Instructional ski programs for children, a learn-to-ski park for beginners only, and the best ski program in the nation for disabled persons. Numerous other activities, restaurants, and lodges nearby. If you're coming from Denver, consider riding the Rio Grande Ski Train; (303) 296-ISKI.

SILVER CREEK RESORT

This newer, smaller ski area is custom-made for families with young children, or for those who want a more intimate setting than Winter Park provides. It features gentler slopes just right for new skiers and snowboarders. There's also an excellent Nordic center for ski touring. If you want to be away from the hustle of a bigger, busier resort, check into Silver Creek. But if you or your adolescent kids are competitive black diamond skiers or off-trail tree bashers, forget it. You'll be much happier up the road at Winter Park's Mary Jane Mountain.

WHERE: 17 miles north of Winter Park on Highway 40; (800) 926-4FUN.

ACTIVITIES: Cross-country and downhill skiing, snowboarding.

FACILITIES: Instruction, Nordic center, restaurant, accessory shop, lodging.

YMCA Snow Mountain Ranch Nordic Center

A 100-kilometer groomed-trail system is open to the public for cross-country skiing; rentals, lessons, and lodging are also available. Snow Mountain Ranch is a YMCA retreat and conference facility located just west of Highway 40 between Winter Park and Silver Creek Ski Areas; (970) 887-2152.

Tubing at Fraser Hill

Tubing is like sledding, only instead of using a toboggan or a wooden sled with runners, you slide down the hill on a big inner tube. Pay by the hour and ride down the hill as often as you please. A tow rope saves you the trouble of trudging up each time. Monday through Friday, 4 to 10 P.M., 10 A.M. to 10 P.M. on weekends. Fraser Tubing Hill is on the south end of Fraser, off Highway 40; (970) 726-5954.

Jim's Sleigh Rides

Afternoon and evening horse-drawn wagon rides on the historic Cozens Homestead Ranch. Most kids will like the horses—and the outdoor bonfire with refreshments. Adolescents may be bored with the slow pace and the passel of other passengers they may be riding with. Very small kids don't get the romance of the whole experience—they just get cold and tired. On Highway 40 in Fraser, next to Cozens Ranch Museum; (970) 726-5527.

Dogsled Rides of Winter Park

A one-hour guided backcountry tour covering 5 miles with eight to ten Siberian Huskies pulling the sled. Each sled can carry two adults and one child. Daily during peak season, from Tuesday through Saturday while the snow lasts. Off Highway 40 in downtown Winter Park; (970) 726-TEAM.

High Country Stampede Summer Rodeo Series

Every Saturday evening from early July through August, amateur cowgirls and boys compete at the John Work Arena in Fraser. For an extra fee you can eat a barbecue dinner; (970) 726-4118 (Fraser Chamber of Commerce).

I-70 Corridor: Eisenhower Tunnel to Frisco

Take an hour and a half drive west of Denver on Interstate 70, and you're in a mountain playground. Five major ski areas are found along or near this corridor, beginning with Loveland Ski Area on the east side of the Eisenhower Tunnel. Even if your family doesn't ski, inexpensive off-season lodging rates at the major resorts make summer and autumn an attractive time for families who want to enjoy organized fun.

Loveland Ski Area

Proximity to Denver, cheaper than average lift tickets, short lift lines, and plenty of white stuff make Loveland popular with Denver area skiers. Linda used to take her kids to Loveland a few times each winter; it was only a forty-five-minute drive from their house in North Denver. Here there are no condominiums, hotels, or convenience stores, but there is a day lodge at the base where you can buy your lunch and warm up with some hot chocolate. There's not much in the way of shopping, but you can buy ski-related items, lip balm, sunscreen, and souvenirs. If you're looking for no-frills skiing in the metropolitan area, we recommend Loveland.

If Loveland has a drawback, it's that it's often bitterly cold and windy. Call ahead for a weather report, and if it sounds tolerable, bundle the kiddies like snowmen. When their cheeks are red and their noses are running, it's time to call it a day.

Where: 50 miles west of Denver on I-70 at the Eisenhower Tunnel; (303) 571-5580 or (800) 736-3SKI.

Activities: Downhill skiing, snowboarding.

Linda's children Mindy and Matt at Loveland Ski Area.

FACILITIES: Instruction, including kid's ski school; cafeteria, rental and repairs, ski accessory and gift shop. Nearest lodging is 10 miles in both directions (Georgetown and Silverthorne).

KEYSTONE MOUNTAIN RESORT

Bob learned to ski at an early age, but Linda learned when she was twenty-seven years old at Keystone. She still remembers the terror or riding the lift for the first time—scarier by far than starting down the face of the mountain (without lessons) under the expert direction of her friend Mary. "It's easy. You'll get the hang of it," she said.

After falling at least forty-six times, she grasped the beginner's snowplow technique Mary demonstrated before she swished down the mountain, not to be seen again until Happy Hour. Linda probably would've given up if it wasn't for the nice little preschoolers who kept stopping and offering her a hand.

"Hey lady, are you okay? You want me to go get the Ski Patrol?" As Mary said, "Anybody can learn to ski."

Keystone has long been considered a prime family ski resort. Not so much for the prices, which are right up there near the top of the list, but for the abundance of planned activities available throughout the self-contained resort. For instance, the three-hour sleigh rides are first-rate, your destination being a heated log cabin complete with juicy steaks (or a vegetarian alternative). These rides are extremely popular, especially during the December holidays, so call early for reservations.

As with most Colorado resorts, there are lots of outdoor activities to be found in the summer as well. Mountain biking is extremely popular, with easy access to Summit County's excellent trail system. From Keystone you can pedal to Lake Dillon Reservoir, to Breckenridge, to Frisco. Or you can stay close to the resort, enjoying the smaller body of water, Keystone Lake. Unlike many resorts, whose extracurricular adventures are provided by outside companies, Keystone runs most of its own activities. This at least provides predictability and consistency in service. You can arrange just about any adventure by calling the Keystone Activities Line at (970) 468-4130.

WHERE: 10 miles east of Dillon on Highway 6 (approximately 65 miles west of Denver); (800) 847-4754. Keystone Activities Hotline: (970) 468-4130.

ACTIVITIES: Downhill and cross-country skiing, snowboarding, ice skating, sleigh rides. An arrangement with Breckenridge and Arapaho Basin lets you ski any of the three facilities on one ticket. In summer, hiking, biking, horseback riding, hay rides, barn dances, and water sports are available. Outdoor festivals include a Fourth of July celebration and children's concerts.

FACILITIES: A full-service resort offering lodging with various activity packages, ski instruction, a kids-only slope and a snowplay area for youngsters, a cross-country ski center and Nordic ski school; snowboard park, restaurant, ski repair, amenities shops. Also, the largest outdoor maintained ice-skating rink in the country.

BRECKENRIDGE MOUNTAIN RESORT

Covering more than 1,500 acres, "Breck" is a popular ski area, particularly among Colorado's young-adult skiers. Receptive to the latest methods of sliding down mountains, this resort was hosting world snowboard championships while other areas were still banning boards.

Breckenridge stands out from other resorts, too, because it's part of a real town with a colorful mining history and personality and not just a resort conceived and built solely for recreation. For nearly a hundred years this town was the site of numerous gold and silver booms and busts, the last being in the 1940s. Colorado's largest gold nugget, a 13-pound rock called Tom's Baby after the lucky guy who found it, was discovered in the mountains near Breckenridge. Today you can tour the Country Boy Mine just east of town on French Gulch Road. The mine is open daily all year, and the guided tour takes about forty-five minutes. Call (970) 453-4405 for more information.

But our favorite outdoor activities in Breckenridge are simple ones. In the summer we like to walk around the quaint and colorful buildings, or ride bikes on the mostly flat paved trail that connects Breckenridge with the towns of Silverthorne, Frisco, and Dillon. We like to watch kids with strange hairdos perform acrobatics in the skateboard park at the recreation center on the north edge of town. Bring your own board—it's free of charge.

WHERE: 85 miles west of Denver. From I-70 take Highway 9 south at Exit 203; (970) 453-5000.

ACTIVITIES: Downhill and cross-country skiing, snowboarding, ice skating; ski programs for kids as young as three. Summer activities include hiking, biking, horseback riding, and riding the alpine slide. Outdoor festivals include The Lighting of Breckenridge, an old-fashioned holiday celebration and tree-lighting ceremony held in early December; (970) 453-6018.

FACILITIES: Full-service resort with custom packages and family discounts available. Ski instruction, lodging, restaurants, and shops in a historic setting. Inexpensive ice skating on Maggie Pond, behind the Bell Tower Mall. Breckenridge Horse Stables and mountain bike rentals at the base of Peak 8 during the summer. A free town trolley makes getting around town easy.

COPPER MOUNTAIN RESORT

Situated at the junction of I-70 and Highway 91, Copper Mountain Resort offers challenging runs for novices, intermediates, and experts. Many Front Range skiers are willing to drive the extra miles past the other ski areas along the I-70 corridor for Copper's excellent runs and generally abundant snow. There are shops, restaurants, a health club, and even a medical office at the base.

One drawback of Copper Mountain, from our point of view, is that all the buildings and condominiums are relatively new and drably uniform-looking. There is no real town in the historical sense. And because of the steep terrain that makes for good downhill skiing, you won't find much in the way of novice cross-country trails here, or beginner mountain-bike routes.

But Copper's activity department really shines during the summer and early fall with lots of regularly scheduled family fun. Chairlift rides, ranger-guided hikes, gold-panning, pony rides, storytelling inside a tepee, kids' fishing, and fly fishing clinics for all ages all are free. Now that's a deal!

WHERE: Exit 195 from I-70, about 10 miles west of Frisco; (800) 458-8386 or (970) 968-2882.

ACTIVITIES: Skiing, snowboarding, ice skating, sleigh rides. Summer activities include horseback riding, hiking, challenging mountain biking, free activities for kids. Outdoor festivals of note are the Michael Martin Murphy West Fest in early September, featuring the music, art, and other culture of the American West.

FACILITIES: A full-service year-round resort with on-site lodging, restaurants, and a health club.

SUMMIT COUNTY RECREATIONAL TRAIL

See the snowcapped peaks of Summit County and tour the ski resorts from the saddle of a bicycle, or on the wheels of in-line skates. Nearly 50 miles of paved paths connect all the major Summit County ski resorts, following what used to be the routes of two 1880s narrow-gauge railways.

With all the bicycle shops, grocery, and convenience stores in the area, you won't have to bring much from home. Just rent it, buy it, eat it, and pedal on. If you're on a tighter budget, bring your own bikes and food. You can even bring a tent, stove, and sleeping bags and set up camp at one of the four Forest Service campgrounds around Dillon Reservoir.

For a short afternoon bike ride, take I-70 to Exit 203 at Frisco, then go left at the stoplight. Park in the large pull-out up the road on the right. Here you can ride 4 miles from Frisco to Dillon along the shoreline of the lake. It's a gently rolling section of paved trail with fabulous views of the mountains and lake. A wildlife-viewing station on the edge of the water gives you an opportunity to see an osprey nest. Be sure to pick up a free trail map at the visitor center in Dillon or Frisco or any of the ski resorts or sport shops in Summit County.

WHERE: Paved pathway connects Keystone with Dillon, Silverthorne, Frisco, Breckenridge, Copper Mountain, and Vail. Contact the Summit County Chamber of Commerce for maps and other information: (970) 668-2051, or (800) 530-3099.

WHEN: Year-round.

ACTIVITIES: Biking is most popular. Also walking, jogging, skating, or snowshoeing.

FACILITIES: Nearly 50 miles of recreational trails, mostly paved. Many nearby rental/repair shops. A biker/hiker-only campground is set up at Peninsula Recreation Area near the south end of Dillon Reservoir, toward Breckenridge; other drive-up campgrounds.

BE SURE TO BRING: Plenty of water, sunscreen, warm hats, and gloves. Layered clothing is best. If you don't pack food, bring money to buy it.

DILLON RESERVOIR

Dillon Reservoir is one of the premier sailing lakes in Colorado. But although there's a sailing school and rental facility at the marina, it's not the best place for youngsters to learn, due to the often gusty winds and always frigid water. If you don't know your port from your starboard, you can rent a pontoon boat and simply paddle around, exploring all the coves and inlets. The reservoir is stocked with brown and rainbow trout, if you like to fish.

But the easiest and least expensive way to enjoy this big, cold mountain reservoir is to stop by the nearest grocery store and get a loaf of bread and some sandwich makings, then stake out one of the picnic sites as your own for the afternoon. After eating you can take a walk along the shore and look for muskrats, frogs, ospreys, and herons.

WHERE: Drive 75 miles west of Denver on I-70 to the Silverthorne exit, then follow the signs south. Also accessible farther west, from Frisco; (970) 468-5400.

WHEN: All year, but marina is only open from late May to late October and campgrounds from May to September. The best times for most families is when these facilities are open.

ACTIVITIES: Walking and biking on paved trail; boating, sailing, fishing, picnicking, summer camping; winter snowshoeing or cross-country skiing. No swimming allowed.

FACILITIES: Marina, Forest Service campgrounds (over two hundred sites), picnic areas, restrooms, paved recreational trail.

BE SURE TO BRING: Warm clothes any time of year. If you're going out on a boat, bring even more. Don't forget sunscreen and hats that won't blow off in a gust of wind.

THE SOUTH-CENTRAL MOUNTAINS

f ski resorts aren't your style, leave behind the organized group activities, the lift lines, and some of the expense. Just a short drive south from the I-70 resorts is breathtaking scenery, including the highest mountain east of California. You'll discover a rich and fascinating history and countless opportunities for adventure. If you still want to ski, you can do so at Ski Cooper, Monarch, or Crested Butte.

LEADVILLE AREA

Surrounded by mountains rich in ores and minerals, the mining town of Leadville is a designated National Historic District. The stories of Horace and Baby Doe Tabor, and countless others who struck it rich then lost it all, are to be found in the museums of Leadville, in the restored hotels and saloons, and in the famous Tabor Opera House and Matchless Mine.

A good time to visit Leadville might be during August's Boom Days, when the town turns back the clock to the 1880s. Mining contests, burro races, carnival rides, a beer garden, and parade are featured. Contact the Leadville Chamber of Commerce for details; (719) 486-3900.

SKI COOPER

If you're looking for a quieter skiing experience, this is it. Cheaper lift tickets, fewer skiers, and no designer skiwear shops are reasons why people choose Cooper over some of Colorado's larger ski resorts. At this small facility featuring an abundance of powdery snow, kids (and parents too) can concentrate on skiing. It's a good environment for developing new skills—snowboarding or telemarking perhaps? An extensive group of trails maintained by the Cooper Nordic Center are easily accessed for those who want to cross-country ski.

Keep in mind that there are no hotels or condos at the base, so if you're planning on staying the night or the week, you'll want to arrange for lodging in nearby Leadville. For some atmosphere and historic charm, try the Delaware Hotel, 700 Harrison Avenue; (719) 486-1418.

WHERE: 10 miles north of Leadville on Highway 24; (719) 486-2277.

ACTIVITIES: Downhill and cross-country skiing; snowboarding.

FACILITIES: Day lodge, cafeteria, rentals, and repairs. Nordic center and trail system.

LEADVILLE, COLORADO & SOUTHERN RAILROAD

One way to really see the surrounding countryside and get a feel of old Leadville is to take a ride on the Leadville, Colorado & Southern Railroad. The train follows a standard-gauge track to a roundhouse at Climax Mine—over 11,000 feet above sea level—and back down to Leadville again. Along the two-and-a-half-hour narrated journey you'll have one stop at the French Gulch Water Tower, where you can deboard for a short break. Don't worry, parents—there are restrooms and concessions on board. Choose between an open car, a covered car, or a fully enclosed car, and feel free to move around if you need to.

WHERE: 326 East Seventh Street in Leadville; (719) 486-3936.

WHEN: Twice daily, from Memorial Day through Labor Day; weekend trips through early autumn.

ACTIVITIES: Two-and-a-half-hour narrated train ride.

FACILITIES: Restrooms, concessions, and gift shop on board.

BE SURE TO BRING: Warm clothing in layers and a pocketful of your own snacks. Photographers, don't forget your cameras.

CAUTIONS: Very young children or fidgety older ones might enjoy a shorter train ride more. (Such as the Georgetown Narrow-Gauge train ride, which is about half as long. See pages 89–91.)

MOUNT ELBERT

If you're only going to climb one of Colorado's fifty-four fourteeners—mountains at least 14,000 feet high—you might as well climb the biggest one. Mount Elbert is the tallest peak in the United States east of California. In fact, in the forty-eight contiguous states, only Mount Whitney is higher—by a mere 62 feet! But though it requires advance planning, good health, and stamina, the hike to the top of Mount Elbert is within most people's reach. (There are many other peaks in Colorado that, though shorter, are much harder to ascend.)

Climbing mountains can be a family activity. In fact, kids lead their parents up fourteeners all the time. (We know because they've passed us on numerous occasions, as we're panting and puffing along. They usually pass us again; we're still on our way up, and they're on their way back down.)

If you and your kids want to climb Mount Elbert, or any of Colorado's mountains, first consult a reliable guidebook, such as *A Climbing Guide to Colorado's Fourteeners* by Walter Borneman and Lyndon Lampert. Be sure to get the appropriate USGS (United States Geological Survey) topographical maps, as well. Make sure everyone is in good shape physically and is mentally up to the challenge. Plan to start your hike at dawn in order to be down below tree line before afternoon thunderstorms threaten. The Forest Service can give you valuable advice about current weather and trail conditions shortly before your climb. Call the Lake County office; (719) 486-0749.

If you just want to get a great view of Mount Elbert, continue south out of Leadville on Highway 24 approximately 10 miles. Watch for a small point-of-interest sign identifying this majestic mountain to the west.

LEADVILLE NATIONAL FISH HATCHERY

The cutthroat trout is the only species of trout native to Colorado. Over the years its numbers have dwindled in Rocky Mountain waters due to vanishing habitat and competition from introduced trout such as rainbows and brookies. Cutthroat trout are raised at the Leadville Fish Hatchery to help replenish the species in rivers and lakes throughout the West.

After looking at the fish exhibits in the visitor center, walk the mile-long self-guided nature trail, a pleasant way to spend an hour out of doors at the base of Mount Massive and learn more about the ecology of rivers and streams in the process.

WHERE: West of Leadville to Highway 300, turn right, following the sign, for about 2 more miles; (719) 486-0189.

WHEN: Daily from 7:30 A.M. to 5:00 P.M. during the summer. Closes at 4 P.M. the rest of the year.

ACTIVITIES: Fish study, nature walk, picnicking.

FACILITIES: Visitor center, interpretive trail, picnic area.

BE SURE TO BRING: Warm layered clothing, water bottles, and a picnic lunch or snack.

BUENA VISTA AREA

A longtime Colorado resident accustomed to spectacular scenery, Linda still catches her breath every time she approaches Buena Vista. *Buena vista* means "good view" in Spanish, and it is aptly named. Driving in from any direction, you'll see the broad, fertile Arkansas Valley spread out before you below the lofty Sawatch Range.

About 115 miles southwest of Denver by Highway 285 or 24, the Buena Vista area makes a good weekend getaway for Front Range families. Driving Highway 24 south from Buena Vista to Salida you'll pass a number of river-rafting companies, private campgrounds, riding stables, and several Forest Service roads leading to more campsites, trailheads, and ghost towns. Here is one of our favorite ways to spend an outdoor weekend in these parts.

Arrive on a Friday afternoon, early enough to set up camp at one of many campgrounds in the San Isabel National Forest—Chalk Lake, for instance, along County Road 162. The next morning take a short hike up Agnes Veille Falls, following the trail north from Chalk Lake Campground. Or hike a short distance along the Colorado Trail, a 469-mile path from Durango to Waterton Canyon, south of Denver. After a picnic lunch, take a short drive up the valley to wander through a living ghost town—St. Elmo. For a more challenging experience, ride mountain bikes up the hard-packed gravel road.

Experienced hikers might want to climb one of the 14,000-foot Collegiate Peaks in the area. Mounts Princeton, Harvard, and Yale are just three of many mountains in the region popular with experienced hikers. Although it's beyond the scope of this guidebook to give specific details on trails, techniques, and safety measures, we encourage any family who is inspired to climb a mountain to do it as long as your kids are persevering enough to enjoy six to eight hours of rigorous hiking with some steep boulder-walking at the top. Be sure to talk with an experienced mountaineer before you go, or invest in a guidebook and the appropriate USGS maps. Also check with the local Forest Service about current weather and trail conditions.

After your hike, bike, or mountain climb, treat yourself and the family to a soak at the Mount Princeton Hot Springs, open to the public for a small fee. Or stay in overnight lodging, then head for home in the morning.

MOUNT PRINCETON HOT SPRINGS RESORT AND STABLES

Nothing fancy here. Just a friendly lodge where you can take a hot soak, or do some laps and let the kids splash in one of three outdoor pools. Even if you're not a guest here, you can use the facilities for a small fee. You can also eat at the restaurant if your camping dishes are all dirty and you're too tired to wash them. What the heck—might as well stay at the lodge too! Guests have free use of the water facilities. Be sure to call ahead; this rustic resort isn't elegant, but it's well attended by vacationers and locals alike.

The Mount Princeton Riding Stables, less than half a mile east of the resort, offers guided rides into the nearby Chalk Cliffs and Collegiate Peak area. We're told your chances of seeing bighorn sheep are pretty good.

WHERE: South of Buena Vista on Highway 24/285 to Nathrop, then 5 miles west on County Road 162; (719) 395-2447 (resort), (719) 395-6498 (stables).

WHEN: Resort is open year-round, daily hours for pools. The stables are open from late May through September, weather permitting.

ACTIVITIES: Horseback riding, swimming, and hot springs soaking. Overnight lodgers have free use of pools, a small fee is charged to nonguests.

FACILITIES: Stables for guided trail rides. Three outdoor swimming pools, including an Olympic-size lap pool, streamside hot pools, and indoor hot tubs. Locker rooms, swimsuit and towel rental, restaurant, and overnight accommodations.

St. Elmo—A Ghost Town

This picturesque mountain town, a mining supply center founded in 1880 and originally called Forest City, was renamed St. Elmo after a nineteenth-century romantic novel. The population peaked at nearly two thousand during the 1880s, but a fire destroyed part of the town in 1890, and it was never entirely rebuilt. Gold and silver prices fell soon after, and the population dwindled to a mere seven in 1930. By 1950 a single person remained, running the Stark General Store. Unfortunately, most of the customers had all died or moved away.

Over the last few decades, however, people have been moving back to St. Elmo a few at a time. They've been restoring some of the cabins on the edge of town and building new Victorian-style mountain homes in the area. Alas, you realize this isn't a true ghost town but rather a picturesque example of a mining-era mountain community with a colorful past. It's a living ghost town. It's easy to spend half an hour walking along the dirt street looking at the weathered wooden buildings, taking pictures, or just wondering what it would have been like to live here in 1880. But be careful which windows you peer inside; you might find yourself looking right into somebody's living room! Respect the privacy of the residents, and don't go inside any of the deserted buildings.

If you want to do more than just stroll down Main Street, camp out at one of many Forest Service campgrounds in the area. The closest is Iron City, which is on the approximate site of an old mining camp just half a mile east on County Road 162. Or bring your mountain bikes and explore the old jeep roads that lead out of St. Elmo. One exhilarating jaunt is to continue northwest out of town by crossing the bridge and pedaling about 8 miles to Tincup Pass on County Road 267. In the winter this trail is popular with cross-country skiers and snowmobilers.

The ghost-town portion of St. Elmo imparts the feel of a nineteenth-century Colorado mining town.

WHERE: 17 miles west of Nathrop on County Road 162.

WHEN: Summer through late fall is usually the best time. In the winter and early spring the road to St. Elmo can be nearly impassable due to snow or mud.

ACTIVITIES: Take photographs or make up stories to go along with the setting. Explore surrounding jeep trails by foot, mountain bike, or four-wheel-drive.

FACILITIES: A Forest Service campground and restroom .5-mile east of St. Elmo.

BE SURE TO BRING: Water, snacks, sun protection, jackets or windbreakers. Bring mountain bikes, four-wheel-drive vehicles, or good hiking shoes if you want to explore the jeep trails beyond the town.

RAFTING THE ARKANSAS RIVER

Brown's Canyon of the Arkansas is by far the most popular stretch of any river in the state, and there's no shortage of rafting companies to take you down this nationally known ribbon of water.

Whatever you do, don't decide to save a few bucks and float it on your own (unless, of course, you're a highly experienced white-water runner yourself). Which Bob wasn't. Nonetheless, he went on a rafting expedition with some devil-may-care friends, each in his own flotation device (the kind you can buy at a blue-light special in the sporting department of K-Mart). This makes about as much sense as jumping out of an airplane with a homemade parachute—something Bob would never do—but somehow he survived the turbulent eddies, the rapids, the sinkholes, the suckholes—and lived to tell the story. But every year the Arkansas River and other Colorado rivers claim several lives. Most of these drownings could have been prevented by following prudent safety measures suggested by reputable river guides.

River guide John Rice says: "Nearly all of Colorado's rivers can be done by novices or families with children—you just have to know which section of the river to do, and when. Where to put in, and when to get out." Which is why you hire a river outfitter to help you select the appropriate adventure for your experience. You don't want to get more than you paid for.

For more information, contact Clear Creek Rafting at (303) 277-9900, or Arkansas Valley Expeditions at (800) 833-RAFT. Age restrictions may apply.

RUBY MOUNTAIN

Linda started collecting rocks in the fifth grade, and she hasn't stopped. It's become a habit, and she still gets a thrill from discovering a crystal in the dirt beneath her feet. The problem rock collectors face is finding places where it's legal to collect. National and state parks are out, as are wilderness areas. To collect on private land you must get permission, which can be difficult.

At Ruby Mountain, one of Colorado's favorite rock-collecting spots, taking rocks home is legal. Although you probably won't find any rubies, you might find small garnets. And if you're really lucky, you might discover prisms of topaz that range in color from light yellow to amber-brown. Some collectors find specimens by rooting through the rocks at the base of the cliffs; most use hammers and chisels to break up the matrix rhyolite. Remember to wear goggles.

A collecting trip here can be a treasure hunt for families with a little knowledge of minerals.

WHERE: Just east of Nathrop, a few miles south of Buena Vista. Go east on County Road 47 and follow the small sign south onto a gravel road. Continue about 2.5 miles to a parking area on the Arkansas River. Ruby Mountain is the big hill to the south. For more information on Ruby Mountain and other nearby BLM campgrounds, contact the Arkansas Headwaters Recreation Area office in Salida, (719) 539-7289.

WHEN: Year-round, though late spring through late fall is generally best. Serious hounds might want to combine a collecting trip with the annual Gem Show in Buena Vista in August; (719) 395-6612.

ACTIVITIES: Mineral collecting, fishing in the Arkansas, picnicking, and camping. A fee is charged.

FACILITIES: Ruby Mountain is partly owned by the Bureau of Land Management and partly by a private party. Both operate riverside campgrounds and allow rock collecting for a small fee. Primitive toilets, picnic tables, and grills.

BE SURE TO BRING: Sunscreen and hat; a pocket-sized mineral guide, collecting sack, hammer, chisel, and protective eyewear; drinking water or a reliable purification method to make the river water potable.

Monarch Ski Resort

Monarch is a favorite among experts who don't want to pay a lot of money to stand in line. The resort also offers one of the lowest-priced learn-to-ski-plus-lodging packages in the state. Or how about the ski and swim package? The swimming happens in the nearby town of Salida, at the state's largest indoor hot springs pool. Snowboarders will appreciate the new snowboard park; lessons and rentals are available. Or maybe you and the kids would like to go on a moonlight ski tour on the Old Monarch Pass Road.

The closest overnight accommodations are 3 miles away toward Salida, at the Monarch Mountain Lodge.

Where: 16 miles west of Poncha Springs on Highway 50; (719) 539-3573.

Activities: Downhill and cross-country skiing, snowboarding, snowcat skiing. Summer activities are much less developed.

Facilities: Rentals, lessons, and instructional programs for children as young as four; affordable ski-and-stay and learn-to-ski packages; snowboard park, groomed cross-country trails; day lodge with cafeteria and bar; nearby overnight lodge (3 miles away).

Area State Parks and National Forests
San Isabel National Forest

We've always had good luck finding nice campsites in one of the many campgrounds in the San Isabel National Forest, west of Buena Vista along the Sawatch Mountain Range.

There are several good campgrounds about 8 miles south and west of Buena Vista, along County Road 162. Mount Princeton, Chalk Lake, Cascade, and Iron City together provide over seventy-five sites. The Collegiate Peaks Campground, about 10.5

miles directly west of Buena Vista on County Road 306, has spaces for more than fifty tents, campers, and trailers. Other Forest Service campgrounds can be discovered by driving gravel county roads—if you have the time and inclination to explore. The campgrounds are generally open from late May to late October; (719) 539-3591, U.S. Forest Service in Salida.

ELK MOUNTAIN LODGE

This intimate guest ranch (thirty guests maximum) offers the usual trail rides, but because the guest roster is so small, the staff is able to take you on "discovery rides," instead of the same old beaten paths the horses can follow with their eyes closed. At this ranch you can also discover archery, trapshooting, and riflery. Open June through September. Seventeen miles from Buena Vista; (719) 539-4430.

OUTDOOR FAIRS AND FESTIVALS

NEW/OLD FASHIONED CHAFFEE COUNTY FAIR

Five days of rodeos, livestock displays, arts and crafts, country-western music, and other traditional county fair fun. Late July in Poncha Springs, south of Buena Vista on Highway 285; (800) 831-8594.

GOLD RUSH DAYS

Gold-panning, crazy races involving beds and outhouses, melodramas, etc. Mid-August in downtown Buena Vista; (800) 831-8594.

CRESTED BUTTE AREA

Crested Butte is a historic coal-mining town. Today it's best known for its skiing, mountain biking, and championship golfing in a picturesque mountain setting.

Off-road bicycling was practically invented in Crested Butte when, in 1975, a few hardy residents pedaled their old-fashioned one-speed bikes 39 miles to Aspen—over 12,705-foot Pearl Pass!

This energetic ride is reenacted every year during Fat Tire Bike Week, in mid-July. If you're adept enough, you're welcome to join them. For intermediate-skilled mountain bikers, there are dozens of other trails in the surrounding Gunnison National Forest, and not all of them are as difficult as Pearl Pass. Hikers who want to get away from bikers and find some solitude will find plenty of opportunity in the four designated wilderness areas nearby.

If you don't want solitude, come to Crested Butte during one of its famous festivals. Fat Tire Week is followed shortly after by Aerial Weekend, an annual event featuring hot-air ballooning, hang gliding, paragliding, ultralight aircraft flying, and skydiving. Nestled in the south-central mountains about 90 miles northwest of Salida and 225 miles southwest of Denver, Crested Butte is out of the way but definitely worth the drive.

SKIING

CRESTED BUTTE MOUNTAIN RESORT

Families can take advantage of the Crested Butte Ski Resort's Kids Ski Free program, or the Learn to Ski Free offer for beginners of any age (restrictions apply). The Butte also traditionally offers great deals for preseason skiing, and since more than half of the trails on the mountain are rated intermediate, this is a good choice for those who are past the snowplow stage. Experts, Extreme Limits is 400 acres of ungroomed, outrageous, double black diamond terrain set aside for you.

But for us, the best reason to ski Crested Butte Mountain is to enjoy the sheer natural beauty of this area. Few other Colorado ski resorts can compare.

WHERE: 2 miles north of downtown, 12 Snowmass Road; (970) 349-2333.

Activities: Downhill skiing, snowboarding.

Facilities: Base lodging, restaurant, and nearby amenities in town.

The Crested Butte Nordic Ski Center

A 20-kilometer groomed track, rentals, and lessons are available at the Crested Butte Athletic Club. Cross-country ski touring is a wonderful way to enjoy winter's beauty in the Gunnison National Forest.

Where: In the historic downtown district, Second and Whiterock Avenue; (970) 349-6201.

Activities: Cross-country skiing.

Facilities: Rentals, lessons, groomed track; hot tub and sauna. Nearby restaurants and lodging.

Area State Parks and National Forests
Gunnison National Forest

Camping, fishing, mountain biking, and backpacking are the best activities to pursue here in the heart of the Elk and West Elk Mountains. Four designated preserves—West Elk, Raggeds, Snowmass–Maroon Bells, and the Collegiate Peaks Wilderness Areas—surround Crested Butte, providing thousands of acres of undeveloped backcountry that is off-limits to motorized vehicles, pets, and bicycles. And there are miles of old logging, mining, and Forest Service roads to be explored by foot, bike, or four-wheel-drive. Those wishing to enjoy these resources are strongly advised to purchase the appropriate USGS topographic maps and to talk with the local Forest Service office for current information. Wilderness adventure in any form is not to be chased on a whim. Life-and-death emergencies can happen, even to the most experienced mountaineer, especially in a remote, rugged, high-altitude environment such as this.

Most families can find their best and safest adventure pitching a tent at one of the Forest Service campgrounds and enjoying its immediate surroundings. Anglers, bring your tackle —there are quite a few fishing opportunities not far off the beaten track. For a complete list of area campgrounds, contact the USFS (U.S. Forest Service) Forest Station in nearby Gunnison at (970) 641-0471.

CEMENT CREEK CAMPGROUND

Thirteen sites for tents or motor homes. Water and primitive toilets are on-site. Open from mid-May to late October; a fee is charged. Bonus: You can hike to two hot springs 2 miles away. Details are on the Forest Service map. The campground is 7 miles south of Crested Butte on Highway 135. Turn east on Cement Creek Road and go 4 miles.

LAKE IRWIN CAMPGROUND

Thirty-one tent and trailer sites. Water and primitive toilets are on-site. The shores of a mountain lake provide a beautiful location at the foot of the Ruby Mountain Range. A half-mile walk to some small waterfalls is a fun afternoon activity here. Open from early June to late October; a fee is charged. West on County Road 12 for 7.2 miles, then north on Forest Service Road 826 for 2.6 miles to the campground.

OUTDOOR FAIRS AND FESTIVALS
MOUNTAIN MAN RENDEZVOUS

Traders, trappers, mountain men and women gather in costume to have some fun, barter their goods, and compete at events such as ax throwing and black-powder shooting. In late June. Contact the Crested Butte Chamber of Commerce; (800) 545-4505 or (970) 349-6438.

FAT TIRE WEEK

Although it's geared toward young adults, Fat Tire Week is one of Crested Butte's most popular events. A week of off-road bicycle tours, clinics, races, and other contests are the highlights. Held in mid-July. Contact the Crested Butte Chamber of Commerce; (800) 545-4505 or (719) 349-6438.

AERIAL WEEKEND

Get up early to watch hot-air balloons take off north of town by the ski resort. In the afternoon you can watch skydivers land their modern wing-type parachutes in the ballpark, competing for the accuracy of home plate. And all day long the skies above Crested Butte are filled with colorful gliders, parachutes, and kites. Games, prizes, and other activities for earth-bound children. Held the last weekend in July. Contact the Crested Butte Chamber of Commerce; (800) 545-4505 or (719) 349-6438.

ALAMOSA AND THE SAN LUIS VALLEY

Ute, fur trappers, Mexicans, Mormons, Zebulon Pike, Union and Confederate soldiers, gold seekers, settlers—they all explored, hunted, defended, or staked claims to this valley over the past few centuries. Colorado's oldest settlement, San Luis, is here in the southern part of the valley not far from the New Mexico state line. San Luis was first settled by Mexicans in 1851; you can still see the Common, or *Vega*—a parcel of land designated for community agricultural use. There's not a lot of commercialized activities here, 212 miles southwest of Denver, but if history and culture interest you it's worth a detour off the main highway just to drive through it. (If it's open, stop at Emma's Hacienda for a good, authentic lunch special.)

The San Luis Valley is rich in natural history, too. The Alamosa and Monte Vista Wildlife Refuges are the best places to catch a glimpse of sandhill cranes and endangered whooping cranes that stop here on their migrations. And the Great Sand Dunes are a marvel of erosion not to be missed.

Centrally located Alamosa, the largest town in the valley, is the logical place to base yourself. Stay the night in one of the roadside motels, or at least stop for gas and lunch at Dairy Queen or Kentucky Fried Chicken.

GREAT SAND DUNES NATIONAL MONUMENT

It's an amazing sight. Even laconic Matt, a hard-to-impress adolescent the first time he saw the big sweeping sand dunes, said "Cool!"

You immediately wonder what caused this Lawrence of Arabia landscape here in the folds of the Rockies. A trip to the visitor center is in order, where you'll learn it was wind blowing eroded glacial and riverbed debris up against the Sangre de Cristo Mountains. As the sun crosses the sky and the cloud formations change, the dunes change color, chameleonlike, and cast sharp shadows in the late afternoon. During the summer and early autumn months, morning and late afternoon are the best times to explore the sand. It's cooler then, the light isn't so blinding, and the chance of getting struck by lightning from an early afternoon thunderhead is lessened.

It's easy to spend the better part of a day here, or several days, if you plan on hiking into the backcountry. Many people driving from the Front Range area try and fit this in with a trip to Mesa Verde, in the far southwest corner of the state. We've done it ourselves. It's possible, but we guarantee, you'll wish you had longer to explore. If time permits, allow a day at the Great Sand Dunes National Monument and spend the night at the campgrounds or in nearby Alamosa before continuing on to Mesa Verde the next day.

THE SAND DUNES

WHERE: From Highway 60 east of Alamosa, go north on Highway 150 and follow signs 16 miles to the park; (719) 378-2312.

Even hard-to-please children are awestruck by the magnificent dunes at the Great Sand Dunes National Monument.

WHEN: Open daily, year-round. Piñon Flats Campground in the monument is open from April to October on a first-come first-served arrangement. It fills quickly during the summer season.

ACTIVITIES: Sight-seeing, natural history study, picnicking, hiking, exploring the dunes, camping.

FACILITIES: Visitor center with interpretive displays and programs, restrooms, campground, gift shop, snacks.

BE SURE TO BRING: Broad-brimmed hat, socks, and shoes! "Don't wear sandals without socks; the sand will burn your feet and ankles," is the "hot" tip from our son, Adam. Also bring water bottles, sunscreen, and snacks.

FORT GARLAND HISTORIC FORT

Built initially to protect encroaching settlers against Native Americans, used as a Union post during the Civil War, and commanded for a year by the legendary Kit Carson, Fort Garland has been reconstructed and serves as a sort of indoor/outdoor western history museum. It makes a good rest stop during a long road trip—especially if you brought some snacks to enjoy in the shade of the central courtyard. Though most families won't want to choose this as their only destination, it could be visited as part of a statewide tour of historic forts. Fort Garland is probably best enjoyed during one of several special events: Rendezvous of Cultures, a two-day festival on Memorial Day weekend, commemorates the Ute, Hispanics, and fur trappers, the major players in the history and settlement of the valley. Over Labor Day weekend you can watch an 1880s military reenactment, and in December there's the Festival of Lights.

WHERE: 26 miles east of Alamosa, 3 blocks south of Highway 160, follow the signs; (719) 379-3512.

WHEN: Open year-round, from April through October 9 A.M. to 5 P.M.; the rest of the year Thursday through Monday, 8 A.M. to 4 P.M.

ACTIVITIES: An indoor/outdoor history museum within the walls of a historic fort. Special activities and demonstrations; call for upcoming events.

FACILITIES: Restrooms and water fountain, gift and book store, guided tours on arrangement.

ALAMOSA—MONTE VISTA NATIONAL WILDLIFE REFUGE

Want to see thirty-five thousand ducks? Come to Monte Vista Wildlife Refuge in the fall. Bored with mallards? Then how about the prospect of spotting a bufflehead, a common snipe, a pair of phalaropes? Or American wigeons, hooded mergansers, and gadwalls? If your timing is right you might also get to hear the eerie barking of the sandhill cranes as they stop to rest and feed on their migratory journey. Even if you don't know the difference between a grebe and a goose, you'll be impressed by this experience. You'll see hundreds of cranes circling, barking, and on the horizon hundreds more in small triangular groups, like specks of pepper blowing on the wind.

If you're really living right, you might be fortunate enough to see rare whooping cranes. We didn't, so I guess we weren't. But we did enjoy a pleasant walk along the Rio Grande with an inspiring view of Mount Blanca. Until small annoying insects distracted us. And a threatening afternoon thunderstorm. Bring citronella and a rain jacket. And be patient.

WHERE: 3 miles southeast of Alamosa and 6 miles south of Monte Vista on Highway 15; (719) 589-4021.

WHEN: Best time to see cranes and many other birds is spring and fall (March through May and September through November) at the Monte Vista Refuge. A Crane Festival is held annually, in March (see page 190). However, eagles are most often spotted during the winter months.

ACTIVITIES: Bird-watching, walking; occasional interpretive programs.

FACILITIES: Visitor centers, restrooms, auto-tour route.

BE SURE TO BRING: Binoculars, telephoto lens, picnic lunch, and drinks. Sunscreen and bug repellent is advised for warm months, and jackets for morning and evening visits. A bird identification book is helpful; bird lists are available at the visitor centers.

CUMBRES & TOLTEC SCENIC RAILROAD

This historic train ride between Antonito, Colorado, and Chama, New Mexico, follows 64 miles of track laid in 1880 as part of the San Juan Mountain Extension of the Denver & Rio Grande Railroad. A daylong journey on the country's longest and highest narrow-gauge steam railroad can be a wonderful excursion—if your kids are good travelers. There is a restroom aboard as well as a snack and souvenir concession, and the train stops midday for lunch. Tunnels and high bridges add excitement to the scenic journey, but if your family can't sit still, this isn't for you.

A menu of excursions is offered: Leave from Antonito or Chama, ride one-way and take a shuttle bus back to your car; or leave from Antonito, ride halfway and return to Antonito. All in all there are eight trips to choose from, and all take six hours or longer. Unless you live nearby, plan to spend the night in Alamosa, Antonito, or Chama.

WHERE: Antonito, about 30 miles south of Alamosa by Highway 285. Or you can board the train across the state line in Chama, New Mexico; (719) 736-5483.

WHEN: Daily, from Memorial Day to mid-October. Call for times and schedule.

ACTIVITIES: Daylong train rides on a historic narrow-gauge railroad. One-way, or halfway and return (approximately six hours).

FACILITIES: Semi- and fully enclosed cars. Restroom, concessions, and souvenirs on board; lunch stop; shuttle ride back to your car.

BE SURE TO BRING: Warm clothes in layers, snacks, and a picnic lunch (or money to buy food and drinks), books, notepads, travel games, or other quiet amusements.

COLORADO ALLIGATOR FARM

It's definitely not a petting zoo. In fact, it's not a zoo at all but a ranch. Of sorts. But instead of the usual cows and chickens you can get to see hybrid fish and alligators who thrive in the geothermally warmed water under the San Luis Valley's steady supply of sunshine.

Of course, we all know how exciting fish are to watch. And if you've never seen alligators in captivity, they tend to lie motionless for hours and you start to wonder if they're stuffed. So you could be disappointed if you were expecting a lot of interaction from the livestock. That is, until feeding time. Then it looks like a scene from *Friday the 13th* as the alligators move with frightening speed to gnash and hack at their dinner—a tasty preparation of fish-farm "by-products."

Though there is a nature trail to walk and native wildlife like waterfowl and small mammals to see, chances are the kids'll mainly want to see the carnivorous reptiles and buy a plastic alligator from the gift shop. Unless you are morally opposed to the idea of raising cold-blooded animals for human consumption, a brief visit to the Colorado Alligator Farm is an interesting diversion if you're in the Alamosa area.

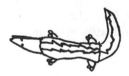

WHERE: 17 miles north of Alamosa on Highway 17; (719) 589-3032.

WHEN: Daily from June through August, 7 A.M. to 7 P.M.; September through May, 10 A.M. to 3 P.M.

ACTIVITIES: See alligators and tilapia fish being raised for harvest. Warm-water fishing, picnicking, and nature walks.

FACILITIES: 2-mile creek wildlife habitat, picnic area, gift shop.

Area State Parks and National Forests
San Luis Lakes State Park

This small state park offers fishing, boating, picnicking, and camping during the warm months. Also water skiing and wind-surfing if you bring your own equipment. During the winter, ice skating, snow tubing, and cross-country skiing can be done if conditions are right. Enjoyed by locals for its fishing and boating opportunities, San Luis Lakes offers traveling families an alternative campsite in case Great Sand Dunes and the nearby RV campgrounds are booked. The park is 20 miles from Alamosa, 8 miles off Highway 17 near Great Sand Dunes National Monument; (719) 378-2020.

Outdoor Fairs and Festivals
Crane Festival

Wildlife exhibits, wetland educational seminars, free buses from town to tour the refuge. Mid-March in Monte Vista; (719) 852-2731.

Rendezvous of Cultures

Festivities depicting the cultures and occupations of the San Luis Valley, specifically Ute, Hispanic, and fur trappers of European descent. Memorial Day weekend at Fort Garland; (719) 379-3512.

WESTERN COLORADO

The West Slope, we call it here, the land west of the Continental Divide. It's a country of forested mountains, broad valleys, dry rocky buttes, and sage. In western Colorado the land has held onto its wildness, resisting development, somehow holding us at bay. The towns out here are fewer, sparser, and rougher around the edges than their Front Range counterparts. On the West Slope you can still catch glimpses of the old American West—those places where nature's rule is supreme, and sometimes extreme. Western Colorado is still the domain of wild animals and plants, a place where the spirits of Native peoples and the shadows of buffalo, grizzly bear, and wolves still roam. It is a place where we are never more than reverent guests, wanting to belong.

Some practical advice: To best explore western Colorado, pick one town each year. Discover that area's treasures—there's more adventure in and around a single western Colorado town than you could possibly experience in a week's time.

If you only have a weekend, our first choice would be to spend it in Glenwood Springs. On I-70, it's less than a three-hour drive from Denver. If you don't have a car, Amtrak and Greyhound make regular stops in Glenwood, and you can rent bikes in town.

Grand Junction also makes a great base for a vacation of any length. It has a commercial airport in addition to train and bus stations. And if you're driving, it's about a four-and-a-half-hour ride from Denver along I-70. There's plenty of lodging and campgrounds, and the weather here is among the mildest in the state.

But we'd have to say that our favorite western town is Steamboat Springs. A little more out of the way than Glenwood or

Grand Junction, Steamboat offers much in the way of hiking, biking, and skiing in a relaxed, low-key environment. With all these choices, you wonder why more families don't explore the great outdoors of western Colorado. And yet, you're kind of glad they don't!

STEAMBOAT SPRINGS AREA

Here's our idea of a perfect Colorado mountain town: Hip enough to sell espresso, latté, and microbrew, but too down-to-earth for a Planet Hollywood or a Mercedes dealership. Called Ski Town, U.S.A. by the marketing folks, this is a community skiers share with local businesspeople, artisans, and ranchers.

If you go to Steamboat you'll immediately notice mink coats are out and plaid flannel shirts are in. This is a genuine town, complete with a high school marching band that performs on skis. It's a town with a couple neighborhood pubs where the local softball teams go for a pitcher of beer after the game—pubs where you can take your kids for a hamburger and not be the only family in the dining room.

Steamboat is not the best place in the state to wear an après-ski outfit or to spot rich and famous people. Your waitress and the lift operator probably live down the street, not in a tent somewhere because they can't afford to live in a million-dollar condo. Let's hope this genuine atmosphere doesn't change as the community grows (which it most certainly is doing).

Steamboat grew up along the Yampa River, in a valley once frequented by the Ute. Nineteenth-century trappers and explorers called it Steamboat Springs because the strange chugging sound one of the springs made sounded like a steamboat. Grading for the railroad silenced the sound, although the namesake water hole still exists. Hundreds of mineral springs are in the area, but many are on private property. (Strawberry Park is a privately owned hot spring many visitors hear about. For a small price, you can camp and soak in one of three pools where bathing suits are optional after dark, and where it occasionally gets a little noisy late at night. Personally, we think Strawberry Park makes a better retreat for young singles or couples than for families with children.)

Skiing became popular early on, first as a method of transportation. Ranchers and townspeople used crude wooden slats to negotiate the deep winter snows. In 1913 a Norwegian named Carl Howelsen moved to town and showed everyone how to ski for fun. He built the country's first ski jump on Emerald Mountain (now called Howelsen Hill), started the Winter Carnival, a Norwegian custom, and inspired local kids to ski competitively. In the decades since, Steamboat Springs has sent more local athletes to the Winter Olympics than any other town in the country. The Winter Carnival Carl Howelsen started has become a Steamboat tradition. Today it's a week of ski competitions, demonstrations, and crazy street entertainment like shovel races and horse-drawn skiers racing down Lincoln Avenue. Not that this town is lacking for winter events that are centered around skiing: Every winter weekend there's a race, a training camp, a happening of some sort.

As much as we like to ski, we prefer summer and autumn in the Yampa Valley (although our young-adult kids might disagree). Hiking trails, picnic spots, and wilderness camping sites are plentiful—many just a short drive from the conveniences of town. May through October can be good months for fishing, rafting, horseback riding, or just exploring. You might want to organize your own photo safari. Wildlife—deer, elk, waterfowl, summer wildflowers, autumn aspen—are all great subjects. But if your timing is bad, you can almost always photograph the hot-air balloons rising daily with the sun over the Yampa Valley. For amateur photographers, it's a guaranteed good shot.

Whatever time of year you go, chances are good we'll see you there.

STEAMBOAT SPRINGS SKI RESORT

As at most Colorado ski resorts, there's ready-made fun to be bought year-round at the ski slopes. In the summer you can take your Aunt Alice from Fort Lauderdale to the top of the mountain on the Silver Bullet gondola. This supersized lift is also the best way to haul mountain bikes to the top of Mount Werner. (To ride the gondola in the summer costs less than half what it does during ski season, but even that's not exactly cheap by our standards.)

Skiing in Steamboat isn't exactly cheap either, but it is family-friendly. In 1981 this was the first resort in the state to offer a "kids ski free" package (with some restrictions). Steamboat's reputation for quality instruction in an atmosphere of fun is well deserved; if you sign your kids up for ski school here, we don't think any of you will be disappointed. Be sure to ask about family packages and any available discounts before you book lodging. Also request a current calendar of events from the lodge, the resort, or the chamber of commerce. If your family likes to watch other skiers—some of them more at home in the saddle than on skis—you'll get a kick out of the annual Cowboy Downhill. In this madcap series of events, professional cowboys compete in a sort of ski rodeo, not quite by the book. Thank goodness Steamboat doesn't take itself too seriously!

WHERE: Follow signs from Highway 40 to Ski Times Square; (970) 879-6111.

ACTIVITIES: In winter, downhill skiing, snowboarding. In summer, hiking, mountain biking, gondola rides.

FACILITIES: Equipment rentals, instruction, shops, restaurants. An excellent ski school and family rates.

HOWELSEN HILL SKI AREA AND PARK

Howelsen Hill is the oldest, largest, and most complete ski-jumping complex in the United States. Owned by the city and operated in conjunction with the Winter Sports Club, the Hill is open to the public except during major competitions. Howelsen

Hill provides for all alpine and Nordic disciplines plus aerial freestyle and snowboarding. The Winter Sports Club here at Howelsen has produced numerous Olympic contenders over the years.

According to the experts, ski jumping is quite safe with proper instruction—and the Hill's safety record is impressive. Kids start out on "small" jumps of 20 or 30 meters, working their way up to the incredible 90-meter monster. Serious injuries are extremely rare.

Whether you want to ski some short runs on an inexpensive lift ticket or watch young athletes launch off a jump, Howelsen Hill is the place to go. And if you weary of downhill skiing, you can explore one of many trails on cross-country skis or snowshoes. You can also take the kids ice skating. The outdoor rink is on the south side of the rodeo grounds.

For a real thrill, try the 4,800-foot bobsled run on a clear, cold winter night. Chickenhearted people take comfort: Sleds are heavily padded and do not need to be steered. Simply hang on tight and scream. One of the few bobsled courses in the country open to the public, this is your big chance to pretend you're all members of the U.S. Olympic Bobsled Team. Open nightly, conditions permitting, through the winter months.

During the summer and early fall you can take a hike or mountain bike on one of Howelsen's many trails. A steep but short climb to the top of Howelsen Hill will give you a breathtaking view of Steamboat Springs and the Yampa Valley. Or stop at the riding stables behind the arena and explore the hill on horseback. Skateboarding, ice skating, tennis, rodeos—Howelsen Hill Park is full of opportunities for year-round fun.

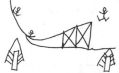

WHERE: Downtown at Fifth Street and River Road. Also accessible from the Yampa Core River Trail; (970) 879-4300.

ACTIVITIES: Downhill and cross-country skiing, ski-jump spectating, snowboarding, night skiing, ice skating, bobsledding. In summer, hiking, mountain biking, tennis, basketball, volleyball, soccer, softball, horseback riding, in-line skating, skateboarding, weekly rodeo.

FACILITIES: Chairlift, ballfields and batting cages, tennis courts, skateboard park, skating rink, bobsled track, horse stables, playground, picnic tables, restrooms, pay phone, food concessions during events.

STEAMBOAT SKI TOURING CENTER

If you're new to the sport of cross-country skiing, the Ski Touring Center is an ideal facility for learning to manage those skinny slats on your feet. It's also the best place for little skiers who aren't quite ready to go bushwhacking in the National Forest—or for parents who don't want to drive too far from town. You'll feel like you're way out in the wilderness because of the woods and creekbeds nearby, but you're really on the edge of civilization. One of the groomed trails traverses a golf course, now hibernating under a couple of feet of snow. An added bonus: You can warm up with a cup of hot chocolate when you're finished, inside at the snack bar.

WHERE: 2000 Clubhouse Drive, follow the signs from Steamboat Boulevard; (970) 879-8180.

ACTIVITIES: Cross-country skiing, lessons, backcountry ski tours.

FACILITIES: 30 kilometers of groomed trails, rentals and sales, refreshments.

SLEIGH RIDES

Several companies near Steamboat Springs can take you on a romantic winter sleigh ride. The destination is usually a cabin or tent in a picturesque location, where you warm your hands on Styrofoam cups of hot chocolate (and in some cases hot toddies or wine). Most rides include a steak, barbecue, or vegetarian dinner.

This adventure is not recommended for toddlers and infants (who have no idea that being outside past their bedtime on a cold dark winter night is romantic). Older children and adults will appreciate mittens, warm hats, sock liners—the whole bit. Here are four local outfits whose horses are raring to go: Sunset Ranch, (970) 879-0945; All Seasons Ranch, (970) 879-2606; Glen Eden Stables, (970) 879-3907; Windwalker Tours, (970) 879-8065.

Dogsledding with Steamboat Sled Dog Express

It seems a bit expensive for an hour-and-a-half ride, considering the dogs aren't making a dime. (They are well cared for, of course. Capable of hauling humans and other heavy loads and bred to thrive in blizzards, the sled dogs actually seem to enjoy their work.) But like hot-air ballooning, it's an extravagant adventure—worth the money, if you have that kind of money to spend. Or this might be the best time ever for a physically disabled child who loves the snow and the wilderness but isn't able to ski or snowshoe.

Where: These guys will pick you up and take you to the backcountry of Routt National Forest, about a forty-five-minute drive from town; (970) 879-4662.

When: Generally open the same season as the ski resort.

Activities: Ninety-minute dogsled rides. Allow four to five hours, however, for automobile transportation to and from the site. Two riders per sled.

Be sure to bring: Warm clothes, including hats and gloves. (The dogs stay warm, but they're working and you're not.)

Tour of Steamboat's Mineral Springs

Since the town is named for one of its many mineral springs, why not visit a few? Most of them aren't springs you can soak in, but by following the map you can make it into a sort of treasure hunt. Children can learn map-reading skills and lead the way. And you'll all lean more about the springs and the town of Steamboat in the process.

Long before any of us were here, the native Ute appreciated the waters for their spiritual and restorative powers. Many of the early white settlers also believed in the healing properties of the warm mineral water. Just after the turn of the century, the Steamboat Springs Sanitarium's Cabin Hotel—a hundred-room lodge—was built along the banks of the Yampa to house travelers who came to "take the cure." Many animals seem to be drawn to the smelly, steaming pools to quench their thirst, but we don't recommend tasting. Certain microscopic organisms thrive in the mineral-laden water—you could end up with diarrhea for your curiosity.

Families interested in geology will want to find out how the springs were formed. In a nutshell, an igneous hot spot deep below the valley heats up groundwater. The steam rises through faults formed during the uplift of the Rocky Mountains, dissolving minerals along the way.

To learn more about the formation or the history of the springs, plan a stop at the library, which happens to be right along your route. You'll find it facing West Lincoln Park and across the river from the spring for which the town was named. Before the railroad was built, this spring made a chugging sound that reminded settlers of the sound an old-fashioned steamboat makes as it paddles along a river. Most kids have never seen a steamboat, but the library is sure to have a book with a picture of one. And just outside, in the shade along the Yampa River, is as good a place as any to eat those peanut butter sandwiches you remembered to pack.

If you want to soak in the springs, end your trip at the Steamboat Springs Health and Recreation Association, 136 Lincoln Avenue. Here you can relax in hot spas, swim in the Olympic-sized pool, or ride the water slide. If you're short on money, you can still get wet in the Heart Spring runoff, across Highway 40 at the Yampa River Park along the Yampa Core River Trail.

Those on foot should set aside most of the day; you'll want to stop frequently along the river, at the various parks, and maybe even at the shops along Lincoln Avenue. If you're touring by bike, plan on two to three hours.

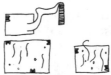

WHERE: There are numerous places to park and start your loop tour. If you want to soak in some springs when your walk or ride is over, we suggest starting at the Steamboat Springs Health and Recreation Center (home of Heart Spring); (970) 879-1828.

WHEN: Year-round.

ACTIVITIES: A 2-mile walk or bicycle tour within the city limits. Soaking, swimming, and sliding into spring water at the Steamboat Springs Health and Recreation Center.

FACILITIES: Restrooms at parks along the way, near to cafés and restaurants. Suit and towel rental at the Health and Recreation Center.

BE SURE TO BRING: A free *Walking Tour of the Springs of Steamboat* guide and map is available at the Health and Recreation Center and at the visitor center at 1255 South Lincoln; (970) 879-0882.

THE YAMPA RIVER CORE TRAIL

This multi-use greenway trail is an ideal way for people of all ages to enjoy nature and get a little exercise without leaving Steamboat. Following the Yampa's course through town, the paved path is dotted with small parks and river access.

Bring bikes from home, or rent them. If you have small children, you can pull them along in a rented carriage that attaches to your bicycle. Or rent in-line skates—now *there's* adventure. Your children can probably teach you the basic skills (unless they're easily humiliated at the sight of mature adults stomping, flailing, and sprawling all over the pavement). Don't forget to request wrist guards, knee pads, shoulder pads—all the protective garb you can get your hands on.

For an old-fashioned dose of refreshment, simply walk along the path for a short distance, enjoying the sights, sounds, and smells of Steamboat's streamside urban park.

WHERE: 3.5 miles long, a paved trail follows the river's course through town. Newcomers can pick it up on the southeast end at Walton Creek Road (Casey's Pond) or on the west side of town at West Lincoln Park. Once you're familiar with the area, you'll find many other access points; (970) 879-4300.

ACTIVITIES: Walking, strolling, biking, skating, picnicking, fishing, wading, tubing, rafting.

FACILITIES: Port-a-lets or restrooms at several parks along the path. Bicycle rentals just off the trail (Sore Saddle Cyclery, Ski Haus, and others). Close to restaurants and grocery stores. Free parking at parks or in some areas at curbside.

RIDING THE YAMPA RIVER

The Yampa River meanders conveniently right through town, providing a handy place to try river rafting or tubing for the first time. Families who require more adrenaline can choose full or multiday trips through the Yampa's wilder Cross Mountain Canyon section, or on the nearby Eagle River.

The Yampa is an excellent river for beginning kayakers to paddle. But even though the Yampa is mild, your first lesson will likely be in an even more mellow body of water—a local swimming pool or fishpond—in order to practice the basic skills.

Tubing down the Yampa is as easy—and refreshing—as it looks.

Tubing takes no experience and is enjoyable for a family with in-between-age kids. We would not take a preschooler or a child small for his age or with physical handicaps tubing. Even though the river is fairly shallow, kids should be big and strong enough to get back on their inner tubes unassisted, in case they tip them over or fall off. But for families with bigger kids it's a great way to spend a few hours on a hot summer day. Springtime tubing can be dangerous due to high water volume from snowmelt and runoff. If in doubt, check with the local Forest Service office; (970) 879-1870.

Sunscreen and hats are necessary for all river activities. Water bottles are a good idea for trips longer than an hour. Water shoes are recommended and can be rented from most of the guide companies, but an old pair of sneakers works too. Since you'll most likely get wet and chilly, bring along some towels, dry clothes, and sweatshirts to leave in the car or at the rental concession.

Here are some reputable outfitters who can safely take you down the river: Rock'n Roll Rubber Rentals: Rents tubes, life vests, and has a complimentary shuttle. On the Yampa River at Eleventh; (970) 846-7777. Buggywhips Rafting: Fifth and Lincoln; (800) 759-0343 or 879-8033. Adventures Wild Rafting: Eighth and Lincoln; (800) 825-3989 or 879-8747. Steamboat Kayak School at Backdoor Sport: 811 Yampa; (970) 879-6249. Barry Smith's Mountain Sports Kayak School at Inside Edge Sports: 1855 Central Park Drive; (970) 879-8794.

THE NATURE CENTER AT CASEY'S POND

Casey's Pond is a fine place for a kid to catch a fish or just watch ducks bob and listen to red-winged blackbirds chirp. This small park features fishing piers and a tiny log cabin that used to house the nature center. (At this writing a new, larger facility is under construction half a mile northeast at Walton Creek Road and Village Drive.) The nature center maintains a good hands-on natural history collection—samples of pinecones, bark, rocks, and feathers—which is sure to expand with the opening of the new building.

Be sure to ask for a schedule of free summer activities happening at the pond and other places around town. Guided hikes and ecotours, fireside talks, fishing derbies—there's something scheduled nearly every day from late May through early September. And if the center is closed, the staff thoughtfully leaves a copy of scheduled activities posted outside.

WHERE: Highway 40 and Walton Creek Road, southeast of ski area; (970) 879-7376.

WHEN: Pond open year-round. Call for nature center hours.

ACTIVITIES: Fishing from the pier at the stocked pond. During the summer, guided hikes, campfire programs, and other activities are coordinated from the nature center.

FACILITIES: Small dirt parking lot and port-a-lets. Nearby fast-food restaurants and grocery stores. Access to Yampa River Core Trail.

BE SURE TO BRING: Fishing tackle and bait.

HORSEBACK RIDING, HAY RIDES, CATTLE DRIVES

Steeped in a culture of ranching, Steamboat Springs has always been a horsey kind of town. There's no shortage of nearby stables and outfitters who advertise horseback riding, from trail rides to overnight backcountry excursions. Some ranches offer riding camps to hone your equestrian skills. One outfit, Steamboat Stables, is conveniently located in town at Howelsen Hill Rodeo Grounds. If time or cash is dwindling, you can take a one-hour ride.

For a longer experience, consider taking part in a cattle drive. Saddleback Ranch is one family-owned and operated outfit that can make you a wrangler for a day. Participants help gather and herd cattle to and from pastures on a working ranch southwest of Steamboat Springs. To pay for the experience of being a ranch hand you must be at least eight years old and comfortable around cows and horses; (970) 879-3711.

Hayrides are good alternatives for young children, or for those a little fearful of large hoofed animals. Most include a barbecue lunch or dinner. Be sure to wear long pants to protect your legs from scratchy hay; if it's an evening ride, bring jackets (not sweaters—you'll be picking hayseeds out for weeks). Here's a sampling of the local ranches where you can ride a horse, a wagon, or a sleigh: Steamboat Stables, (970) 879-2306; All Seasons Ranch, (970) 879-2606; Elk River Guest Ranch, (970) 879-6220; Vista Verde Guest Ranch, (800) 526-RIDE or 879-3858.

HOT-AIR BALLOONING

If you are staying in one of the condominiums or motels on the southeast side of town near the ski resort, you are likely to be awakened in the morning by a whooshing sound. Sounds kind of like a dragon breathing on your window pane. Get up and look out—you'll be surprised to see a big hot-air balloon in your face. Wave to the passengers, wake up the kids, put the coffee on. Grab a coat and camera and go outside, you'll probably see a few more. What dazzling circus colors!

Don't go back to bed. Stick around to watch them land. It can get exciting. There's no steering or brakes, so it takes a skillful pilot to set the basket down, gently, in the chosen spot. A ground crew follows each balloon to help with landing and deflating the great beast when it settles with a sigh.

Watching is free, but if you'd like to go up, plan on spending quite a bit more than you'd spend on a lift ticket. Several reputable companies operate here year-round, depending on weather.

The trouble with ballooning is that you must get up so darn early to catch the air while it's still and cold. Dress warmly and don't forget gloves and hat, which are sometimes appropriate in the summer. Ask about lower children's rates and family packages. (If you're skydivers, as we are, ask about the one-way discount.) Balloons Over Steamboat, (970) 879-3298, and Pegasus Balloons, (970) 879-9191, are two companies that have been floating over the Yampa Valley for years.

Hikes and Kid-Size Mountain Climbs
Fish Creek Falls

Here's a great Steamboat outing you can do on the spur of the moment, no planning involved. It's on the outskirts of town, and you can view the falls in an hour's time or less by walking along a nature trail to an overlook. But why rush it if you don't have to? Stop at the grocery store for some deli sandwiches and film. If you're not into photography, you might want to bring a sketch pad or notebook instead. Kids can trace leaves, write down birds they identify, or sketch the impressive falls. The paved, self-guided trail with interpretive brochures provides a good introduction to the area's natural history; during the summer, rangers host guided walks on a scheduled basis.

If your family is ready for more adventure, the trail to the base of the falls gives access to Long Lake Trail, which leads 6 miles to a cold mountain lake near the Continental Divide. This is a good destination for an older child's first backpacking trip. Be sure to get advice and a map from the local Forest Service office (see phone number below).

WHERE: 3 miles outside of town on Fish Creek Falls Road. Follow the signs from Highway 40, east downtown Steamboat; (970) 879-1870.

WHEN: Year-round. The falls are most impressive in the late spring during runoff, when the volume of water is higher. During the winter the road to Fish Creek Falls may be difficult to travel because of snow.

ACTIVITIES: Sight-seeing, nature study, picnicking, hiking.

FACILITIES: Restrooms, picnic tables, interpretive nature trail, all wheelchair accessible. No overnight camping here.

BE SURE TO BRING: A camera, sketchpads or notebooks, and pens to record your impressions.

RABBIT EARS PEAK

The hike up to Rabbit Ears Peak is one of my favorite walks in Colorado. It's a great adventure for kids because there's a definite destination—an ancient rock formation resembling the appendages of a chocolate Easter rabbit someone has nibbled on. There's a spectacular view and a sense of accomplishment for having reached it.

It's a 2.5-mile hike one way to "the Ears," with a 1,000-foot gain in elevation, but that's well within the ability of most fit families. Unless you're very speedy and don't stop for snacks and snapshots and to examine animal tracks in the mud or tie shoes, you should allow at least four hours for the round-trip. Keep your eyes open for deer and smaller mammals, keep your ears alert for the cries of hawks and eagles circling above.

The geology of the area is quite interesting, a mixture of sedimentary rock with igneous intrusions. Near the top you can spot good examples of volcanic pumice and ancient Precambrian granite. Midway, nice pieces of quartz and chert can be found.

During the summer months, expect a profusion of wildflowers. September and October are crisp and colorful. Expect mud in the springtime, or deep, wet snow. In winter you'll need snowshoes or cross-country skis. Be prepared for some background buzzing and whining—the nearby Dumont Lake Campground area is a popular spot for snowmobilers.

WHERE: About 18 miles southeast of Steamboat Springs on the north side of Highway 40; follow the sign to Lake Dumont, going past the Lake Dumont Campground and turning left at the Rabbit Ears Monument. Follow this dirt road a short distance to Forest Service Road 291. Park here and follow the hiking-trail signs along an old jeep road; (970) 879-1870 (Forest Service office, Steamboat Springs).

ACTIVITIES: Hiking, mountain biking, nearby camping. In winter this area is popular with snowmobilers and cross-country skiers.

FACILITIES: Nearby campgrounds and picnic areas with latrines. No facilities along the trail, so pack out your toilet paper and other trash.

BE SURE TO BRING: Sturdy shoes, snacks, water, sunscreen, a windbreaker or rain slicker. Dress in layers—it's cold and windy at the top.

CAUTIONS: Toward the top the trail steepens and is very slippery, wet or dry. Afternoon lightning strikes are not uncommon any time of year, so hike early in the day. Beware of the crumbly rock that forms the ears. Climbing them is tempting but extremely dangerous.

_____

HAHN'S PEAK

I've heard that some of Butch Cassidy's gang once escaped from the Hahn's Peak jail. And a local man, Billy Baxter, was incarcerated here for shooting an unarmed resident. When vigilantes from the Yampa Valley came to string Billy up, the Hahn's Peak sheriff ran them off. It sounds like a chapter from a western novel! You can visit that jail, at the historical Society Museum on Hahn's Peak's Main Street.

Established in the 1860s, the town of Hahn's Peak is an interesting place to stroll around. This community was once the seat of Routt County. Columbine—the cluster of mostly deserted cabins a short distance north—was a mining camp. Although neither one is a ghost town (people still live here), both have the feel of the Old West. The smell of gold lingers.

You'll undoubtedly want to climb Hahn's Peak. This pointed precipice looks just like a five-year-old's drawing of a mountain. And although it may appear intimidating, requiring a climb of nearly 1,500 feet, it's easily hiked by those with stout legs and determination.

On the walk up keep your eyes peeled for gold. We doubt you'll find any, but it keeps the enthusiasm up. And maybe you'll be luckier than we were. Except for some conglomerates at the base and some tiny quartz crystals along the way, all we saw were tons of lichen-covered boulders. The remains of old mining shacks are interesting discoveries along the trail. They're great to photograph and for making up stories about the folks who built them, but stay out, in case what's left of the walls falls in on you.

If you make it to the top you'll want to check out the lookout station. The views from up here are incredible: To the southwest is Steamboat Lake, dappled with cloud shadows. Sharp eyes can pick out sailboats if the wind is right. Far to the southeast you can see the mountains of Rocky Mountain National Park. To the north, Wyoming!

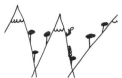

WHERE: 24 miles north of town on Routt County Road 129. The small town called Hahn's Peak is opposite the entrance to Steamboat Lake State Park. Hahn's Peak Ranger Office, (970) 879-1870.

WHEN: Summer and autumn are the best months.

ACTIVITIES: Sight-seeing, hiking, nearby camping. (Forget snowshoeing or Nordic skiing unless you are an expert and don't mind avalanches.)

FACILITIES: Nearest bathrooms are at gas stations near the village of Hahn's Peak. When climbing the peak, you'll have to use bushes (bring a bag to pack out your toilet paper). Nearby campsites at Hahn's Peak Lake, Steamboat Reservoir, and Pearl Lake State Park.

BE SURE TO BRING: A USGS topographic map of Hahn's Peak, or talk to a ranger before hiking. Numerous Forest Service roads and old jeep trails can be confusing. Water, sun protection, warm clothes, rain jackets, and snacks. Also toilet paper and a trash bag to pack it out.

CAUTIONS: This hike is recommended for well-conditioned families with school-age kids. Be careful—it's easy to twist an ankle on the rocky scree at the summit. Hike early to avoid afternoon thunderstorms. People have been killed by lightning on this peak.

AREA STATE PARKS AND NATIONAL FORESTS
STAGECOACH STATE PARK

One hundred campsites around a reservoir with fishing, swimming, and a full-service marina offering rentals. Water sports of all sorts are enjoyed here. Cold-weather activities include winter camping, cross-country skiing, snowshoeing, and ice fishing. The park is 12 miles southwest of Steamboat. To get there, follow signs from Highway 40 to County Road 131 to County Road 14; (970) 736-2436.

Steamboat Lake State Park

A huge reservoir with a swim beach, boat ramp, and full-service marina, including equipment rentals. Over 180 campsites are spaced well apart and graced with wildflowers during the summer months. This is a good place for bigger kids to ride their bikes without getting lost. Easy cross-country skiing in winter. Outfitters are nearby for horseback riding by the day or half-day. The park is 27 miles north of Steamboat, just off County Road 129; (970) 879-3922.

Pearl Lake State Park

Features fishing and no-wake boating. This park is smaller and sometimes quieter than the other two state parks in this area. Year-round camping and winter activities such as ski touring and snowshoeing can be done here as well. Follow the sign from County Road 129 just a few miles southeast of Steamboat Lake State Park; (970) 879-3922.

Routt National Forest

Surrounding Steamboat Springs, Routt National Forest provides hiking, biking, fishing, and camping opportunities. The Mount Zirkel Wilderness Area is backcountry set aside for low-impact hiking, fishing, and primitive camping. Access is near Slavonia, about 30 miles north via Highway 129 and Forest Service Road 400.

A number of campgrounds can be found within twenty minutes of downtown Steamboat. Here is a sampling.

Dumont Lake, Meadows, and Walton Creek Campgrounds

Watch for signs along Rabbit Ears Pass southeast of Steamboat on Highway 40. About one hundred sites among the three campgrounds. Generally open July through late October.

Hahn's Peak Lake

A popular campground with thirty-five sites for tents and motor homes near the historic town of Hahn's Peak. Generally open mid-June to late October. The campground is 33 miles north of Steamboat off Route 129.

Dry Lake

Closer to town but smaller (only eight sites) and less developed. No water here; no reservations and no fee. Drive 2 miles out of town on Strawberry Park Road, then 2 miles north on County Road 36, and 2 miles east on Forest Service Road 60 (Buffalo Pass Road).

For more information, contact the Forest Service at (970) 879-1870. The totally unprepared can rent camping equipment from Ski Haus, Highway 40 and Pine Grove Road, by Safeway; (970) 879-0385.

Outdoor Fairs and Festivals

Yampa River Festival

River races and rodeos, kayak clinics, children's activities, food, music. In mid-June; (970) 879-4300.

Steamboat Springs ProRodeo Series

Traditional rodeo events, spectator activities, and a barbecue. Every Friday and Saturday night at 7:30, from mid-June through mid-August at the Howelsen Hill Rodeo Grounds, Romick Arena; (970) 879-0880.

Rainbow Weekend Hot-Air Balloon Rodeo

Aerial competitions provide colorful amusement for spectators in mid-July; (970) 879-9008.

Winter Carnival

A hockey tournament, ski-jumping competitions, ice-sculpture contests, parades, snow-shovel races, lots more! Based on a Norwegian tradition, this Steamboat festival began in 1914. In early February; (970) 879-0880.

In Case of Bad Weather

Tread of Pioneers Museum

Lots of artifacts and memorabilia from early ranchers, native Ute, and early skiers. Downtown at 800 Oak Street; (970) 879-2214.

Steamboat Springs Health and Recreation Center

Hot Springs, water slide, lap pool, and fitness center. Open daily, year-round, regardless of weather. 136 Lincoln Avenue; (970) 879-1828.

The Northwest Corner

The northwest corner of our state is not widely promoted. Frankly, there's not much out there. Just sagebrush, shadscale and creosote bushes; unfettered rivers and wetlands alive with trout, ducks, and geese; herds of deer, pronghorn, elk, moose, and bighorn sheep; golden eagles, red-tailed hawks, and burrowing owls trying to make a living on prairie dogs and mice; ancient geologic formations, fossils—and a legacy of ranchers, Ute, and prehistoric Fremont. On the other hand, we guess there's a lot out there, depending on what you're looking for.

Dinosaur National Monument

Dinosaur National Monument is not exactly on your way home from tee-ball practice, so you'll have to do a little planning and preparation to visit. It's not a "let it happen" kind of experience. But if you appreciate minimally developed parks without all the souvenir shops, fast-food stands, and convenience camping, a trip to Dinosaur is worth the effort.

Although the really cool stuff (the dinosaur fossils) are found in the quarry just across the state line in the Utah section of the park, the Colorado side offers the best camping, hiking, and river-floating opportunities. So of course you'll want to cross over to visit the quarry and see the excellent museum there, but you'll also want to do some exploring on the Colorado side.

The Cold Desert Interpretive Trail behind the visitor center just east of the town of Dinosaur is a good way to stretch your legs after the long car ride. The path is very short, just a quarter-mile. If you walk it you'll learn to identify desert plants like greasewood and galleta grass, and learn why each grows where it does. Your eyes will become acquainted with the nuances of a cold desert life zone such as this. Your nose will pick up the sharp, pleasant smell of sage and rabbitbrush. Your ears will notice a definite lack of noise, the predominant sound being the wind in the brush. And if it's early morning or evening, your skin will probably prickle with goose bumps from the chilly air.

A slightly longer walk would be the Harpers Corner Trail— 1 interpretive mile. The trailhead is easy to find. Just follow Harpers Corner self-guiding scenic drive from the visitor center and monument headquarters. There are some good picnic spots along the drive, if you remembered to bring food from home or the nearest town.

If you want to enjoy the mighty Yampa, one of the West's last undammed rivers, one of the best ways is by raft. Adventure Bound Rafting in Grand Junction offers multiday rafting trips recommended for families with older children who enjoy primitive camping and have had some prior paddling experience; (970) 241-5633.

WHERE: 295 miles from Denver via Highway 40, 2 miles east of the town of Dinosaur; (970) 374-2216.

WHEN: Monument open year-round. Visitor's center open daily during the summer, limited hours off-season.

ACTIVITIES: Hiking, camping, river floating, fishing, learning about dinosaurs and paleontology. Park Service programs and activities are sometimes offered during the summer months.

FACILITIES: Visitor center with educational displays, interpretive trails, and six campgrounds. Nearest gas, food, and lodging are found in the towns of Dinosaur and Rangely, or in Vernal, Utah.

Camping is advised because there's not much in the way of lodging close at hand.

BE SURE TO BRING: Water, picnic food, warm clothes worn in layers. This national monument is remote, and most of the campgrounds are primitive.

CANYON PINTADO

It's a little like a giant Where's Waldo? puzzle, looking for the ancient rock art of Canyon Pintado. You have a map and a description of what you're looking for. Animals, strange symbols, and figures etched into or painted on the canyon walls. But like Waldo, the images you're looking for aren't readily apparent.

The explorer-priests Dominguez and Escalante were the first Europeans to discover the rock art, back in 1776. Escalante wrote, "We saw crudely painted three shields . . . and the blade of a lance. Farther down on the north side we saw another painting which crudely represented two men fighting." It is thought the paintings and carvings were made by the Fremont people, who roamed this region from A.D. 700 until the mid-1100s.

See who can be the first in your family to spot them. It's harder than it sounds, but fun if you like petroglyphs. Morning or late afternoon provides the best light for viewing, not to mention the coolest temperatures during the summer months. Be sure to get a map from the chamber of commerce in Rangely, or at the BLM office in Grand Junction (the Bureau of Land Management oversees Pintado Canyon).

A trip through the canyon takes anywhere from an hour and a half to four, depending on how long it takes you to spot the glyphs. A good three-day loop trip would be to visit Dinosaur National Monument by way of Highway 40 (camping there overnight), then exploring Canyon Pintado on your way to Grand Junction, where you can spend the following night.

WHERE: South of Rangely, along Highway 139. Contacts: Rangely Chamber of Commerce, (970) 675-5290, or Grand Junction BLM office, (970) 244-3000.

WHEN: Year-round, but can be brutally hot during midsummer.

ACTIVITIES: Finding ancient Fremont rock drawings, short hikes or bike rides on BLM land, and primitive camping in an area rich in petroglyphs, deer, oil, and natural gas.

FACILITIES: None in the canyon. This is not a park. Stock up on everything in or before the small town of Rangely, or in Grand Junction if you're coming up from the south.

BE SURE TO BRING: A map from the Rangely Chamber of Commerce, the Colorado Welcome Center in Dinosaur, or the BLM office in Grand Junction. Wear sturdy shoes, long pants, hat, and sunscreen for protection. Take plenty of water and snacks.

GLENWOOD SPRINGS AREA

This is the weekend getaway many Colorado families choose—it's relatively inexpensive and easy to get to by car or by train. Once there, you can play in the 15-mile long Glenwood Canyon, at Ski Sunlight, in the remote White River National Forest, or just relax in one of the largest hot mineral pools in the world. Perhaps most rewarding is to combine some physical challenge with some dissolute soaking and enjoy the best of both worlds.

The famous hot springs for which the town is named were once sacred to the Ute, who believed them to have healing and restorative powers. The Ute introduced them to early explorers, and the word spread. The name Glenwood comes from Glenwood,

Iowa, the hometown of an early settler (who had little imagination or he would have called it something a little more evocative). Walter Devereux, an Aspen engineer who made a fortune in silver, bought the hot springs and incorporated the town. With the help of foreign investors he built an elegant resort, attracting wealthy guests from all over the world. Kings, dukes, U.S. presidents, actors, actresses, and infamous gangsters stayed at the Glenwood Springs Resort during its heyday.

Today a large part of the charm of Glenwood is its connection with history, although some claim both the pool and neighboring landmark Hotel Colorado are in need of a facelift. It's true, they both show signs of age. But to us the lines and wrinkles are signs of character, not blemishes. If the resort is ever totally renovated and updated, it may not be any different than dozens of other slick modern resorts. We like Glenwood Springs just the way it is—a charming middle-class vacation town. It may be less chic, but it's also less expensive and pretentious than the place called Aspen 40 miles to the southeast. We recommend Glenwood as a base station for families looking for simple outdoor adventures. Two suggestions are to drive and camp, or take the train and stay at the Hotel Colorado. One is rugged, one romantic, and both are loaded with potential for fun.

Glenwood Springs Hot Springs Lodge and Pool

As hot-spring swimming pools go, this one is the mother of all—it's over two blocks long! Heated to 90 degrees, the temperature is just right for year-round swimming. Since it'll take the kids longer to get cold, you're sure to get your money's worth.

Some adults may prefer the smaller, steamier "therapeutic" pool, maintained at 104 degrees. This pool is for relaxing, not romping. For parents who need even more of a retreat, the adjacent Yampah Hot Springs Vapor Caves is a separate facility offering private hot tubs, facials, massages, and other therapies.

Most kids will be content to spend the day in the big pool and riding the water slide. There are plenty of places to eat, including the on-site restaurant, and other cafés are within walking distance.

Many people go to Glenwood Springs just for the swimming pool while others feel compelled to earn their enjoyment by spending the day skiing, rafting, or hiking before they indulge in a hot soak. In any case, don't miss it. The price is reasonable, the kids will love it, and who knows what restorative powers those steaming, odiferous waters hold?

WHERE: 401 River Road, north on the Grand Avenue exit from I-70; (970) 945-7131.

WHEN: Swim year-round daily until 10 P.M.; closed second Wednesday of the month from September through May.

ACTIVITIES: Swimming and soaking in warm mineral water. Also amusements such as miniature golf, arcade, water slide.

FACILITIES: Two heated pools, water slide, restaurant, gift shop, swimsuit and towel rentals, locker rooms, athletic club, and moderately priced lodging just across the street. For reservations at the Glenwood Hot Springs Lodge, call (800) 537-SWIM or (970) 945-6571.

BE SURE TO BRING: Sunscreen any time of year (unless you're soaking by starlight). If you forget it, you can buy it there.

GLENWOOD CANYON RECREATION TRAIL

With the deep red cliffs on either side of the roiling Colorado River, the Glenwood Canyon captivates you even as you're driving through it. You can't wait to park the car, get out, and explore it. The recently completed 18-mile recreational trail that parallels the river provides an easy route.

Geology buffs will try to read the eons in the 1,800-foot cliffs where ancient Precambrian granite lies next to newer sedimen-

The Glenwood Canyon Recreation Trail offers eighteen miles of opportunities to explore the captivating Glenwood Canyon.

tary formations. Locomotive enthusiasts will enjoy the trains that run on the riverside track, first laid in 1887 by the Denver & Rio Grande Railroad. Technical minds will appreciate the engineering and construction marvel of the canyon's highway. River enthusiasts will salivate at the challenges the swift-flowing Colorado presents. Whatever your interest, you'll find this canyon amazing.

You can reach the trail from any of the four canyon parking plazas off I-70 east of town. Exit 129, the Bair Ranch exit and Rest Area, provides parking, restrooms, and a riverside hiking loop in addition to trail access at the eastern end of the canyon. Nearer to town, Exit 119 (No Name Rest Area) offers restrooms and a nearby campground. In town, you can get on the path just east of the Yampah Spa and Vapor Caves, 709 East Sixth Street. Bicycles and in-line skates can be rented at numerous shops in town, including Rock Gardens Camping and Rafting, 2 miles east of town at Exit 119, just off the trail; (970) 945-6737. Also BSR Sports, 210 Seventh Street; (970) 945-7317.

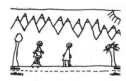

WHERE: Just east of Glenwood Springs, alongside the Colorado River. For more information, contact the Visitor Center at Eleventh and Grand Streets; (970) 945-6589.

WHEN: Year-round, weather permitting.

ACTIVITIES: Easy-grade biking, in-line skating, jogging, walking, picnicking; access to numerous other side trails.

FACILITIES: Parking areas, restrooms, water, and landscaped picnic areas along the way. Wheelchair-accessible paved path.

BE SURE TO BRING: Sun protection, water bottles, and snacks.

WALKS AND HIKES
HANGING LAKE

It's a fairly steep "Are we there yet?" climb, but very rewarding. You know it's rewarding because everybody who passes you on the way down tells you it is. Soon your expectations are way out of control. It better be really awesome, you're thinking, wishing you'd brought more water and maybe a candy bar or two. But the sight of dozens of other families, babies in backpacks, and grandparents with walking sticks toiling up the trail ahead serves as a shaming device to keep you going.

Although steep and somewhat crowded, this is never a boring hike. A sparkling stream with the picturesque name Dead Horse Creek stays beside you most of the way. If you get hot you can splash some Dead Horse water on your face. Fossil fanatics, keep your eyes peeled for some crinoids embedded in boulders and cliffs along the way. The specimens are way too big to take home but are fun to spot.

Adventurous kids will love the end of the climb, just before reaching the much-anticipated lake. Here you must negotiate some steep and rocky steps cut out of the granite that are precariously close to a great vertical drop. This presents a small challenge for those afraid of heights. Mothers, be prepared for some heart flutter as you watch your youngster who seems barely capable of climbing the school-bus steps lead the way.

The scene at the top would be surprising if you hadn't been expecting it. Lakes are generally found in valley floors or in mountain cirques scoured by glaciers, not along steep streambeds. Hanging Lake and its waterfall were created by an ancient geologic fault that dropped the lake from its former location.

You'll find a boardwalk over the edge of the lake, and benches to rest on. Those who haven't spent all their energy will want to climb a short distance above the falls to see Spouting Rock, where Dead Horse Creek dramatically enters the canyon from underground. From this vantage point you also get a bird's-eye view of Hanging Lake below. There's not a lot more to do here except explore the banks and try to go behind the waterfall. (Be careful, the rocks are slippery.)

On the trek back down you can give smug encouragement to the Johnny-come-latelys huffing and puffing up the trail. "You're almost there! It's really worth it," you'll say. And you're right. It is!

WHERE: 10 miles east of Glenwood Springs; follow the signs from I-70 Exit 125 eastbound, or Exit 121 westbound.

WHEN: Summer and fall are best for most people. The trail can be slippery under snow, ice, and mud.

ACTIVITIES: One of Colorado's most photographed places, involves a hike of 1.2 miles one-way, uphill. (Feels much farther, frankly.) Nearly 1,000 feet in elevation gain, and from our observations, small tots who start out walking will end up being carried.

FACILITIES: Parking, restrooms, and water fountain near trailhead at the Hanging Lake Rest Area. Several benches and one shelter along the trail. Not wheelchair accessible.

BE SURE TO BRING: Sturdy, nonslip hiking shoes and water. Small first-aid kit with moleskin or bandages for blisters. A snack to eat at Hanging Lake is a good reward for young walkers. (And old walkers, too, says Bob. We didn't bring any food and were ravenous by the time we got back to the car.)

PIONEER CEMETERY AND DOC HOLLIDAY'S GRAVE

Everybody loves a good bad guy, we guess. Romanticized by western novels and movies, Doc Holliday was a southern gentleman/dentist/gambler who was also handy with a gun. He associated with Wyatt Earp and his brothers down in Tombstone. Holliday died in Glenwood Springs, having come here to the hot mineral springs to take the cure for his consumption, as tuberculosis was then called. The cure didn't work. He is purportedly buried in the Pioneer Cemetery (once known as the Linwood Cemetery) in a grave that is kept secret. What you will see is a headstone and memorial on the west side of the cemetery, near the American flag. (Bear left as you enter the gate.) Holliday's dry sense of humor is evident by his chosen epitaph, and it's up to you to speculate on the actual burial site.

Get your imagination working on the walk up. Sagebrush, juniper, and mountain mahogany line the dirt road. You can practically hear the horses' hooves, the jingle of the harness rings, the creaking wagon carrying Doc's wooden coffin to its resting place. You can picture yourself as one of the few people who followed the hearse up the dusty hill.

Though Doc's monument is the big draw, there are lots of interesting people buried here who, though less famous, made more lasting contributions to the town and surrounding valley. An interpretive sign educates sight-seers about the hard lives and early deaths of the immigrants who settled here, and the Ute who hunted here.

Although visits to cemeteries can be sobering and thought-provoking, those families with an imagination will find the short hike to Pioneer Cemetery a fun and interesting outing of one to two hours.

WHERE: Trailhead approximately two blocks behind the Glenwood Springs Chamber and Visitors Center (Eleventh Street and Grand Avenue). Take Eleventh Street east to Bennett and walk a short distance until you reach a sign that marks the trail; (970) 945-6589.

WHEN: Year-round. Avoid midday in midsummer because of intense heat and bright sun.

ACTIVITIES: A climb of about half a mile to a historic cemetery with a great view. Easily hiked by anyone in good health, even young children.

FACILITIES: Restrooms and drinking fountain at the nearby Visitor Center.

BE SURE TO BRING: Sun protection and water. Even though it's a short walk, it's all uphill. A picnic in the cemetery, or in the small shady park behind the Visitor Center, might be fun.

RAFTING THE COLORADO AND ROARING FORK RIVERS

The Colorado and Roaring Fork Rivers present rafters with a dilemma: Which river to float? Depending on conditions and your family's experience level, there's a stretch of water for you. The Glenwood Canyon typically provides some of the wildest, whitest water, and the Roaring Fork south of Glenwood usually offers more mellow terrain. The season is generally Memorial Day through the end of September, and the following companies represent just a few of the many licensed outfitters.

ROCK GARDENS RAFTING AND CAMPGROUND

Specializes in family floats of varying lengths; takes kids who weigh at least 40 pounds. And if you're camping, it's right along the bike path through Glenwood Canyon. Open April through mid-October; the start and end of the season are weather-dependent. Located 2 miles east of town off I-70 Exit 119 (No Name exit); (970) 945-6737.

BLUE SKY ADVENTURES, INC.

Conveniently based in the lobby of the Hotel Colorado, this company has been in operation since the mid-seventies and offers both half-day and full-day trips; (970) 945-6605.

SKI SUNLIGHT

The appeal of Ski Sunlight is the price—cheap compared to bigger, busier Colorado resorts. Most of the runs are intermediate, and the laid-back, friendly atmosphere here lends itself to good times and happy memories. Sunlight offers snowboard lessons, rentals, and a snowboard park for those who want to enjoy this once radical, now almost mainstream sport. Sunlight's Nordic center is excellent—30 kilometers of groomed trails across varying terrain—and two wayside cabins to warm up in. You can even arrange to spend the night in one of the cabins. Though they seem remote, they're less than a mile from the trailhead—close enough for even a family of novice skiers to take advantage of. Or, if you don't want to spend the night in the backcountry, take advantage of one of the guided moonlight ski tours and just sip hot chocolate by the cabin's fireplace before returning to your cozy warm motel room or your own cabin for the night.

WHERE: 10 miles south of Glenwood Springs on Four Mile Road (County Road 117); (800) 445-7931 or (970) 945-7491.

ACTIVITIES: Downhill and Nordic skiing, snowboarding, ice skating near the base at the Bavarian Inn. In summer, weekend western show and barbecue, horseback riding, hayrides, nearby in-line skating, hiking, and biking.

FACILITIES: Kids-ski programs and discounts for ages three to fourteen, a designated kids hill; low-cost packages, including beginner deals, ski-lodge-hotsprings combo, downhill/Nordic tickets. Nordic center has 30 kilometers of groomed trails and two cabins. Free shuttle bus from downtown. Summer facilities include food concessions and riding stables. Year-round lodging such as the Hideout Cabins and Campground, 3 miles south of town on County Road 117 (Ski Sunlight Road); (970) 945-5621.

AREA STATE PARKS AND NATIONAL FORESTS

RIFLE GAP STATE RECREATION AREA

Year-round camping and fishing are this park's highlights. Other water activities include swimming, water skiing, and scuba diving. But bring your own toys—there's no marina and no equipment rentals. Some big kids seem to like riding their bikes around the reservoir and on the nearby county road. A nearby eighteen-hole golf course will keep some parents and adolescents amused. In winter you can go ice skating, cross-country skiing, or snow tubing. About 35 miles from Glenwood Springs, 7 miles north of Rifle on Highway 325; (970) 625-1607.

RIFLE FALLS STATE PARK

Year-round camping and a self-guided nature trail over and above Rifle Falls are the highlights here. Wildlife in the immediate area include mammals such as beaver, chipmunks, weasels, and bobcats. A variety of birds, from great blue herons to hummingbirds, can be spotted. About 3 miles beyond Rifle Gap on Highway 325; (970) 625-1607.

HARVEY GAP STATE PARK

This is a day-use only park. Fishing is the primary activity; windsurfing and scuba diving are also done here. Go past Rifle Gap on Highway 325 to Highway 226. Turn right and go 4 miles to County Road 237. Follow the signs to the park, 1 mile south; (970) 625-1607.

THE WHITE RIVER NATIONAL FOREST

This national forest shoulders Glenwood Springs to the north, offering lots of opportunities for hiking, mountain biking, and semiprimitive camping. The Flat Tops Wilderness Area is in the northern part of this preserve. This protected environment offers remote fishing, wildlife-viewing, hiking, and primitive camping. Contact the White River ranger station in Glenwood Springs for maps and specific details; (970) 945-2521.

OUTDOOR FAIRS AND FESTIVALS

SKI SPREE

Competitive and just-for-fun events, including a mountain-bike race on snow. Midwinter in Glenwood Springs and at Ski Sunlight; (800) 445-7931 or (970) 945-7491.

EASTER AT SKI SUNLIGHT

Sunday sunrise service, reduced lift fare, and Easter egg hunt. March or April, on Easter Sunday; (800) 445-7931 or (970) 945-7491.

STRAWBERRY DAYS

Since the turn of the century, Glenwood Springs has been hosting this outdoor event featuring arts, crafts, a carnival, sporting contests, a parade—and free strawberries and ice cream! Mid-June, on the south end of town at Sayre Park; Grand Avenue and Hyland Park Drive; (970) 945-6589.

IN CASE OF BAD WEATHER

FRONTIER HISTORICAL MUSEUM

Find out about the role coal played in the valley, and see artifacts from Theodore Roosevelt's visits to Glenwood Springs. Kids under twelve admitted free. Monday through Saturday from 1 to 4 P.M. during the summer, Thursday through Saturday during the rest of the year. 1001 Colorado Avenue; (970) 945-4448 or 945-8465.

HOTEL COLORADO

Even if you aren't a guest at this fine old hotel, at least step inside and look around the lobby. Or have a meal in the Devereux

Restaurant (breakfast is the least expensive meal). Although it's a little down in the heels, this historic resort is full of colorful history. Some well-known past guests include Teddy Roosevelt and William Howard Taft. 526 Pine Street; (970) 945-6511, or (303) 623-3400 from the Denver area.

GRAND JUNCTION AREA

Dinosaur bones. Red rocks, sheer cliffs, and a river. Orchards and estate wineries. The biggest mesa in the world. Grand Junction is a great place to explore.

Named for the junction of two rivers, the Gunnison and the Colorado (once known as the Grand River), Grand Junction is a city big enough to offer all the amenities of lodging, gas, grocery stores, sporting shops, and restaurants, yet it's not urbane enough to cause parking hassles or polluted skies. There's so much to do around here if you like the outdoors, and it's easy to get to by car, train, bus, or commercial airline.

Our own favorite weekend in Grand Junction includes one-day hiking in the Colorado National Monument or on the Grand Mesa, a few hours spent at the Jurassic museums of Devil's Canyon and Dinosaur Valley, and one day touring the vineyards of nearby Palisade to sample the latest vintage. (You could easily spend a week on Grand Mesa alone.)

Whatever you decide to do on your Grand Junction adventure, be sure to stop at the visitor center on Horizon Drive, just off Interstate 70. After collecting a fistful of maps and flyers, continue west on Horizon, following the signs to the ranger's station and the BLM office. Here you can get topographic maps and the latest information about camping, hiking, and biking in the national forest and on BLM land.

If you're like us, you'll return to Grand Junction again and again to enjoy its Grand Mesa, its red canyons, its vineyards and rivers.

COLORADO NATIONAL MONUMENT

Sunrise. A porcelain sky, empty but for two jet contrails like woolly eyebrows above the cliffs. A raven rises—the sound of wings cutting the cool air. The sandstone turns a dozen shades of pink as first light appears over the mesa. These are impressions of Colorado National Monument at daybreak.

This is our state's own intimate Grand Canyon, carved by the same river. It's dry, rugged land dominated by voluptuous red rock, studded with dwarfed juniper and piñon trees. Your eyes can't get enough of it. You somehow want to be a part of it.

Most people drive through the monument in their vehicles, stopping at a few of the scenic overlooks to pan the horizon with their video cameras. Although it's a very short drive from Grand Junction and can be "done" in a couple of hours by car, what fun is that? If possible, make a day of it. Plan to stop at the visitor center to see the displays and ask about trails—more than half a dozen of them within the monument, from short nature walks to overnight backpacks. We enjoyed Otto's Trail—an easy mile walk with stunning views of canyon walls, Grand Mesa to the east, the chalky Book Cliffs to the north, and the whole Colorado River Valley.

Early morning and late afternoon are the best times to hike: It's cooler, and the angle of the sun makes sight-seeing better. Keep your eyes peeled for golden eagles, red-tailed hawks, peregrine falcons, mule deer—and watch for mountain lion tracks. The monument is also a great place to spot small reptiles: collared and sagebrush lizards, whiptails, and bull snakes are common here. Off-road bicycling is not permitted. Road cycling through the monument is strenuous and dangerous, due to the road's narrow shoulder and motorists distracted by the scenery.

WHERE: 10 miles west of Grand Junction on Highway 340. From I-70, take Exit 21 (Grand Junction) or 19 (Fruita) and follow the signs; (970) 858-3617.

WHEN: Open all year, but summers here can be very hot. In our opinion, autumn, winter, and spring are the best times of year.

ACTIVITIES: Sight-seeing, hiking, on-road biking, camping, picnicking. Scheduled ranger-led walks and campfire talks in the summer and fall.

FACILITIES: Visitor center, restrooms, campgrounds, and trails, some with wheelchair access.

BE SURE TO BRING: Sunscreen and hats, water bottles, sturdy hiking shoes, snacks.

DINOSAUR WALKS IN DINOSAUR VALLEY

Okay, it takes a little imagination, but these short, self-guided walking tours through excavation sites in the Grand Junction area are fascinating to some of us. Important discoveries have been made at these separated areas, and who knows what other fossilized bones lie beneath our feet, yet to be found? At Dinosaur Hill, an apatosaurus skeleton was found that is on display at the Field Museum of Natural History in Chicago. Riggs Hill is where Elmer Riggs came across the first-known brachiosaurus skeleton. At Rabbit Valley, bones are still being excavated. The Bureau of Land Management oversees these quarries and trails, and in conjunction with the Museum of Western Colorado has provided a brochure and trail map for each of the three sites.

We walked Dinosaur Hill shortly before sunset in September. It was still noticeably hot. Bob, who is slightly less enthralled by sandstone formations than Linda, was a good sport nonetheless. But he points out that kids should realize they probably won't find any brontosaurus femurs poking out of the dirt, and even if they did, it's against the law to take them! We met up with a mother and her two young boys, who were having more fun spotting rabbits and lizards than in reading about and imagining bones. For Linda, the 1-mile self-guided trail was just about the right length to survive without water, which we forgot to bring.

Guided maps are sometimes available at the trailhead, but often the supplies run out. To make certain you get a map and trail guide, contact the Dinosaur Valley Museum, (970) 241-9210, or the Bureau of Land Management, (970) 244-3000.

WHERE: Riggs Hill is on South Broadway at Meadows Way, on the west side of Grand Junction; .75-mile loop trail. Dinosaur Hill is 1.5 miles south of Fruita on Highway 340; 1-mile loop trail. Trail Through Time at Rabbit Valley is 25 miles west of Grand Junction on I-70, Exit 2; 1.5-mile trail. For more information, contact the Dinosaur Valley Museum, (970) 241-9210 or (970) 243-DINO.

WHEN: Year-round. The temperature can get extremely hot during the summer, so if that's when you're visiting, walk early in the day.

ACTIVITIES: Self-guided trails through excavation sites where dinosaur fossils have been found.

FACILITIES: Not wheelchair accessible. Restroom and covered picnic tables; guided maps available at the Dinosaur Valley Museum in Grand Junction at Fourth and Main.

BE SURE TO BRING: "Bring water, sunscreen, and hats. And walk when the weather is cool—say, mid-January. Otherwise, it's a death march," says Bob.

DINOSAUR VALLEY MUSEUM OF WESTERN COLORADO

Before going off to the dinosaur digs, spend an hour or more at Dinosaur Valley Museum so you can better appreciate your outdoor walks. At this downtown Grand Junction museum you can watch scientists and volunteers prepare fossil specimens in the laboratory. There's also an excellent collection of dinosaur tracks and casts on display. A walk-through diorama with half-size animated dinosaurs will captivate even preschoolers. But the highlight of Dinosaur Valley Museum for some youngsters will be a toss-up between the joy-stick-controlled giant T-Rex and the fossilized dinosaur turds.

WHERE: 326 Main Street; (970) 241-9210 or 243-DINO.

WHEN: Tuesday through Saturday, 10:00 A.M. to 4:30 P.M. During the summer it's open daily from 9 A.M. to 5 P.M.

ACTIVITIES: Museum and fossil-preparation demonstrations.

FACILITIES: Restrooms, gift shop, trail maps for area dinosaur walks. Street parking only; be prepared to walk a block or more.

POWDERHORN SKI RESORT

Powderhorn is one of the least-frequented ski areas in the state. Many Colorado skiers have no idea where it is. Maybe because it's rather small (less than 600 acres), or because its peak elevation is less than 10,000 feet, or because it's not located near a trendy, hip development where movie stars have built million-dollar mountain retreats. But guess what? The prices are some of the lowest in the state, and the snow can be some of the best. Twenty percent of the runs are designed for beginners, 50 percent for intermediate skiers, which makes it perfect for those of us who aren't NASTAR rated.

A Nordic center grooms 12 kilometers of trails within the boundaries and offers rentals and lessons. More experienced ski-touring families can use the lifts to reach a good trail system in the Grand Mesa backcountry.

Although the Mesa probably gets more snowmobilers than skiers, it's possible to find peace, quiet, and an ocean of powder at Powderhorn.

WHERE: About 35 miles east of Grand Junction on the Grand Mesa. From I-70 Exit 49, follow Highway 65 about 20 miles through Grand Mesa National Forest; (800) 241-6997.

ACTIVITIES: Downhill and cross-country skiing, snowboarding, sleigh rides. In summer, hiking, mountain biking, wildlife tours.

FACILITIES: Limited overnight accommodations at the base; two nearby lodges; Alexander Lake, Grand Mesa, and Spruce Lodges rent cabins year-round. Rentals and instruction, warm-up lodge and cafeteria, ski instruction, kids' programs, and snowboard park.

BIKING THE ORCHARDS AND VINEYARDS OF PALISADE

What a great way to spend an afternoon! Bring your own bicycles and tour the orchards and vineyards of Palisade. You'll feel like you're visiting the vineyards of Burgundy. (Well, not quite, says Bob, pointing out the stark cliffs and dry mesas.) When you get thirsty you can stop at one of half a dozen wineries and sample their vintage. Kids and teetotalers are offered tastes of nonalcoholic juices. One winery specializes in mead—wine made from honey.

Fruit and grapes grown in Colorado? Believe it or not, it's nothing new. In the nineteenth century, when the Grand River Valley was settled, fruit trees and wine grapes were important crops for the pioneer farmers. The climate here is tempered by the surrounding landforms and is generally milder than much of the state. Prohibition destroyed the fledgling wine industry until the late 1960s, when a few brave souls began to grow grapes and make Colorado wine once more. Today local wineries are gaining a lot of well-deserved recognition for their fine vintages, and Palisade has been designated a unique viticultural area—just as the Napa Valley is.

There are several fruit stands and wineries you can visit in one afternoon. Carlson makes good fruit wines, and the winery is quaintly picturesque. Don't miss Colorado Cellars—a real family operation. You're likely to see the Turley boys at work or at play in Mom and Dad's cellar or out in the vineyards. And if you consider yourself a connoisseur, be sure to stop for a taste at both Plum Creek and Grande River Vineyards wineries.

The whole valley is one beautiful picnic spot. Find a tree or use one of the picnic tables most of the wineries provide. Bring a tablecloth, water bottles, and some bug repellent—just in case. Some wineries will even prepare a picnic lunch for you for a reasonable fee, if you call in advance. If you like any of the wine you taste, it's courteous to buy a bottle. If you don't have enough room in your backpacks or saddle bags, have the vintner ship it to your house.

Contact the Palisade Chamber of Commerce or any of the wineries for more information. Children should know the rules of riding on a paved road and have some biking experience. Although you'll be riding on quaint country roads, you're sharing them with cars, trucks, and John Deere tractors. And of course, wine country can be toured by automobile as well as by bike.

WHERE: In and around Palisade, 12 miles east of Grand Junction, Exit 42 from I-70. Contact the Palisade Chamber of Commerce at (970) 464-7458. Grande River Vineyards, 787 37.3 Road; (970) 464-5867. Plum Creek, 3708 G Road; (970) 464-PLUM. Colorado Cellars, 3553 E Road; (970) 464-7921. Carlson Vineyards, 461 35 Road; (970) 464-5554. Confre Cellars, 3701 G Road; (970) 464-7899.

WHEN: The wineries are open year-round, though hours will vary greatly. The Colorado Mountain Winefest is held in late September in Palisade. It's a fun event, and all the wineries sponsor booths, open houses of their facilities, and activities for the kids, too. But if you prefer to avoid the crowds and have a serious discussion with the vintner about winemaking methods, visit during the winter when he or she is not quite so busy.

ACTIVITIES: Bicycling, wine tasting, informal tours, picnicking.

FACILITIES: Restrooms and gift shops at the wineries; a nearby market for picnic supplies. No bike rentals in Palisade.

BE SURE TO BRING: Sun protection, water bottles, and helmets if biking.

RIVER RAFTING

The Grand Valley rivers offer rafters a choice—a picnic or a panic, depending on the stretch and the time of year. Through the valley of peaches and wine grapes, from Palisade to Fruita, the Colorado River is lazy and brown. Those with a low tolerance for excitement might try this run. Farther west toward Utah this same river wakes up again at Horsethief and Ruby Canyons before really getting wild and white at Westwater Canyon in Utah.

Tom Kleinschnitz has been rafting since he was a kid and since 1971 has managed Grand Junction's Adventure Bound Rafting Company. Tom says you shouldn't take kids of any age on a passive trip where they're merely rowed down the river. They'll soon be bored and fidgety and, of course, so will you. "What you gotta do," he says, "is tire the little tykes out so they'll go to bed early and not make a lot of noise around the campfire." (We're with you, Tom!) He says inflatable kayaks, which his company has been using since about 1985 in conjunction with the big oared boats, give kids a chance to maneuver and row themselves where the river conditions are suitable. When the water gets whiter and wilder, you pull in the inflatables and ride in the oared raft. A lot of other companies are now picking up on that trend.

"The inflatables allow us a tremendous versatility, and that's what makes our ticket fly," says Tom, who has taken experienced families with teenagers on powerful class IV and V rapids, as well as six-year-old first-timers on gentler stretches of the Colorado.

For a three- or four-day remote experience on the Yampa, Colorado's last unfettered river, consider going up to Dinosaur National Monument with Adventure Bound.

With the weather and topography of western Colorado, the rafting season here tends to be much longer than in the central part of the state. It's usually possible to run some portion of some river year-round—if you're willing to put up with frigid water, says Tom.

Colorado's rivers can be dangerous, especially during spring runoff and at other times when the water level is high. For your safety, always raft with a licensed river outfitter such as Adventure Bound. In Grand Junction at 2392 H Road; (970) 245-5428.

GRAND JUNCTION AIRPORT: WALKER MEMORIAL FIELD

Looking for some simple, free activity that doesn't require much planning? Spend an hour at Walker Memorial Field watching airplanes and jets take off and land against the stark background of the Book Cliffs. Outside the terminal a small park features a Blue Angel jet, and there's a tiny shaded picnic area nearby. If you didn't bring a picnic, you can eat inside at the airport cafeteria. Also inside are some good rock and mineral displays and a large pterodactyl model hanging from the ceiling. After lunch, stop at the nearby BLM and forest service offices to plan your next adventure.

WHERE: North Grand Junction, at the far northeast end of Horizon Drive; (970) 244-9100.

WHEN: Year-round, daylight hours.

ACTIVITIES: Free aircraft observation.

FACILITIES: Picnic tables, restrooms, cafeteria, museum exhibits, and gift shop inside.

CONFLUENCE PARK AND FORT UNCOMPAHGRE

You can easily spend an entire summer day here in this community called Delta, south of Grand Junction. Long, hot days are great for swimming, and Delta's Confluence Park even has a beach! It may not be Waikiki, but there's plenty of water and sand. If your kids are like ours, they'll cheerfully spend all day in the water if you let them. But try to keep them out long enough to explore some other attractions.

Set aside an hour for visiting Fort Uncompahgre, the outdoor living history museum just east of the lake. Summer hours are 10 A.M. to 5 P.M. Wednesday through Sunday. We suggest going early and saving the swimming for the long, hot afternoon.

The tour of the fort is a bit long for preschoolers, but it's so well done we highly recommend it for adults and school-age kids. You start the tour inside a cool, dark adobe building where a bearded mountain man in dirty buckskin explains how he tans his hides. This guy is no actor! Ed Maddox and his wife really live this life. From his hat to his leather boots, every article of clothing was hand-made by Ed and his wife using methods typical of the 1820–1840 period. The musty air of the adobe is filled with the smells of wood smoke, animal hides, and sage. The sage is used to ward off evil spirits (and, we suspect, for its clean, sharp smell).

Fort Uncompahgre is a replica of the trading post Antoine Robidoux built about 1825 somewhere around here, although the exact location can only be speculated on. The reproduction is typical of and true to what is known about western trading posts of the fur-trapping era, which reached its height in the 1830s and early 1840s. It's built around a central courtyard where chickens roam about, pecking and scratching for bugs and seeds. We followed the mountain man from cool dark building to cool dark building, learning the purpose of each and getting a feel for what it might have been like to live here. Ed's mountain dog knew the routine—he led the way, stopped at each point of interest, and lay in the shade while Ed talked. (The mountain cats, of course, never left their napping spots inside the tanning shed on stacks of fur pelts.)

While Ed related colorful facts, stories, and interesting lore of the nineteenth century, we must say that the absolute highlight of the tour was the ax-throwing contest. Big kids, little kids, and old people like us all got to try our hand at this game. (We know—all those years of telling them never to throw sharp objects, down the drain. You even set a bad example by doing it yourself. Worst of all, you're sure to be beaten handily by some pigeon-toed six-year-old in a sundress!)

A good follow-up to Fort Uncompahgre's living history lesson is eating a picnic lunch under a cottonwood tree at the adjacent park. If you forgot to pack the watercress and goat cheese sandwiches, you can probably make do with Colonel Sanders or a Happy Meal. (Both fast-food restaurants are an ax throw away.) Following lunch, take a nature walk on the north side of the lake, keeping eyes open for herons and other waterfowl among the cattails. As soon as the kids tire of bird-watching, head for the beach. You'll be more than ready, if it's a hot summer day in Delta.

If time allows, plan on staying until evening to watch a lively performance of Thunder Mountain Lives Tonight! (Thunder Mountain is another name for the Grand Mesa, which played a major role in Delta's history.) This nationally renowned act is staged by a huge cast of mostly local talent who, through song, dance, story, and humor, portray the people who once inhabited this region. The show is performed Tuesdays through Saturdays at 8 P.M. from July 4 until Labor Day. Bring sweatshirts; although you've been fighting heat exhaustion all day, you're going to be shivering after the stars come out. It's also wise to make reservations for the show before your visit, and to plan on staying the night at one of the nearby motels on Highway 50 or the KOA campground a mile east of town on Highway 92. For more information about the show, contact the Delta Chamber of Commerce; (800) 228-7009 or (970) 874-8616.

WHERE: 40 miles south of Grand Junction in Delta, on Gunnison River Drive, just west of Main Street; (970) 874-0923.

WHEN: Park is open year-round; some activities are seasonal.

ACTIVITIES: Swimming, paddling, fishing, volleyball, picnicking, tennis, bird-watching, biking, skating, horse shows, and summer evening performances of Thunder Mountain Lives Tonight! In winter, ice skating, fishing, tennis.

FACILITIES: Swim beach and separate shallow wading beach; food concessions and paddle boat rental; tennis courts, horse arena (but no horse rentals), 3 miles of gravel and paved trails, outdoor amphitheater, volleyball nets, indoor recreation center. At Fort Uncompahgre, a gift shop and book store.

BE SURE TO BRING: Suits, towels, and whatever toys or sporting equipment you want. (No marina or rentals.) And definitely bring sunscreen, sun hats, and water bottles or a cooler full of drinks.

BLACK CANYON OF THE GUNNISON NATIONAL MONUMENT

An hour's drive southeast of Grand Junction is the deep, raw gorge called The Black Canyon of the Gunnison, carved by the Gunnison River. Though the views from the rim are striking, only highly experienced hikers should actually go down into this steep and occasionally treacherous canyon. A visitor center is open during the summer months, and there are several short nature trails on both the north and south rims, but in our opinion there are not enough activities suited to children for families to plan a vacation here.

If you want to see this impressive but formidable and nearly inaccessible geologic feature, you could stop on your way to or from Grand Junction. If you're driving from eastern Colorado, use Highway 50 to reach the south rim (the more-visited one). Or visit the north rim by way of Highway 133 south of Carbondale to Highway 92 at Hotchkiss. Both of these routes are less direct and slower but more picturesque than driving Interstate 70. If you're not able to incorporate the canyon as a stop on your driving route, you'll have to decide if an awesome view and a nature walk is worth the hour's drive from Grand Junction. On the other hand, if you are an experienced hiker and your adolescent kids are accustomed to rugged tracks, a trip down into the canyon could be a fantastic backpacking expedition.

WHERE: About 60 miles southeast of Grand Junction by Highway 50, six miles east of Montrose. May also be reached from the north rim, south of Hotchkiss; (970) 249-7036.

WHEN: Visitor center open Memorial Day to mid-September.

ACTIVITIES: Sight-seeing, nature walks, hiking, camping, interpretive displays, and seasonal guided activities.

FACILITIES: Visitor center, restrooms, water, and several campgrounds on both sides of the canyon. Primitive tent sites can be found down in the canyon near the river's edge.

AREA STATE PARKS AND NATIONAL FORESTS
COLORADO RIVER STATE PARK

Picnic sites, river access, and multi-use trail. This park is still being developed; the trail will eventually be 25 miles long and connect with the longer Tabegauche Trail. Also in progress, the Tabegauche will connect Grand Junction with Ouray, more than 100 miles south. Day use only. At 32 Road and Colorado River; (970) 464-0548.

HIGHLINE STATE PARK

Two fishing lakes, a playground, and shade trees make this a desirable camping spot. Twenty-five sites, some wheelchair accessible, are open year-round, with limited winter facilities. Drive west of Grand Junction on I-70 to the Loma exit (County Road 139), then north for 6 miles, following the signs; (970) 858-7208.

ISLAND ACRES STATE PARK

Camping on thirty-two sites within 1 mile of a coffee shop and store. Close to Grand Junction, yet seemingly remote. Closer yet to the orchards, vineyards, and wineries of Palisade. Bring bikes and tour. Open year-round. The park is 5 miles east of Palisade, take Exit 47 from I-70; (970) 464-0548.

VEGA STATE PARK

Although it's a bit of a drive from Grand Junction, this state park is a good destination for families who like winter sports best of all. There are over one hundred all-season campsites for tents and motor homes, and miles of trails for snowmobiling, cross-country skiing, or snowshoeing. When the reservoir freezes over you can ice-fish and ice skate. For any winter activity you must bring your own equipment. If you don't like cold-weather camping, the warmer months offer camping, boating, and fishing. Real cattle drives pass through here occasionally in the spring and fall, adding a little excitement. Although there isn't much in the way of ranger programs and other organized activities, a self-guided nature trail with interpretive view stations will take you on a learning adventure through aspen groves. Those with mountain bikes can bring them and explore a separate trail for dirt bikes and snowmobiles. The park is 12 miles east of Collbran on Mesa County Road 330; (970) 487-3407.

GRAND MESA NATIONAL FOREST

Thunder Mountain, it was once called. An evocative name for a massive block of rock topped by lava that has eroded more slowly than the surrounding and underlying sedimentary rock.

But Grand Mesa isn't just any block of rock: It's the tallest flat-top mountain in the world.

September is a great time to explore the Mesa, by bicycle, foot, or horseback. As fall turns, the plateau is colored with yellow aspen and rusty red Gambel oak. Above, the sky is nearly always blue. Of course, summer and winter are fine seasons too. Wildflowers or snow, hiking boots or snowshoes, fat-tire bikes or snowmobiles—take your pick.

You'll find about two dozen established and regularly maintained trails—five of them under 3 miles long. Lost Lake Trail, starting at Glacier Springs picnic ground, is a stimulating mile and a half that can be hiked or biked on a limited time budget. Mesa Lakes Shore Trail is a gravel path that runs around a lake—one of the hundreds of lakes, ponds, and puddles on this table-top mountain. The total mileage is about a mile and a half, with benches for the faint of heart to rest on. But you probably won't need to rest, because there's not much elevation change.

Hardier hikers might prefer to explore part or all of the Craig Crest National Recreation Trail, an exhilarating route restricted to pedestrians and equestrians. There's a 4-mile easy-grade loop you can do in an afternoon. You'll find spectacular views from this rocky trail—and if you're fortunate you'll hear elk bugling during the autumn months. Primitive camping is allowed 300 feet or more off the trail. The west trailhead parking lot is located next to Island Lake, off Highway 65, and detailed maps can be obtained from the Forest Service visitor center or the ranger station in Grand Junction.

Grand Mesa is a popular place to throw a line any time. There are so many lakes stocked with fish, it's not hard to find your own special spot. In winter, tons of snow attracts cross-country skiers and snowmobilers, who share the open spaces and miles of forest trails on the top.

More than fifteen campgrounds with the national forest provide over three hundred camping sites, some primitive and some with full amenities. Here are a sampling for which no reservations are necessary.

Carp Lake: Twenty sites for tents or motor homes. Water lovers, you can rent boats, and there's a store and coffee shop nearby. Open late June to mid-October. North of Cedaredge 16 miles on Highway 65.

Little Bear: Thirty-six developed sites near the shores of Island Lake, not far from Carp Lake Campground. Open from late June through October 15. North of Cedaredge 16 miles on Highway 65, then .5-mile west on Forest Service Road 116.

Island Lake: Over eighty sites—half for tents, half for motor homes—near the shores of Island Lake. Open late June to mid-October. Same directions as for Little Bear Campground, but half a mile farther on Forest Service Road 116.

Kiser Creek: A less-frequented camp with twelve sites for tents, trailers, or small motor homes on Kiser Creek, near Eggleston Lake. Open late June to late September. North of Cedaredge 16 miles on Highway 65, then east on Forest Service Road 121 for 3 miles, then .1-mile south on Forest Service Road 123.

No matter what you're looking for in the way of outdoor fun, Grand Mesa National Forest has much to offer.

WHERE: 30 miles east of Grand Junction; take Exit 49 off I-70 to Highway 65, or Highway 50 south to Delta and Highway 65. National Forest Service office, (970) 242-8211.

WHEN: Summer and fall are best for hiking and biking.

ACTIVITIES: Camping, skiing, snowmobiling, mountain biking, horseback riding.

FACILITIES: Visitor center at Ward Lake Campground, where you can get maps, books, and species checklists. Convenience stores, canoe and rowboat rentals, restaurants, campgrounds, lodges and rental cabins, picnic grounds, restrooms. Many camping and picnic facilities are wheelchair accessible.

BE SURE TO: Contact the ranger station or visitor's center for maps, fishing and hunting rules, cabin rental information.

Outdoor Fairs and Festivals

Applefest in Cedaredge

A Main Street celebration in this Grand Mesa town celebrating the apple harvest. This is probably the best time to explore the Grand Mesa as well. In early October; (970) 856-6961.

Winefest

Besides wine tasting, winemaking seminars, food stands, and live bands, there are fun and games for kids too at this September festival in Palisade. A fee is charged. For more information call the Colorado Wine Industry Development Board; (970) 523-1232.

In Case of Bad Weather

Devil's Canyon Science and Learning Center

Don't wait for bad weather—it seldom comes to Grand Junction. Make time to see this! Devil's Canyon may not be suitable for sensitive preschoolers who tend to have nightmares after seeing large lifelike prehistoric beasts gnashing their teeth and whipping their very realistic tails. Older kids love it—they line up and wait their turn to have a Jurassic monster spit at them. Serious-minded family members can watch researchers whittle and brush away at dinosaur bones; you can even view a monitor showing microfossils under a scientist's microscope. Open daily except major holidays from 9 A.M. to 6 P.M. A fee is charged. On the south side of the intersection of I-70 and Highway 340 near Fruita; (970) 858-7282.

DooZoo Children's Museum

Children's museums everywhere are a great place to spend a rainy, dreary afternoon. In Grand Junction, where the weather is usually sunny, you might go on a blistering summer afternoon instead. The DooZoo is located along the main outdoor shopping mall, near a treasure of a bookstore, various coffee shops, and restaurants—and not far from the Dinosaur Valley Museum. Open mid-May through November 1, Tuesday through Saturday. Call for current hours. A fee is charged. 635 Main Street in Grand Junction; (970) 241-5225.

COLORADO'S
SOUTHWEST CORNER

Until 1880 the southwest corner of Colorado was a land few whites had seen. The rugged San Juan Mountains and the remote Uncompahgre Plateau belonged to the Ute, who had lived in this region for centuries.

In 1870, however, gold was discovered near what would become Silverton, high in the San Juans. This discovery was followed by silver, and later lead, zinc, copper, and tellurium. Silverton, Ouray, and Telluride sprang into being. A new treaty was drawn up and enforced by the United States government, who now wanted the Ute out of this mineral-rich land. By 1882 a railroad connected Silverton with Durango and provided a more efficient means of moving the ore out of the mountains. Towns grew to supply the miners, then highways grew to supply the towns.

Today, gold, silver, and other minerals are still being mined in the San Juans. And you can still ride the old train from Durango, a town growing by leaps and bounds, to Silverton, a step back in time of about a hundred years, it seems. The former mining town of Telluride rose from the ashes in the 1970s to become a ski resort and celebrity vacationland, pricing much of the local workforce out of housing in the process. As for the Native people, the Mountain Ute and Southern Ute are the only Native American tribes remaining in Colorado today. They live a modern lifestyle yet retain some of their traditional customs on a fragment of the land they once roamed.

Southwest Colorado is a rich land—rich in history, in natural resources, in mountainous beauty and wild spirit. We only hope that as more people visit here and more families call it home, these gifts will be preserved for future generations.

242

OURAY AREA

This mountain town is named after the Ute leader Ouray, who lived during the middle and later part of the nineteenth century. Born of a Ute mother and a half-Ute half–Jicarilla Apache father, Ouray was never formally educated. Still, he was a highly intelligent person who spoke four languages and loved to converse. Ouray was recognized by the United States government as the overall leader of the seven Ute tribes. In 1868 he negotiated a treaty considered to be one of the most favorable ever gained by an Indian group, an agreement that barred settlers from entering the entire West Slope of the Colorado Rockies! Obviously, this treaty was not honored for long; as soon as gold and silver were discovered in the San Juans, the agreement was redefined and prospectors poured in. Ouray's influence did keep his people free for a long time—the Ute were one of the last Native American tribes to be sent to the reservations.

But Ouray's leadership was not fully accepted by many of his own people. According to historian and author Charles Marsh, centralized power was foreign to the Ute, who weren't accustomed to being under the rule of a supreme chief. Not all Ute people agreed with Ouray, who believed the only way to save the few thousand remaining Ute was to negotiate with the encroaching whites and to abide by agreements that forced the Ute to give up land they had roamed and hunted on for generations in exchange for protection and assistance.

Ouray today is a town whose economy is based on tourism and outdoor recreation. The buildings are charmingly restored to enhance the architecture of the Victorian period, when silver and gold ruled. The only real evidence of the man whose name the town took is nearly 40 miles north, in Montrose at the Ute Indian Museum and Ouray Memorial Park. Here his wife, Chipeta, is buried. Ouray himself is buried at Ignacio, Colorado, on the Southern Ute Indian Reservation.

Ouray Hot Springs Pool and Fitness Center

Here's a wonderful place for a swim and a workout, a picnic in the park, or for a relaxing soak after a day spent exploring. Be sure to ask about "full moon nights," when extended hours allow you to bask in the hot mineral water under the milky light of a San Juan moon. (Put the kids to bed and sneak back, just the two of you . . .)

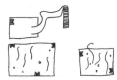

Where: North end of Ouray, on Main Street; (970) 325-4738.

When: Year-round (often closed Tuesdays for cleaning). Summer hours are 10 A.M. to 10 P.M., usually closes earlier during the winter.

Activities: Soaking, swimming, and playing, aerobics and weight lifting, picnicking.

Facilities: Three separate sections of a huge pool provide three different temperatures. Rentals of suits, towels, water toys. Fitness center, park, and playground.

Exploring Jeep Roads in the High Country

Ouray has proclaimed itself jeep capital of the world. If you want to bounce around old mining roads in a four-wheel-drive vehicle, this is a popular place to do it during the summer and early autumn.

Five hundred miles of off-road trails lead through forests and over mountain passes to old camps and ghost towns. The trails have colorfully romantic names like Cinnamon Pass, Last Dollar Road, Yankee Boy Basin, Black Bear Road. During the summer months and into early autumn you can take a guided tour of these trails in an open multipassenger vehicle. Or you can rent your own four-wheel-drive and see if you can get the family good and lost up in the mountains. ("Honey, don't you think we should pull over and ask for directions?") There are at least half a dozen companies in town that will take you for a tour or rent you a vehicle. Colorado West Jeep Tours and Rentals will do both, with half-day and full-day rates from May through mid-October. 440 Main Street; (800) 648-JEEP or (970) 325-4014.

I think most kids would enjoy a four-wheeling trip more if they were allowed to drive their own vehicles, rather than sitting in the back seat, trying not to get carsick. Although a thirteen-year-old can't drive a jeep, she can drive an all-terrain vehicle (ATV). Ouray Mountain Sport offers guided tours of the mountains and mining camps where everyone drives their own Polaris ATV. It's fairly safe and easy—no shifting required. In case you're not familiar with them, all-terrain vehicles resemble riding lawnmowers with fat tires, minus the blade. These tours are offered during the summer months only and are secondary to the company's primary business, which is mountain bikes and related outdoor equipment.

Most trails in the area are not recommended for beginning mountain bikers or families with young children, due to the steep, rugged terrain. The River Road is one exception. Following the old railroad grade to Ridgway, this is a scenic 11-mile ride along the Uncompahgre River, downhill. Pedaling back to Ouray is harder because it's all uphill, nearly 1,000 feet in elevation gain. For more information on this and other trails, contact Ouray Mountain Sport, 722 Main Street; (970) 325-4284.

HORSEBACK RIDING

Riding is a good alternative for those who want to explore the mountains, but not by motorized vehicle. And in Ouray you don't have to go far to find a stable. Here are two local outfitters.

OURAY LIVERY BARN

For more than twenty-five years the Linscotts have offered trail rides into the nearby mountains, starting from downtown Ouray. Memorial Day through Labor Day. 834 Main Street; (970) 325-4606.

SAN JUAN MOUNTAIN OUTFITTERS AT POLLY'S MOTEL AND RV PARK

Summer trail rides and fall hunting trips start from this motel/campground. (Especially convenient if you happen to be spending the night here.) Just north of town at 1805 Highway 550; (800) 331-3015 or (970) 626-5360.

BOX CANYON FALLS

Box Canyon Falls is not just another waterfall. Keep this in mind when you're wondering whether or not you should pay the small fee the city charges to see it. This thundering rush of water seems to be blasted out of the mountains with dynamite. The sheer power of the water is what impressed us, even more than the 285-foot drop. Be prepared to reach for your little one's hand, to still your own heart.

After climbing the stairs and walking out on a fenced catwalk to catch a faceful of mist and an earful of sound, take the short but steep trail up to an old steel bridge that spans the canyon. (Yes it's old, but it seems sturdy enough.) From here you'll have a bird's-eye view of the falls and the town below. You'll have to explain to the kids why you can't throw rocks off it, which is what they instinctively want to do. When the thrill of heights wears off, you can enjoy a picnic lunch if you don't mind the brazen chipmunks who beg for a handout. Unless you're dining on pinecones, you shouldn't feed them.

Plan on spending half an hour to forty-five minutes here, longer if you brought a picnic. It's easily combined with another nearby activity, such as the Bachelor-Syracuse Mine Tour, or swimming at the Ouray Hot Springs Pool.

WHERE: .5-mile south of Ouray, off Highway 550; (970) 325-4464.

WHEN: Mid-May to mid-October, 8 A.M. until dark. The earlier in the year you go, the greater the force of the waterfall.

ACTIVITIES: Sight-seeing, short hike, picnicking. A small fee is charged.

FACILITIES: Restrooms, picnic tables, concession stand; stairs and wooden catwalk to falls.

BACHELOR-SYRACUSE MINE TOUR

If you haven't seen a real Colorado gold and silver mine, the Bachelor-Syracuse is only a few miles away on Gold Hill and well worth a visit. Actually the mine is not on Gold Hill, it's 3,350 feet *inside* Gold Hill! (That's horizontally, not vertically.) A guided tour on a train called a "trammer" takes you into the dark heart of the working mine (named for the three bachelor men who discovered silver in 1884, and for their Syracuse, New York, investors.) Besides ninety million dollars worth of silver, this mine has also produced gold, lead, zinc, and copper over the years. On the tour you'll get to see how explosives are used, which will immediately engage any young minds that have begun to wander.

After the trammer brings you back to the light of day, you and the kids can try to get rich quick by panning for gold in the stream. Don't be bashful; an instructor will show you how it's done. Best of all, you get to keep what's in the bottom of your pan, be it gold, fool's gold, or, in our case, mud.

When your hands get too cold to pan anymore, the kids can shop for a souvenir. Maybe you'll want to shop for a souvenir too. ("Oh, look Honey, they sell real gold and silver jewelry here . . .")

If there's any money left, you can have lunch at the outdoor café. You can even have breakfast—it's served all day, at unbeatable prices (biscuits and gravy, Linda's favorite comfort food).\

WHERE: About 2 miles north of Ouray. Follow the signs from County Road 14; (970) 325-0220.

WHEN: Daily, from May 20 through September 15 (closed July 4). Tours hourly on the hour beginning at 10 A.M., and at 9 A.M. from mid-June through August.

ACTIVITIES: Guided tour inside a working gold and silver mine; gold-panning with instruction, blacksmith shop and demonstration.

FACILITIES: Restrooms, gift shop, outdoor café.

BE SURE TO BRING: Wear sturdy shoes and bring a sweatshirt or coat for the 50-degree temperature inside the mine. Money or credit cards for the gift shop. Reservations are recommended.

AREA STATE PARKS AND NATIONAL FORESTS

RIDGWAY STATE RECREATION AREA

This is one of Colorado's newest state parks, and it features water sports and year-round camping in over 180 spaces, including ten walk-in tent sites. Modern restrooms, showers, and laundry facilities are convenient, and most of the park is wheelchair accessible. The reservoir is the big draw. Fishing, boating, water skiing, sailing, and windsurfing are all done here. A full-service marina provides paddleboat and pontoon rentals, supplies, and a snack bar. Swimming is allowed too, in one designated area. Four miles of paved multi-use trails (no motorized vehicles) round out this park's features. There are no bike-rental concessions yet, so bring your own. Ten miles north of Ouray on Highway 550; (970) 626-5822.

UNCOMPAHGRE NATIONAL FOREST

Surrounding Ouray, the Uncompahgre National Forest is a magnet for drivers of off-road vehicles, hard-core mountain bikers, and conditioned hikers. Two designated wilderness areas, Mount Sneffels and Big Blue, offer remote backcountry for those who want to escape the sights and sounds of civilization, including jeeps and bicycles. This is rugged land; there are relatively few established campgrounds in the Uncompahgre

National Forest. The only one close to Ouray is Amphitheater Campground, with fifteen tent sites and twelve sites for small motor homes. Piped water and pit toilets are the facilities. Open late May to early September. One mile south of Ouray on Highway 550, then .5-mile east on Forest Service Road 885; (970) 249-9631. There are several private campgrounds on the outskirts of Ouray just off Highway 550.

San Juan Guest Ranch

With room for thirty-two guests in their beautiful lodge near the Mount Sneffels Wilderness Area, this intimate guest ranch offers a comprehensive riding program, guided jeep tours to ghost towns and abandoned gold mines, weekly overnighters and cookouts, fishing, and a trap and rifle range.

Although there are supervised activities for kids of all ages, we think this ranch is particularly suited for families with kids old enough to appreciate the rugged four-wheeling adventures and the history of the area's gold and silver mining, and who can perhaps even develop their skills on the trap and rifle range (they must be at least ten years old). Open June through December. Bed-and-breakfast facilities during the winter months. San Juan Guest Ranch is 4 miles north of Ouray; (800) 331-3015 or (970) 626-5360.

Outdoor Fairs and Festivals
Ouray Fourth of July Celebration

Pancake breakfast, races, kids' games, barbecue, firefighter water fights, and of course a parade and fireworks. A townwide celebration, mostly within walking distance; (800) 228-1876, or (970) 325-4746 (Ouray Chamber Resort Association).

In Case of Bad Weather
Ute Indian Museum in Montrose

Chief Ouray, Chipeta, Ignacio, Colorow, Buckskin Charlie: These famed nineteenth-century Ute and their people are remembered in an impressive collection of Ute tribal life. This is the only museum in Colorado dedicated to a single Native American nation. Outside the building on museum grounds is Chipeta's gravesite and the ruins of Ouray's government-built home. Open Memorial Day through Labor Day, Monday through Saturday from 10 A.M. to 5 P.M., Sunday from 1 to 5 P.M. Modified hours through September. A fee is charged. Located on the south side of Montrose off Highway 550 at 17253 Chipeta Drive; (970) 249-3098.

TRAIL TOWN

Just a short drive north to Ridgway you'll find a few hours of diversion at Trail Town—an emporium of false-front western shops, food, and seasonal entertainment for kids. The Memory Makers, storytelling historians and entertainers, are based here and offer activities such as tepee sleepovers and council fire pow-wows. Contact Memory Makers Rick or Dawn Bresett at (970) 249-8715; for information about shopping at Trail Town, call the Ridgway Chamber of Commerce at (970) 626-5181.

DURANGO AREA

Durango was conceived by the Denver & Rio Grande Company and was born a full-fledged railroad town in 1880. Trains were needed to haul precious ore out of the mountains and to bring supplies, miners, and settlers into the valley. These days you can still visit the old roundhouse and ride the train over the pass to Silverton, but one look around Durango will convince you times have changed: Bicycles have replaced locomotives in some sort of strange transportation devolution. With bike racks on every other car, parking lots look like herds of grazing elk. Vigorous-looking people zip around town wearing tight black pants and canoe-like helmets—you know you're not in Kansas anymore. Bicycle lanes connect Durango with Silverton, 45 miles north, and countless off-road trails wind into the San Juans, offering challenging mountain-bike adventures. In 1991 the first-ever Mountain Bike

World Championships were held in this very town, producing nearly as much of a fever as when gold was discovered.

If you'd rather walk than pedal, there are numerous trails to explore. The volunteer-blazed Colorado Trail has its beginning here, and though you might not be up for hiking 469 miles to South Denver, where it eventually ends up, you could walk a mile or two of it. And if walking's too slow, there's river rafting in the summer and skiing during the winter. In any case, this is an active town for active people.

Even though there are lots of motels, hotels, and inns, be sure to arrange lodging ahead of time or you may find yourself driving from no vacancy sign to no vacancy sign. Campgrounds are less likely to be completely filled, but you would be wise to make reservations or at least have a Plan B in mind. If your budget allows, we highly recommend a night's stay at the historic Strater Hotel. There's so much atmosphere and elegant Old West charm, you'll feel like a character in a Louis L'Amour novel. (Louis used to come here frequently, we're told, to soak up some of that same atmosphere.) If you can't afford to check in, at least step inside to check out the lobby and the saloon.

Your very first stop, however, should be the visitors center at Gateway Park (south end of town, Highway 160 and Gateway Drive). Here you can chat with local folk who can tell you what events are going on around town and help you make lodging or camping arrangements, if needed. Outside in Gateway Park you can stretch your legs and watch kayakers and rafters float by on the Las Animas River; it'll get you pumped for your own personal adventure in Durango.

The Durango & Silverton Narrow-Gauge Railroad

To get a real appreciation of the area's history, take an excursion on the Durango-Silverton train. These antique locomotives carry about 200,000 passengers every summer on sight-seeing excursions. Hikers going into remote wilderness areas also ride the train to reach backcountry trails. One train each day is equipped with lifts and adequate seating for wheelchairs.

If you plan on making the 90-mile round trip, prepare for an eight-hour day! This includes the two-hour layover in Silverton, where you can shop, eat, and catch a mock gunfight or two in the street. Even though this is a fun and interesting way to travel, it makes for a long, tiring excursion if you have preschoolers—or even fidgety fifth graders. One option is to make arrangements to stay a night or two in Silverton before returning to Durango on the train. If you've had enough of scenic train rides, you can return by the Durango and Silverton bus.

If you're spending a day or two in Silverton, you'll have time to take a tour of the Old Hundred Gold Mine. Unless you've already toured other Colorado mines, this is a fun way to learn a little about mining, minerals, and history. There's a campground on the edge of town, or, if you can afford to do it, spend the night in one of two old Victorian period hotels. (The rates are fairly reasonable, as far as hotels go.) The Grand Imperial at 1219 Greene Street looks and feels like the real thing. Built in 1883, it is just slightly down in the heels, enough to give it some real atmosphere. (If TVs and telephones are crucial to your sense of atmosphere, skip this place.) Even if you aren't lodging here, consider having a meal at the restaurant, the Gold King Dining Room, just to admire the beautiful antique bar and the tin-tiled ceiling.

A tad more elegant is the Wyman Hotel, a block up the street. Recently restored, this old hotel mixes antiques and atmosphere with modern amenities like VCRs.

If a train ride to Silverton is in your vacation plans, call and order your tickets well in advance. Although there's sometimes room for standby passengers, Murphy's Law applies.

WHERE: Depot at 479 Main Avenue. Parking lot just west, next to McDonalds. The train goes to Silverton and back, a 90-mile round-trip. Durango & Silverton Narrow-Gauge Railroad: (970) 247-2733.

WHEN: May through October. (Fall is perhaps the most spectacular time, with crisp colors and cool mountain air.) There is also a winter holiday train to Cascade Canyon (52 miles round-trip) that runs late November through December.

ACTIVITIES: A train ride to Silverton and back, about eight hours round-trip including a 2-hour layover.

FACILITIES: Handicap accessible. Open gondola cars and enclosed coaches. Concession cars sell snacks and train souvenirs. Restaurants, shopping, sight-seeing, and lodging in Silverton.

BE SURE TO BRING: Sweaters, coats, and hats, good walking shoes for sightseeing in Silverton, something for kids to do on the way (most kids tire of looking at the scenery, breathtaking as it is). Don't wear your Sunday best—the coal-fired train throws cinders that can blacken clothing.

PURGATORY SKI RESORT

Purgatory has a diverse mix of runs to suit beginners, intermediates, and advanced skiers, and enough of the white stuff to make it worth your while. Across the highway from the main ski resort is the Purgatory Ski Touring Center, with more than 15 kilometers of cross-country trails. Lessons, rentals, and tours are available. If you're not staying at the base, a ski bus makes several runs a day from downtown Durango.

In the summer, mountain biking is the chief activity here. Those new to the sport of pedaling fat-tire bikes along rocky roads would do well to start out at Purgatory Resort, which, like most Colorado ski resorts, becomes a biking playground when the snow melts. The convenience of being able to rent equipment here, of using well-marked and maintained trails, of lift service up the hard part of the ride, not to mention nearby lodging and camping, make it a good choice for families. (You can save money by bringing your own bikes and camping.) When you're ready to venture off the ski area (it'll likely take you more than a week to explore all the trails here) the local experts at any bike shop in town can provide you with ideas, maps, and directions.

WHERE: 25 miles north of Durango on Highway 550; (800) 525-0892 or (970) 247-9000.

ACTIVITIES: Downhill and cross-country skiing, snowboarding. In summer, mountain biking, hiking, and riding the alpine slide.

FACILITIES: A small base village offers lodging, dining, rentals, and shops; instruction, SKIwee program for little kids, children's terrain park, and a snowboard park. Several packages are available, including kids under twelve ski free (restrictions and blackout periods apply), and four-day packages that allow you to trade a day of skiing for one of many other activities in the area (such as a ride on the narrow-gauge railroad, a sleigh ride, a tour of Mesa Verde, and others).

RAFTING THE ANIMAS AND PIEDRA RIVERS

The upper Animas and nearby Piedra Rivers are tumultuous, giving experienced river runners class IV and V runs for their money. For those of us not yet ready for ultrawhite water, lower sections of the Las Animas offer plenty of excitement in a safer environment. Though even preschoolers may go rafting, little kids tend to be far more susceptible to hypothermia than we realize. The frigid water temperatures of spring runoff are not only miserable but can be dangerous. It's far wiser to wait until the height of summer to take small children on the river. Even wiser might be to wait until they're old enough to take part in the paddling—seven or eight years old at least. For adolescents who like a challenge, this can be an ideal family adventure. For more information, contact one of several rafting companies in the area.

Mountain Waters Rafting is one such local outfit, recommended by professional rafters for its experience and safety record in accommodating families with children.

WHERE: Mountain Waters Rafting, 108 West College Drive; (970) 259-4191.

WHEN: Generally from late May through early September, depending on weather and river conditions.

ACTIVITIES: River rafting for all experience levels.

FACILITIES: Full-day, half-day, economy, and dinner trips; all equipment is provided, including appropriately sized life vests. Inflatable kayaks are also available.

BE SURE TO BRING: Dry clothes to change into—you're likely to get splashed. Silk or polypropylene undershirts with long sleeves help keep little kids warm on the river and also protect them from the sun. It sounds strange, but when you're rafting you can be shivering at the same time you're getting sunburned.

GATEWAY PARK

If you're just passing through Durango on your way to or from Mesa Verde, this park is an excellent place to get a glimpse of the area without spending money, and without fighting for a parking space on Main Avenue. Be sure to go inside the visitor center to pick up some brochures and other advice. If you're staying a while, the 3-mile paved path that passes the park is ideal for families with young cyclists. You can also jog, skate, wheel a baby stroller or wheelchair, or relax on the grass and enjoy the sights, sounds, and smells of the river without going far from town.

WHERE: Highway 160 and Gateway Drive at the south end of town; (800) 525-8855 or (970) 247-0312 (Durango Chamber Resort Association).

WHEN: Visitor center open daily from 8 A.M. to 5 P.M., year-round; longer summer hours.

ACTIVITIES: Biking, strolling, picnicking, river-watching.

FACILITIES: Visitor center, restrooms, shady grass and picnic tables, 3-mile paved trail.

AREA STATE PARKS AND NATIONAL FORESTS
MANCOS STATE PARK

Thirty-three year-round campsites around a small lake make this a desirable spot for those wanting to escape the activity of Durango. Even though it's close to Mesa Verde, if the national park is your prime destination, you'll probably want to camp at Mesa Verde's excellent campground. To get to Mancos State Park, go west on Highway 160 to Mancos, north on Highway 184 to County Road 42 (Forest Service Road 561), then east for 4 miles to the park entrance; (970) 883-2208.

NAVAJO LAKE STATE PARK

This park on the border of Colorado and New Mexico features a year-round campground on Navajo Lake with seventy sites and a marina that is open from March to November. For more information, see page 266. On Highway 151 southeast of Ignacio; (970) 883-2208.

SAN JUAN NATIONAL FOREST

You'll find several Forest Service campgrounds near Purgatory Ski Resort, which doubles as a mountain-bike resort in the summer and early autumn. Contact the ranger station for more Forest Service campgrounds and trail maps; (970) 247-4874.

PURGATORY CAMPGROUND

Fourteen sites close to hiking and biking trails, and access to the Weminuche Wilderness. Just off Highway 550 near the resort; look for the National Forest Campground sign. Generally open late May to November. A fee is charged.

SIG CREEK

Near Purgatory Campground, this one is a little more obscure. Nine sites, open late May to November, conditions permitting. Off Highway 550, 6 miles west on Forest Service Road 2578. A fee is charged.

JUNCTION CREEK CAMPGROUND

Thirty-four sites, some wheelchair accessible, close to downtown Durango. Has showers, firewood, a café, and a nearby laundromat and convenience store. Open late May to mid-November. Go 1 mile north on 550, 3.5 miles northwest on County Road 204, then 1.5 miles northwest on Forest Service Road 2574. A fee is charged.

GUEST RANCHES

LAKE MANCOS RANCH

This ranch features organized programs for "Yearling" kids through "Maverick" teenagers. Any child, of any age, who has an interest in horses can ride, and there's an end-of-the-week horse show to show off new skills. Teenagers have taco parties, volleyball games, jeep trips, and fireside talks. They might be so busy having fun that you'll hardly see them all week. Sounds tempting. Early June through late September (September is for adults only). Lake Mancos Ranch is just north of the town of Mancos; (800) 325-WHOA or (970) 533-7900.

COLORADO TRAILS RANCH

This ranch has been around since 1960 and gets high marks for its riding program, its well-cared-for horses, and its children's programs. Three fully supervised youth groups, loosely designated as 5 to 9, 9 to 13, and 13 to 18, are kept busy, but the program is flexible and competition is deemphasized. Here, fun comes first. In addition to all the regular dude ranch activities, you can country line-dance, watch a show put on by the staff, play Ping-Pong or shoot pool in the ruckus room—you gotta wonder when you sleep around here! Early June through late September, with some weeks for adult guests only. Colorado Trails Ranch is near Durango on County Road 240; (800) 323-DUDE or (970) 247-5055.

OUTDOOR FAIRS AND FESTIVALS
UTE BEAR DANCE

This festival dates back hundreds of years and is still an important festivity in Ute culture. Somewhat like a Sadie Hawkins dance, the girls take the lead by asking the boys to dance. And if asked, you can't refuse! Traditional dress is worn, and other activities and entertainment take place over this two-day event. Held in late spring, generally the first weekend in June. The public is welcome. Held on Ute tribal grounds near Ignacio. Contact the Tribal Affairs Office for more information; (970) 563-4525.

THE DURANGO PRO RODEO SERIES

This summer rodeo features Tuesday- and Wednesday-night competitions from June through September. Special events such as the Durango Cowgirl Classic in July and the Durango Ghost Dancer All-Indian Rodeo on Labor Day weekend are worth getting tickets to. Regular rodeo performances start at 7:30 P.M. and are preceded by a barbecue. A fee is charged. For more information, call the La Plata County Fairgrounds at Twenty-Fifth and Main; (970) 247-1666.

IN CASE OF BAD WEATHER
TRIMBLE HOT SPRINGS

An Olympic-size outdoor pool, small outdoor hot pool, 2 private tubs, bathhouse, locker rooms, nursery, and snack bar. Daily from 7 A.M. to 10 P.M. in summer, 8 A.M. to 11 P.M. in winter. 6475 County Road 203, 6 miles north of Durango off Highway 550; (970) 247-0111.

ANIMAS SCHOOL MUSEUM

This is a small seasonal museum featuring a turn-of-the-century schoolroom as well as other artifacts and memorabilia of the Durango area. Open during the summer months Monday through Friday from 10 A.M. to 6 P.M., Saturday and Sunday from 11 A.M. to 4 P.M. A fee is charged. Thirty-first Street and West Second Avenue; (970) 259-2402.

PAGOSA SPRINGS AREA

Pagosa Springs is named for the Ute word *Pagosah*, which translates to "land of healing water," or "boiling waters," depending on who you ask. A story that may be more legend than fact tells how the Ute battled with the Navajo to win the rights for the spring. In 1866 the two tribes decided to settle their long dispute with a good old-fashioned fight to the death—and to the victor would belong the spoils. The Navajo chose their fiercest fighter, while the Ute chose a white man, Colonel Albert Pfeiffer, a friend of Kit Carson's. Pfeiffer accepted the honor of defending the Ute, and as the story goes, both combatants were stripped to the waist with one hand tied behind their backs. Pfeiffer threw his trusty bowie knife at the Navajo and killed him. The Ute now had full control over the springs (well, at least until white settlers moved in). There's a monument dedicated to the battle on the north side of Highway 60 about 4 miles west of Pagosa. This site was selected by Pfeiffer's granddaughters, who believed the fight occurred a few hundred yards south of here.

Many people pass right by the monument without stopping, in fact just blowing right through Pagosa Springs on their way to and from Mesa Verde or Durango. They don't know what they're missing. The hiking, mountain biking, horseback riding, camping, and skiing opportunities in this area are many, and are usually less crowded than those in the Durango area. The chamber of commerce can give you detailed information on trails, as can Juan's Mountain Sports, located next to the hot springs; (800) 955-1273 and (970) 264-4730.

Even if Pagosa Springs isn't your final destination, at least plan a rest stop here. Have a picnic in the park at the Chamber of Commerce Visitor Center on the southwest bank of the San Juan River. We once spent a pleasant hour here, just watching two boys fishing. If you take a little more time you can soak in one of the hot-spring-fed pools a short distance from here. (By this time you're so relaxed that you might as well spend the night.)

The Hot Springs of Pagosa
Great Pagosa Spring

The Great Pagosa Spring is the hottest and largest geothermal spring in the world. No one knows exactly how deep it is—it's been measured to 850 feet, and that wasn't the bottom! Not just a big hot tub, this special spring has been a part of the community's history and culture, and today it is used to heat some of the town's buildings.

From the Pagosa Springs Visitor Center it's a short walk south on Hot Springs Boulevard to the Great Pagosa Spring. You'll notice it's enclosed by a fence for your safety. Interpretive signs describe the geologic formation. At over 150 degrees, the mother of them all is too hot and too deep for bathing, but the water is used to heat other nearby pools that are open for soaking.

The Spring Inn

Eleven natural hot-spring tubs are open here year-round, day and night. The tubs vary in temperature, so take your pick of a warm soak or a lobster boil. Locker rooms and showers are included. The tubs are free for guests, with a small charge for nonguests. If your kids are the rambunctious type (what, my little darlings?), you might be better off taking them to the outdoor warm pool at the nearby Spa Motel, where they can splash and whoop it up a little more. In downtown Pagosa at 165 Hot Springs Boulevard; (800) 225-0934 or (970) 264-4168.

THE SPA MOTEL AND HOT MINERAL BATHS

A large, year-round outdoor swimming pool (maintained at 88 degrees) and indoor men's and women's segregated hot pools and sauna are here. A swimming pool is open to the public for a fee; it's complimentary for motel guests. On the corner of San Juan Street and Hot Springs Boulevard; (800) 832-5523 or (970) 264-5910.

WATERFALLS AND SHORT HIKES

More than twenty-five good-sized year-round waterfalls can be found near Pagosa Springs. Following are a few of the most accessible ones.

TREASURE FALLS

A .25-mile interpretive trail to the bridge at the base of a 100-foot waterfall. (It's likely to be frozen in winter.) A restroom is near the parking area. Fourteen miles west of town on Highway 160.

PIEDRA FALLS

North on Piedra Road (Forest Road 631) about 17 miles to the Sportsman's Supply Junction. Then follow Middle Fork Road (Forest Road 636) for 2 miles, take the first road to the right (Forest Road 637), and follow it to the end. (Don't attempt this in wet, muddy conditions.) Walk up the river to a headgate where the trail begins. The falls are about a half-hour walk upstream.

FOURMILE FALLS

Drive north 9 miles on Fourmile Road (Forest Road 645). Turn right at the junction and go 5 miles to the trailhead. The trail follows Fourmile Creek and is bordered by aspens and spruce. A 300-foot waterfall on your left is your reward. The walk is about 3 miles each way and is an easy-to-moderate grade. Because of the golden aspen, mid-September is usually a colorful time to visit. But to witness greater water volume, early summer is best. This trail continues past the falls another 4 miles to Fourmile Lake.

The Continental Divide Trail at Wolf Creek Pass offers hiking as easy or as difficult as you want to make it.

CONTINENTAL DIVIDE TRAIL

This trail is about 20 miles east of Pagosa Springs, at the summit of Wolf Creek Pass. Look for the parking lot and the big brown sign. The trail, named for the backbone of the continent, has its beginnings at the Mexican and Canadian borders. Okay, you're probably not going to hike the entire 3,102-mile trail. Well, not this year, anyway. But you might want to walk a little piece of it, just to get the feel. Heavy snows in winter make snowshoes or skis necessary, so summer and early autumn are the best seasons for most families. The hike is easy to difficult, depending on how far you go.

HORSEBACK RIDING

There are a dozen outfitters in the area who will take you on a trail ride, and no shortage of beautiful trails to explore. The riding season depends on the amount of snowfall in any given year but generally runs from late May through October. Following are several companies close to town that offer something a little different.

WILDERNESS WEST

This one is family-owned and operated, and close enough to town to combine with an evening soak in a hot spring. Kent Gordon and his family feature full-day trips and longer rides into the backcountry. Give them advance notice and they can customize your trail ride to your needs and desires. You can go on a photo safari, bow-hunt, fish, pan for gold, or just ride. "We have our own piece of wilderness up there where you almost never see another soul," says Kent. Wilderness West accommodates greenhorns, but they especially shine if you're looking for much more than plodding around the pasture for an hour or two. (Beware: They're also horse traders and have dozens of horses for sale at all times. They even offer a "horse sharing program," which is kind of like a four-legged time-share. Horse lovers of the family will surely fall in love with one.) Call (970) 264-4252.

DIAMOND HITCH STABLES AND OUTFITTERS

Trail rides from one hour to half a day, as well as overnight pack trips. Also breakfast rides for early risers, pony rides for kids too little to trail-ride, western riding lessons for the dedicated, and a farm-animal zoo for all to enjoy. Call (970) 731-RIDE.

ASTRADDLE A SADDLE

Besides trail rides and a catchy name, these guys offer dinner sleigh rides, sled-dog rides, and summer wagon rides and barbecues. The owner-operators are fourth-generation residents of the area, so we suspect they know the trails pretty well. Call (970) 731-5076.

CHIMNEY ROCK ARCHAEOLOGICAL SITE

Who knows what the Ancient Ones called these prominent rocky projections that we now call Chimney Rock? Many people have never even heard of this place, yet it is the most spectacular Anasazi building site in all the Four Corners region, according to William Ferguson and Arthur Robin, authors of *Anasazi Ruins of the Southwest in Color.*

Although Chimney Rock pueblo hasn't been excavated as fully as Mesa Verde, it is equally interesting. Built on a narrow ridge 1,000 feet above the valley floor, under the towering pinnacles of Chimney Rock, this pueblo, it is estimated, may have housed as many as two thousand people around the year A.D. 1000. Religion and astronomy seem to have been the focus here, according to recent studies.

You wonder how they did it. All the mud, loose rock, and water for building had to be hauled 1,000 feet up the steep slope from the banks of the Piedra River! But of utmost interest to Anasazi aficionados is the building style: It's more like that of Chaco Canyon, 80 miles south in New Mexico, than that of Mesa Verde and other nearby sites. Archaeologist Frank Eddy, who excavated Chimney Rock, suggests parts of the pueblo were constructed by priests from Chaco Canyon who migrated north about 1076. Whether they came to proselytize and convert or because they were exiled from Chaco, who knows? But fifty years later the entire district was abandoned for reasons that are not at all clear to us.

Chimney Rock is open only to guided tours between May 15 and September 15. For exact dates and times of tours, which vary from season to season, call the Pagosa Ranger District at (970) 264-2268.

WHERE: 17 miles west of Pagosa Springs on Highway 160, then 3.5 miles south on Highway 151.

WHEN: By reservation, May 15 through September 15; off-season tours may be possible by special request. Morning or late-afternoon tours are usually more comfortable, because the sunlight is less harsh at those times. Call for current schedules; (970) 264-2268.

ACTIVITIES: Guided tours of Anasazi ruins. Tours are limited to thirty people per day.

FACILITIES: A minimally developed site. There is a restroom at the visitor center.

BE SURE TO BRING: Drinking water (there is none on the site). Also good walking shoes and sun protection for the 1.5-mile guided walk. Best for families with school-age kids.

WOLF CREEK SKI AREA

One of the oldest ski areas in the state, minimally developed Wolf Creek simply offers the most snow for the lowest prices. The average annual snowfall is over 450 inches! Although there's no lodging here, Pagosa Springs is only about 25 miles west, if you don't mind the drive.

WHERE: 25 miles northeast of Pagosa Springs on Highway 160; (970) 264-5639.

ACTIVITIES: Downhill skiing, nearby cross-country trails. No organized summer activities, although hikers and mountain bikers can explore the trails.

FACILITIES: Two cafeterias, bar, picnic building; rental shop, lessons; "Wolf Pup" classes for kids five to eight and "Hotshots" program for ages nine to twelve.

CROSS-COUNTRY SKIING AT ALPEN HAUS TOURING CENTER

During the winter season you can ski on the snow-blanketed Pagosa Springs Golf Course. These gentle, well-groomed trails provide enough exercise and snow-covered excitement for some of us. Alpen Haus incorporates beautiful mountain views with a restaurant and lodging facilities.

WHERE: Fairfield Pagosa Resort. Go west on Highway 160 3 miles from Pagosa Springs, then right onto Piñon Causeway to the golf course clubhouse; (970) 731-4141, ext. 2021.

ACTIVITIES: Cross-country skiing open to the public. The usual season is November through March, the rest of the year it's a private golf course.

FACILITIES: A 12-kilometer trail system; rentals, lessons, restaurant, and lodging. After the snow melts it's a twenty-seven-hole private golf course open to members and guests only.

AREA STATE PARKS AND NATIONAL FORESTS
NAVAJO LAKE STATE PARK

Features a year-round campground with seventy sites, showers, and flush toilets; a marina is open from March to November where you can rent boats and fishing gear, buy ice and supplies. And how convenient—a 3,000-foot airstrip so you can fly your Piper in and pitch a tarp over the wing. You can even rent a houseboat for the weekend. Other activities at this remote park include hiking an old stagecoach road and an abandoned narrow-gauge railroad bed, and spying on waterfowl, raptors, songbirds, and game birds such as doves, grouse, and turkeys. At the visitors center you can see Native artifacts unearthed from this region. Winter brings snowmobilers and ice fishers. Snowshoeing and ski touring are also possible if you bring your own stuff. Year-round camping. The park is 37 miles south of Pagosa Springs off Highway 151; (970) 883-2208.

SAN JUAN NATIONAL FOREST

Many opportunities for uncrowded car camping or wilderness backpacking can be found in this national forest that surrounds Pagosa Springs. Many Forest Service roads off Highway 160 lead to campgrounds. For more information, contact the Pagosa Ranger District at Second and Pagosa Street; (970) 264-2268. Following are a few campgrounds we've found that offer good river fishing and hiking trails.

East Fork Campground: This one is just off the main drag—a good choice if it's getting late or you're tired of driving and just want to pitch your tent. Open mid-May to mid-November. It's 9.7 miles northeast of Pagosa Springs on Highway 160, then .8-mile east on Forest Service Road 667; (970) 264-2268.

West Fork Campground: Twenty-eight sites for tents or motor homes. Open mid-May to mid-November. Go 13.7 miles northeast of town on Highway 160, then 1.6 miles north on Forest Service Road 684; (970) 264-2268.

Wolf Creek: Twenty-six creekside sites for tents or motor homes, with trailheads (and trail maps) to Windy Pass and Treasure Mountain. Open mid-May to mid-November. Follow directions for West Fork Campground, but go only .5-mile north on Forest Service Road 684; (970) 264-2268.

You'll find lots of private campgrounds along Highway 160 both east and west of Pagosa Springs. Most offer extras like playgrounds, swimming pools, and game rooms. For those who would like to camp out on the Southern Ute Indian Reservation try Lake Capote. No Colorado license is required for trout fishing in Lake Capote. Boat and fishing equipment rentals are available at the marina. Tent sites, motor home sites, showers, and modern restroom facilities are available too. Nature trails, birdwatching, or tours of the nearby Chimney Rock ruins with a Ute guide are available here. Camping begins in April on weekends, then daily from mid-May through early September. Lake Capote is 17 miles west of Pagosa Springs on the Southern Ute Indian Reservation; (970) 731-5256.

Outdoor Fairs and Festivals
Mountain Man Encampment

Organized by the Wolf Creek Muzzleloaders of Pagosa Springs, this rendezvous is held on a three-day weekend in June. South on Hot Springs Boulevard, then east on Spring Street.

Contact the chamber of commerce at (800) 252-2204 or (970) 264-2360.

RED RYDER RODEO

The oldest community event of the summer, this is a traditional rodeo with arts and crafts, a parade, a carnival, and fireworks. Held at the Red Ryder Rodeo Arena, which is named for an old comic strip character made famous by resident western artist Fred Harman. On July 4 weekend. For details, call the chamber of commerce at (800) 252-2204 or (970) 264-2360.

ARCHULETA COUNTY FAIR

Features a Kid's Wild and Woolly Rodeo and tethered-hot-air balloon rides. In early August. Call the extension building for more information; (970) 264-5931.

COLORFEST

Hot-air balloons, mountain-bike races, and a bluegrass concert are some of the outdoor activities at this townwide celebration. Also an integral part of Colorfest are the aspen trees, which are usually decked out in gold, pale yellow, russet, and bronze leaves. In late September. Details are available from the chamber of commerce; (800) 252-2204 or (970) 264-2360.

IN CASE OF BAD WEATHER
SAN JUAN HISTORICAL MUSEUM

Enjoy displays depicting life in the 1800s as it was lived in southwest Colorado. An old-fashioned dentist's office, a one-horse sleigh, and the fire department's water hose are some of the artifacts you can see. From Memorial Day until Labor Day, Tuesday through Saturday from 11 A.M. to 5 P.M. There is a small fee.

MESA VERDE NATIONAL PARK AND ENVIRONS

Mesa Verde is one of Linda's favorite places anywhere, as her youngest son, Matt, can attest. He was nine or ten when she first took him to witness the amazing Cliff Palace, to hike Petroglyph Point Trail, to camp out under the stars of ancient Hovenweep. Although he apparently didn't catch the same archaeological bug that afflicts his mother, he had fun, he says, and "learned a lot."

Mesa Verde is a national park rich in archaeological treasures—the remains of a civilization that evolved over a thousand years in the dry, harsh climate of southwest Colorado. We call the people of this civilization the Anasazi, which is a Navajo word meaning "enemy" or according to some sources "ancient people." It is believed the Anasazi eventually migrated south into New Mexico's Rio Grande area, becoming the ancestors of today's Hopi, Zuni, and other Pueblo people.

At Mesa Verde you can see ruins and artifacts from the time when the Ancient Ones wove utilitarian baskets and lived in pit houses on top of the mesa to the height of their civilization, when they crafted stylized pottery and lived in magnificent dwellings built into the walls of the cliffs. If you weren't fascinated by pre-Columbian American history before you came, you will at least be intrigued by it after you leave. If we were allowed to return to only one national park in the whole United States, it would be Mesa Verde. You could easily spend a week in the area (we could spend months) exploring all the park has to offer and the many other points of archaeological and geological interest in the immediate area. If you only have a day or two, don't despair, you'll be able to see enough to give you an appreciation for the park, and the inspiration to return someday.

But don't try to "do" all of Mesa Verde in a single afternoon. This is not a drive-through park. It takes time to see the dozens of excavated major sites, the hundreds of unexcavated smaller ones. It takes time to study the museum exhibits, browse the

The cliffs of Mesa Verde are as beautiful and mysterious as the archaeological secrets they shelter.

book store, walk the trails. You have to get out of the car many times, out in the hot summer sun or the chill winter wind. Out in the same conditions the Ancient Ones endured. If all you have is an afternoon, we advise you make some choices instead of trying to see it all. Consider passing up the two biggest attractions—guided tours of Cliff House and Balcony Palace. For these you must stand in line to buy tickets. Due to ever-increasing numbers of visitors, the Park Service has limited access to these sites to help preserve them and to help you get the most from your visit. Although tickets only cost a dollar each, the time you spend in line to buy them, then waiting for your group to go, could take up a significant portion of the time you have to explore the park. If you are staying more than one day at Mesa Verde, however, a guided tour through one of these famous sites is definitely worthwhile.

If you have one day or less to spend at Mesa Verde, the following are our suggestions for apportioning the time.

Ruins Road Self-Guided Driving Loop

If you really are just driving through (which is better than not seeing the park at all but still takes at least three hours), use the map given to you at the entrance gate to find Ruins Road. There are several stops along here with interpretive signs and brochures to explain what you're seeing. Most impressive is the Sun Point Overlook, where, upon getting out of your car and walking a very short distance, you will have an incredible view of Cliff Palace, Sun Temple, and eleven other sites.

Spruce Tree House

If you have most of one day to spend, be sure to stop at Spruce Tree House, park headquarters, and the Chapin Museum. Here you can take a self-guided tour of the third-largest and one of the best-preserved pueblos in the park. It involves a half-mile round-trip walk that can be hot and dry, so wear a hat and carry water bottles, even though there is a water fountain at the trailhead. Every time we've been here a ranger has given informal tours that you can join in and cut out of at will. This is nice, with children's attention spans being what they are. Here too, you can climb down into a real *kiva*—an underground room that was used for ceremonial purposes.

There are two hiking trails from Spruce Tree House: Spruce Canyon Trail (2 miles) and Petroglyph Point Trail (3 miles). Matt and Linda hiked the Petroglyph Trail to see the rock carvings, the highlight of a magnificent desert walk. In 1942, Hopi Indians from Arizona, thought to be descendants of Anasazi, studied this rock art, and their interpretations are given in the trail guide.

Chapin Mesa Museum

Time spent in the Chapin Mesa Museum and book store here is recommended. If you're like our family, you could spend an hour in the book store alone! Besides dozens of books on archaeology, there's an excellent natural history section and a large children's section. We watched a young girl count out dollar bills from a wrinkled envelope to buy an armful of books. Her father said she'd been saving her allowance for six months. Here at the bookstore you can also buy National Park "passports," which can be stamped with the Mesa Verde seal. If you plan on visiting other national parks over the next few years, this might be a fun souvenir for the kids. If you're not a bibliophile or a museum addict, you'll at least enjoy the shelter from the sometimes extreme weather outside (summer heat, winter cold). There's a snack bar, gift shop, and restrooms here too.

WETHERHILL MESA

Here's a less-frequented area of the park for those of us who have an aversion to crowds. Four major sites are located here, including Long House, the second largest of the cliff dwellings, and one of the best preserved. Here too, you can ride a minitrain to see some of the excavated sites, an activity the kids might enjoy. There's no charge for the train, and it's wheelchair accessible. Wetherhill Mesa is only open during the summer months.

WHERE: 37 miles southwest of Durango and 10 miles east of Cortez. Follow the sign from Highway 160. Park headquarters and the closest major points of interest are 21 miles off the main highway; (970) 529-4465.

WHEN: Open 365 days a year. Camping, lodging, and gasoline are not available inside the park during the winter months. Expect heavy crowds during the summer; autumn and spring are ideal times to visit.

ACTIVITIES: Exploring archaeological artifacts and ruins, hiking (limited to established trails), picnicking. Camping at designated facility only.

FACILITIES: Visitor centers offer a variety of tours and programs; museums, gift shops, food concessions, picnic grounds, laundromat; seasonal lodge, campground, and gasoline sales.

BE SURE TO BRING: Sunscreen and hats any time of year, water bottles, good walking shoes. Even though there are snack shops and restaurants, you could be forty-five minutes away from one when everybody gets hungry, so a cooler filled with snacks and cold drinks comes in handy.

LODGING AND CAMPING IN THE PARK

FAR VIEW LODGE

This is the only indoor lodging within the park. It is aptly named, for the view from your private balcony is indeed far— you can see well into New Mexico. The proximity to the major ruins make staying overnight here really desirable; if you lodge in nearby Cortez, it takes nearly an hour of driving just to reach the ruins. Rates at the Far View Lodge are reasonable, and there's a restaurant for convenience. (And if someone in the family complains about the lack of televisions or telephones, take them out on the balcony to look at a jillion stars above, or a scattering of lights miles south, across the state line.) Open from mid-April to mid-October, reservations recommended. Call the Far View Visitor Center at (970) 533-7731 or 529-4421.

THE MOREFIELD CAMPGROUND

This is Mesa Verde's only campground, but it's huge. Thoughtfully designed, the sites are spaced well apart and are wheelchair accessible. With five hundred sites, you're likely to find a spot even on the weekend. But it's first-come first-served, so get there early to have the best selection. We found it to be surprisingly quiet and peaceful here, in spite of the large numbers of campers. Deer often visit the grounds and can be seen most often in the early morning or late afternoon. A grocery store, laundromat, and a restaurant that serves a cheap pancake breakfast are nearby. Older kids can ride around the paved campground roads on their bicycles (off-road riding is prohibited). There are several hiking trails near the campground and nightly educational campfire talks are given throughout the summer.

The campground is open mid-April through mid-October, and no other camping is allowed in the park. Follow the signs from the entrance gate. No reservations, but for information call (970) 529-4461.

CROW CANYON ARCHAEOLOGICAL CENTER

It's not cheap, digging in the dirt for pots, or trying to grind hard corn with a stone mano and metate. But the experience may be worth it if you want a really intensive immersion into the ways of the Ancient Ones. If the multiday programs aren't in your time or money budget, consider enrolling in a day program, offered during the summer months. For about the same price as lift tickets, your family can discover archaeology together with real hands-on experience—like making pottery and baskets, grinding corn with a stone, or throwing a primitive weapon called an *atlatl*.

Crow Canyon is a private organization dedicated to archaeological research, experiential learning, and public consciousness of North America's archaeological heritage. It is funded by private gifts and by tuition.

WHERE: North of Cortez, 23390 County Road K; (800) 422-8975 or (970) 565-8975.

WHEN: Most programs are scheduled for late spring through autumn.

ACTIVITIES: Day- and weeklong archaeological and cultural exploration programs.

FACILITIES: Lodging, meals, and transportation for extended programs.

BE SURE TO BRING: Sun protection, water bottles, and patience. Recommended for older kids and adults with a passion for archaeology.

Other Archaeological Sites and Activities

Cortez Center Museum and Cultural Park

Through a partnership with the University of Colorado, this museum offers exhibits of the Anasazi civilization. Additionally, Native craft demonstrations and dances are featured regularly. Free outdoor performances given by Native American dancers in traditional costume are a favorite among visitors and locals alike. Bring a picnic dinner. Memorial Day through Labor Day, Monday through Friday at 7 P.M. At 25 North Market Street, Cortez; (970) 565-1151.

Anasazi Heritage Center and Nearby Ruins

The half-mile paved trail to the Dominguez-Escalante Ruins is a pleasant walk except during the heat of the day. Although it's a small, undramatic site, excavation here revealed the burial of an ancient thirty-five-year-old woman of high status. It is speculated she was a distinguished visitor from the great city of Chaco in New Mexico. Make time to tour the Heritage Center, an excellent museum operated by the Bureau of Land Management. Your kids are sure to appreciate the interactive computers, the microscopes, the loom, and other hands-on exhibits depicting the life and times of the Ancient Ones. Ruins open daily, from 8 A.M. to 5 P.M. The center closes earlier during the winter. Located 10 miles north of Cortez on Highway 184; (970) 882-4811.

Ute Mountain Tribal Park

These ruins, far less visited and less reconstructed than those of Mesa Verde, give us a glimpse of what all the pueblo sites must have looked like when they were first discovered. Especially worth seeing is Lion Canyon, which contains several spectacular cliff dwellings, such as the well-preserved Eagle Nest House. All trips are to remote areas, and all are by guide only. It is important to bring adequate food, water, and appropriate clothing. This tour is not suitable for young children but could be ideal for adolescents and adults looking for a different kind of adventure. Full- and half-day guided tours year-round, weather permitting. Reservations are necessary. Tribal Park headquarters are 20 miles south of Cortez off Highway 666; (800) 847-5485 or (970) 565-3751, ext. 282.

HOVENWEEP NATIONAL MONUMENT

Hovenweep—even the name is hauntingly beautiful. It is a Ute word meaning "deserted valley." (At last, an ancient site that carries its Native name, instead of that of the white explorer who "discovered" it!) This is our favorite place among many in the region. It's remote, and the dirt roads seem endless when you're driving them, but worth every mile if you're really into ruins. Midday can be ruthlessly hot during the summer months; fall and winter are more comfortable times for hiking. A primitive campground makes spending the night inviting. If you have preschoolers or fidgety older kids, or if you aren't crazy about piles of crumbling rocks on the precipices of dry desert canyons, skip this place. But if you're looking for an out-of-the-way adventure, work it into your trip. Park and campground are open year-round, but when the dirt roads are snowy or muddy you risk getting stuck. About 42 miles from Cortez. Drive west on Highway 666 for 3 miles, turn right on McElmo Canyon Road, and follow small signs to Hovenweep—the actual site is just over the state line in Utah. No telephone service here; call Mesa Verde National Park at (970) 529-4461.

FOUR CORNERS MONUMENT

Take a trip to Four Corners—you can pass it off as a geography lesson. You'll need *some* excuse, because the Four Corners Monument is 38 miles from Cortez, which is probably not on your way home. But where else can you be in four different states at once? (And can you name those states without looking on a map?) To actually *be* in four different places at the same time you first have to pay a small token for the privilege. You may actually have to wait in line. (While you're waiting you'll notice some nearby stands where Ute and Navajo are selling arts and crafts. You'll also notice they take credit cards.) When your turn comes you step up on a platform that has the crucial intersecting lines drawn on it, you bend over, and you put a hand or a foot in each state. Of course, someone in your family will take a picture of you in this pose, which will undoubtedly become a treasured family keepsake. But it's worth it. With hands-on learning like that, the kids should all ace geography! The Four Corners Monument is 38 miles southwest of Cortez off Highway 160. There is no telephone and no facilities.

Appendix A:
Activity Resources

Astronomy

Gates Planetarium at the Colorado Museum of Natural History, Denver; (303) 370-6351

Sommers-Bausch Observatory and Fiske Planetarium at the University of Colorado, Boulder; (303) 492-5002

U.S. Air Force Academy Planetarium in Colorado Springs; (719) 333-2778

Bicycling

Bicycle Colorado; (800) 997-BIKE or (970) 256-7340

Bird-Watching

Binoculars, a field guide, a sighting journal, and information from these experts should start young ornithologists off right.

National Audubon Society (Colorado); (303) 696-0877

Colorado Bird Observatory, 13401 Picadilly Road, Brighton, CO 80601; (303) 659-4348

Wild Bird Center, 1641 28th Street, Boulder, CO 80301; (303) 442-1322

Camping

To find thousands of designated campsites and more opportunities for backcountry camping, contact these organizations.

Colorado Association of Campgrounds, Cabins and Lodges, 5101 Pennsylvania Avenue, Boulder, CO 80303; (303) 499-9343

Bureau of Land Management, 2850 Youngfield Street, Lakewood, CO 80215; (303) 239-3600

277

U.S. Forest Service, Rocky Mountain Region Headquarters, 740 Simms, Box 25127, Lakewood, CO 80225; (303) 275-5353

See also Colorado State Parks, below.

Colorado State Parks and Recreation Areas

The state parks offer one of the best values in outdoor entertainment. Consider buying an annual pass—for less than fifty dollars you can go as many times as you like in a year. Call (303) 866-3437, or 1 (800) 678-CAMP after April 1.

Dinosaurs

This is a great state in which to discover dinosaurs. Here are several museums and organizations that specialize in paleontology.

Friends of Dinosaur Ridge, P.O. Box 564, Morrison, CO 80465; (303) 697-DINO

Denver Museum of Natural History, Earth Sciences Department, 2001 Colorado Boulevard, Denver, CO 80205; (303) 370-6473

Dinosaur Valley, 362 Main Street, Grand Junction, CO 80501; (970) 243-3466

University of Colorado Henderson Museum, Fifteenth and Broadway, Boulder, CO 80302; (303) 492-6892

Ghost Towns

Nearly every Colorado town has its historical society and museum where you can learn nore about towns and settlements of yesteryear. One guidebook to help is *Colorado Ghost Towns and Mining Camps* by Sandra Dallas, University of Oklahoma Press, 1985.

Guest Ranches

Prices and packages for Colorado guest ranches vary considerably. Contact the Colorado Dude and Guest Ranch Association for a complete list of member ranches, with current rates.

Colorado Dude and Guest Ranch Association, P.O. Box 300, Tabernash, CO 80478; (970) 887-3128

Hiking

Colorado Mountain Club, 710 10th Street, Golden, CO 80401; (303) 279-5643
The Colorado Trail Foundation, P.O. Box 260876, Lakewood, CO 80226; (303) 526-0809

Horseback Riding

Colorado Horsemen's Council, P.O. Box 1125, Arvada, CO 80001; (303) 279-4546

Hunting and Fishing Trips

Colorado Outfitters Association, Aurora, CO; (303) 841-7760

Mountain Biking

See Bicycling

Mountain Climbing

Colorado Mountain Club, 710 10th Street, Golden, CO 80401; (303) 279-5643

National Parks and Monuments

National Park Service, P.O. Box 25287, 12795 West Alameda Parkway, Lakewood, CO 80225; (303) 969-2000

Native Americans

Ute Mountain Tribal Park; (800) 847-5485, (970) 565-3751, or (970) 565-9653
Southern Ute Cultural Center and Museum; (970) 563-9583

Railroads

Cumbres & Toltec Scenic Railroad: (719) 376-5483
Durango & Silverton Narrow Gauge Railroad Co., 479 Main Avenue, Durango, CO; (970) 247-2733
Georgetown Narrow Gauge Railroad: (303) 670-1686 (Denver Metro) or (303) 569-2403 (local)
SKI TRAIN: (303) 296-4754

River Rafting

Adventure Bound Rafting Co., 2392 H Road, Grand Junction, CO 81505; (970) 245-5428 or (800) 423-4668. Or visit the website: www.raft-colorado.com

Arkansas Valley Expeditions: (800) 833-RAFT (7238)

Blue Sky Adventures, Inc., P.O. Box 1566, Glenwood Springs, CO 81602; (970) 945-6605

Clear Creek Rafting, 18301 West Colfax Avenue, Building U-3, Heritage Square, Golden, CO; (303) 277-9900

Mountain Water Rafting, 108 West College Drive, Durango, CO; (970) 259-4191

Rock Gardens Rafting and Campground, 1308 County Road 129, No Name, CO 81601; (970) 945-6737

Wanderlust Adventure, 3500 Bingham Hill Road, Fort Collins, CO 80521; (800) 745-7238 or (970) 484-1219

Rock Collecting

Colorado Museum of Natural History, Earth Sciences Department, 2001 Colorado Boulevard, Denver, CO 80205; (303) 370-6473

Colorado School of Mines Geology Museum, Golden, CO; (303) 273-3815

Denver Gem and Mineral Show, P.O. Box 621444, Littleton, CO 80162; (303) 233-2516

Colorado's BLM and USFS personnel and lands provide good information and opportunities for amateur collectors. Contact the Bureau of Land Management at (303) 239-3600; the U.S. Forest Service at (303) 275-5353

Rodeos

National Little Britches Rodeo Association, 1045 West Rio Grande, Colorado Springs, CO 80906; (719) 389-0333

Pro Rodeo Cowboys Association, 101 Pro Rodeo Drive, Colorado Springs, CO 80919; (719) 593-8840

Scuba Diving

For a landlocked state, there are a huge number of certified scuba divers in Colorado, and quite a few dive shops as well. These dive shops and many others offer introductory classes as well as full certification programs.

PADI International (Professional Association of Diving Instructors), 1251 East Dyer Road, #100, Santa Ana, CA 92705; (800) 729-7234, http://www.padi.com

Colorado Scuba Center, 1432 South Wadsworth Boulevard, Lakewood, CO 80232; (303) 986-0007

Rocky Mountain Diving Center, 1737 Fifteenth Street, Boulder, CO 80302; (303) 449-8606 or (800) 678-8606

Skiing, Cross-Country

Colorado Cross-Country Ski Association, P.O. Box 169, Winter Park, CO 80482; (970) 887-2152

Skiing, Downhill

Colorado Ski Country USA, 1560 Broadway, Suite 2000, Denver, CO 80202; (303) 837-0793

For snow reports, call (303) 825-SNOW (7669)

Skydiving

Sorry kids, but you have to be eighteen years old to skydive at a center approved by the United States Parachute Association. To find out the location of approved centers in your area, contact the USPA at 1440 Duke Street, Alexandria, VA 22314; (703) 836-3495.

Snowmobiling

Colorado State Snowmobile Association, P.O. Box 588, Silverton, CO 81433; (800) 235-4480

Volunteering

Volunteers for Outdoor Colorado, 600 South Manon Parkway, Denver, CO 80209; (303) 715-1010

WHEELCHAIR ACCESSIBILITY

Wilderness on Wheels; (303) 988-2212

National Sports Center for the Disabled; (303) 892-0961

WILDLIFE

Colorado Bat Society, 1085 14th Street, Suite 1337, Denver, CO 80302

National Audubon Society, Rocky Mountain Regional Office, 4150 Darley Avenue, Suite 5, Boulder, CO 80303; (303) 499-0219

Watchable Wildlife Program, 6060 Broadway, Denver, CO 80216; (303) 291-7518

U.S. Fish and Wildlife Service, P.O. Box 25486, DFC, Denver, CO 80225; (303) 236-8145

Illustration by Cheryl Duff, third grade

Appendix B: Best Activities for Tots Ages 2-5

Most preschoolers love to venture outside, but it usually means a little more work for the adults. To have the most fun with tots we recommend staying close to home and keeping your adventures short. Plan to be back before naptime or bedtime, and provide for meals and frequent snacks.

Nearby urban parks and designated open space lands are some of the best places to take tots because they don't usually require long car rides or much preparation. Here you'll find picnic tables and restrooms, playgrounds with swing sets and jungle gyms, and large expanses of grass for running and rolling. And since most city and county parks are free, you'll definitely get your money's worth.

Zoos are exciting places for families with preschoolers, but don't try to see every animal every trip. In our experience, it's better to leave before the fussing and whining start—and certainly before the crying begins. Preserve the experience by reading animal picture books together, playing with animal toys, and looking at photographs or postcards of zoo animals. With your help, preschoolers can make their own picture book by drawing their favorite animals in a composition book or taping in pictures from magazines.

Very short hikes are good adventures for most tots. Choose paved trails to begin with and take a wagon, stroller, or child carrier for when they get tired. Don't try to teach too much; we've seen overzealous parents quizzing their offspring every step of the walk, trying to inspire an inquiring mind—and missing the point entirely. Tots will gain more if you let them enjoy the sensual pleasures of being outdoors. The inquisitiveness will follow.

If you enjoy camping, chances are good your young children will, too. For the first few times choose campgrounds close to home with plenty of amenities. Use well-insulated sleeping bags and ground pads and dress small children in several layers, including warm hats and sleepers with feet. Silk and fleece are two insulating fabrics that are light and soft against young skin. Colorado nights can be cold even in mid-summer so consider putting small children to bed between two adults for extra insulation. You may end up with your toddler snuggling next to you inside your sleeping bag. If you found you haven't prepared enough for the weather, get in the car and drive home or to the closest motel. Resist the potentially deadly temptation to warm up in a running car; you may fall asleep and be overcome by carbon monoxide poisoning.

We've found that county fairs and small-town events are the best outdoor festivals to take tots to. These fairs feature farm animals, miniature carnival rides, music, and a variety of new sights, sounds, and smells for young senses. Parking is generally free and closer at hand; smaller crowds and simpler entertainment make for a more toddler-friendly experience than most of the bigger extravaganzas provide.

Any outdoor activity with small children requires preparation on the part of the adults in charge. Sun protection in the form of hats, long sleeves, and sunscreen for sensitive skin is critical any time of year in Colorado. Not only does tender young skin burn more easily, but children's greater surface area sets them up for rapid dehydration. Many an outing has ended prematurely with fatigue and crankiness, not caused by over-exertion but from fluid loss. Colorado's intense sunshine, high altitude, and dry air all hasten the dehydration that normally occurs when we play outdoors. Besides hats and appropriate clothing, make sure your kids are drinking plenty of fluids. Pint size plastic water bottles work great—bring along several for each tot and quart-size bottles for the adults. You'll know your wee one is drinking enough fluids if you're having to change diapers or "go potty" every hour. Since most kids aren't big water drinkers you'll have better luck if you fill the bottles with diluted fruit juice such as unsweetened apple or pineapple juice.

If you introduce children to outdoor fun when they are toddlers, chances are they will better appreciate and enjoy nature for many years to come. It worked for us, anyway!

Here are what we consider to be Colorado's best outdoor activities and destinations for families with tots:

NORTHEASTERN PLAINS

COLORADO'S FRONT RANGE

COLORADO'S SOUTHWEST CORNER

Illustration by Kendra Cooper, first grade

Appendix C: Best Activities for Teens

The teen years can be difficult ones for kids and parents alike. Adolescence may start as early as age ten or eleven and may last a decade. Some parents claim their children "breezed through" the teenage years, but ours were prone to frequent attacks of embarrassment, boredom, apathy, fault-finding, and rebelliousness. It sometimes seemed as if they led a parallel existence with the rest of us; near us in person but miles away in thought.

In spite of mood swings, loud music, and occasional sleepless nights, we survived the rites of passage of five adolescents, and even enjoyed those tumultuous years. We had many successful family adventures with our teenagers. Here, we pass on some of our strategies for planning a family outing with teenagers:

1. Let adolescents help with the planning—but reserve the last word and final authority, especially where safety is an issue.
2. Allow your teenager to invite a friend along to share the adventure; you'll all have more fun.
3. Give teens a significant share of the chores involved. Preparing the picnic lunch, packing the car, navigating, taking their turn behind the wheel (assuming they have a drivers license!), and carrying their own gear are all necessary parts of a family adventure. The more involved they are, the more responsibility they'll assume for their own good time and their own well-being.
4. Allow young adults their private thoughts and respect their need for personal space. Let them be moody and sullen now and then; it'll pass. Don't try to create a perfect experience for them, and don't apologize for bad weather, crowded campgrounds, or other events beyond your control.

5. Do whatever you can to keep your perspective and your sense of humor so that someday you'll all look back on these experiences with pleasure.

6. Many teens, though not all, are attracted to sports that are perceived as exciting or risky. Activities like wilderness camping, hiking, river rafting, scuba diving, sailing, and mountain climbing can inspire confidence, camaraderie, and team spirit in teens—even when the team is their own family. If you are fortunate enough to be able to try some of these adventures as a family, you'll have the opportunity to grow closer to your children even as they are growing up and becoming adults.

7. Consider individual or family lessons in one of the activities mentioned above or in specialized skills like mountain biking, archery, kayaking, rock climbing, in-line skating, horseback riding, tennis, or golf. But don't coerce teens or any unwilling family member into doing something they fear or have no interest in. If you hear the call of the wild but your teenager hears the amplified sounds of guitars or would rather curl up on the couch with the latest sword-and-sorcery novel, your best family outing this year might be a concert at Red Rocks or an afternoon spent at the Tattered Cover book store.

8. Multi-use trails, state parks, and reservoirs are great places to enjoy the outdoors with your teenager. Here, you can be near one another yet do your own thing. Adolescents are free to pedal, skate, or swim away when they need a little distance from their parents (don't worry, they'll be back as soon as the hot dogs are ready and the picnic table set!).

Here are what we consider to be Colorado's best outdoor activities and destinations for families with teenagers:

NORTHEASTERN PLAINS

Greeley Area:

Denver Broncos Summer Training Camp	13
Greeley Independence Stampede	18

COLORADO'S FRONT RANGE

Illustration by Alexandra Joyce, fourth grade

REFERENCES

Bird, Isabella L. *A Lady's Life in the Rocky Mountains.* Norman: University of Oklahoma Press, 1960.

Borneman, Walter R., and Lyndon J. Lampert. *A Climbing Guide to Colorado's Fourteeners.* Boulder, Colo.: Pruett Publishing, 1984.

Chronic, John, and Halka Chronic. *Prairie, Peak and Plateau: A Guide to the Geology of Colorado.* Colorado Geologic Survey Bulletin. Denver, Colo., 1972.

Collison, Linda, and Bob Russell. *Rocky Mountain Wineries: A Travel Guide to the Wayside Vineyards.* Boulder, Colo.: Pruett Publishing, 1994.

Ellis, Reuben. Ed. *Stories and Stone: Writing the Anasazi Homeland.* Boulder, Colo.: Pruett Publishing, 1997.

Ferguson, William M., and Arthur H. Rohn. *Anasazi Ruins of the Southwest in Color.* Albuquerque: University of New Mexico Press, 1986.

Frazier, Deborah. *Colorado's Hot Springs.* Boulder, Colo.: Pruett Publishing, 1996.

Marsh, Charles S. *People of the Shining Mountains.* Boulder, Colo.: Pruett Publishing, 1982.

Robertson, Janet. *The Magnificent Mountain Women.* Lincoln: University of Nebraska Press, 1990.

Ryter, Derek. *Mountain Biking Colorado's La Platas: Great Rides Between Durango and Telluride.* Boulder, Colo.: Pruett Publishing, 1995.

Sprague, Marshall. *Colorado: A History.* New York: Norton, 1976.

Ubbelohde, Carl, Maxine Benson, and Duane A. Smith. *A Colorado History, Seventh Edition.* Boulder, Colo.: Pruett Publishing, 1995.

Underhill, Ruth. *Life in the Pueblos.* Santa Fe, N. Mex.: Ancient City Press, 1991.

Voynick, Stephen M. *Colorado Rock Hounding.* Missoula, Mont.: Mountain Press, 1994.

INDEX